Gluten-Free Girl Every Day

Gluten-Free Girl Every Day

Gluten-Free Girl
Every Day

Shauna James Ahern with Daniel Ahern

Photography by Penny De Los Santos

Houghton Mifflin Harcourt

This book is printed on acid-free paper. ∞

Copyright © 2013 by Shauna James Ahern and Daniel Ahern. All rights reserved.

Photography Copyright © 2013 by Penny De Los Santos

Cover design by Suzanne Sunwoo

Cover image by Penny De Los Santos

Interior design by Kara Plikaitis

Food styling by Karen Shinto

Prop styling by Anne Trenner-Mishka

Published by Houghton Mifflin Harcourt Publishing Company, New York, New York

Published simultaneously in Canada.

For information about permission to reproduce selections from this book, write to Permissions, Houghton Mifflin Harcourt Publishing Company, 215 Park Avenue South, New York, New York 10003.

www.hmhbooks.com

Library of Congress Cataloging-in-Publication Data

Ahern, Shauna James.

 Gluten-free girl every day / Shauna James Ahern, with Daniel Ahern; photography by Penny De Los Santos.

  p. cm.

 Includes index.

 ISBN 978-1-118-11521-3 (cloth); 978-1-118-39491-5 (ebk); 978-1-118-39492-2 (ebk); 978-1-118-39493-9 (ebk)

1. Gluten-free diet--Recipes. I. Ahern, Daniel, 1968- II. Title.

 RM237.86.A339 2013

 641.5'638--dc23

                          2012030520

Printed in China

C&C 10 9 8 7 6 5 4 3 2 1

For Danny, who is my loyal, indispensible partner in everything, including the creation of this book.

For Lucy, who is all joy.

CONTENTS

ACKNOWLEDGMENTS

Thank you.

Thank you to the farmers and food makers on Vashon Island and in Washington State, who not only provided the produce and salmon that made these recipes possible but also inspire us every week with their celery root and Japanese cucumbers.

Thank you to our legion of practical, loving friends, who listened to us wonder about what to cook, ate our meals, and gave us feedback on recipes that seemed too elaborate to make on a weeknight. (None of those recipes is in this book.)

Thank you to Tara Barker, Charissa Luke, Lisa Stander Horel, and Erin Swing Romanos, who helped us with all the baked goods, particularly the sandwich bread. We wanted to nail that one, make it foolproof, and you folks helped us do it.

Thank you to Tracy Chastain and Kim Malone, who meticulously tested nearly every recipe in this book, making the millet skillet bread and quinoa sweet potato stew much better, in particular. These two took notes, took photographs, and took the time to make our lives much easier. We owe you two a Vitamix blender and a dozen cookies every week for years.

Thank you to Anna Painter, whose friendship and fine mind helped make every one of the recipes in the dessert chapter what they are. Anna, I owe you some peanut butter and jam bars.

Thank you to my brother, Andy James, who sat down with me at the table one day and said, "Listen, I don't cook according to ingredient, the way you do. I think about the kind of dinner I want to make. Why don't you structure the book according to types of meals: breakfast for dinner, rice and beans, one-pot meals." He was right, of course.

Thank you to Gypsy Lovett, who gave us feedback on recipes that didn't work, let us use her home for a Thanksgiving feast photo shoot, and cheered us on with good advice and stories.

Thank you to Penny De Los Santos for the stunning photography, Anne Treanor Miska for the gorgeous props, and Karen Shinto for her ninja skills at food styling. Thank you to Molly Wizenberg and Brandon Pettit, dear friends who allowed us to invade their home for a week to make the photographs for this book.

Thank you to Stacey Glick, who continues to be the best agent we could ever imagine.

Thank you to Justin Schwartz, whose friendship and enormously high expectations of the quality of work we can do informs everything here.

Thank you to Lucy, who brings more joy than she could possibly know.

Thank you to Danny, whose voice and food authority is in every single recipe in this book. Life without gluten? No big deal. Life without you? I can't even imagine it.

And finally, thank you to every reader of *Gluten-Free Girl and the Chef*. You have made our lives what they are.

welcome to our
KITCHEN

come on in

WE'RE MAKING GRILLED ANCHOVIES WITH AVOCADO AND GINGER-SCALLION sauce. See the five kids over there at the table? They're shaping the sticky rice into little boats. Yep, there's rice all over the floor. We'll get that later. Here in the kitchen, Danny and our friends, Tami and Alejandra, are slicing strawberries while I pat the dough for shortcake into a smooth round. Cutting out biscuits is one of my favorite actions. So soothing. We're laughing and drinking iced tea. Now Lucy is telling Johnny not to play with her toys. Josie and Cisco go outside to unearth the dirt from the pots of herbs. The baby needs feeding. The wailing begins. Hey kids, it's time to eat!

They pile into the kitchen, and I hand them little packages of sticky rice, bits of anchovy, slices of avocado, and drips of ginger-scallion sauce. Everyone goes quiet. Each kid wants another one. Raena eats four. For a few moments, the sun is shining through the window, the kids are happy and chewing, and all is right with the world. Mayhem will ensue again but this moment is still.

This is why I love cooking so much. A good meal can change someone's day. Cooking is the most deeply creative act with the most practical application.

I came to cooking later in life than I did writing. From the time I could clutch a pen, I started forming words and trying to turn them into sentences that made sense. There were so many poor poems and wretched short stories on the way to essays that weren't too terrible. It's said that it takes ten thousand hours of doing something to become quite competent at it. Not a genius—just good. I've put in those hours in writing, and I'm planning on ten thousand more. And while I love the grateful responses I sometimes get from people who read my books, I love the act of writing even more. It's hard, slogging work, putting words on the page, like laying down bricks and hoping they're not too lopsided. I love this work.

But cooking? Cooking's much more fun. Cooking can be deeply contemplative, if you have an empty house, a clean kitchen, and an entire afternoon to make that complex bread recipe. Does that happen often in my life anymore? Not really. Usually, the counters are covered in vegetables we just brought home from the farmers' market. They all need washing and slicing and putting away. Danny gets an idea to make vegetable pot au feu, a dish he hadn't made since culinary school twenty years ago. And our three-year-old daughter, Lucy, wants me to play Candy Land with her at the same time she's saying, "But I'm so very hungry, Mama." Time for food. Now.

Real cooking rarely looks like it belongs in the pages of a glossy food magazine. I discover that I've run out of onions—how did we run out of onions?—when I'm about to make a big pot of tortilla soup. Fishing through the spice cupboard for the onion powder I bought for these kinds of emergencies, I'm reminded again that I really should come up with some sort of system for keeping the spices organized. Oh man, I left the skillet on, and it's smoking. Honey, what did you say? You want to watch the Wiggles? Not right now, okay?

Like most people, I dream of a spacious white kitchen with an island made of reclaimed wood, open shelves with matching dishes, and countertops that gleam. But you know what's wrong with those kitchens? Nobody's cooking in them. If you cook, you make a mess. You clean it up so you can cook again and make another mess. It's an endless cycle, one that I've learned to complete most days. But I'm willing to admit that there are nights I'm too tired to do the dishes again and leave them for the morning.

I'd rather have dirty dishes than give up cooking.

For me (and my husband and our friends and probably for you who are reading), cooking is a way of connecting with the people I love. Slicing garlic and ginger releases their scents into the air—hours later I can still smell them on my hands. I know I've done something good. Taking the time to mix together tamari, rice wine vinegar, dry sherry, and sesame oil, then nestling the pieces of chicken breast I chopped up just before, letting the bowl sit by the stove for a while, means that our dinner will be full of big flavors. Sometimes cooking is about waiting. Slicing the napa cabbage and putting a pile of it on the plate, ready for the hot wok, gives an order to my day. This, at least, I can do.

Mostly, though, cooking is what leads us to the table. Danny, Lucy, and I sit at the table, talking, watching the steam rise off our plates of chicken stir-fry. We each say something that has made us grateful for the day. We raise our glasses in the air and clink. (Lucy loves saying "CHEERS!") We take a moment to say how happy we are to be there. And then we dive in.

In the end, cooking is about the eating.

how we eat now

OUR FIRST COOKBOOK, *Gluten-Free Girl and the Chef: A Love Story with 100 Tempting Recipes*, was a portrait of a love affair, both with each other and every possible ingredient and technique we could use. It's the story of a chef and food writer, first in love, with all the time in the world to make meals at midnight.

Now, we live on a small rural island, a fifteen-minute ferry ride from Seattle. Our food shopping adventures are mostly limited to the local grocery store, the tiny Saturday farmers' market, and the rural farm stands where we gather produce and put our money in a coffee can, on the honor system. We're stuck during the winter, when nothing much is growing. That's when we're especially grateful to have a well-stocked pantry. Vashon is an island made up of food lovers—we've had friends take us geoduck hunting, offer us hazelnuts from their tree, and leave bunches of kale on our porch when we return from trips instead of flowers. We're part of a goat cheese CSA on the island. Family friends have a pork party every year after they slaughter their pigs. Most everyone gardens. People cook here, daily.

I've had two great cooking teachers in my life. My husband, Danny, who is a talented restaurant chef with more than twenty years of experience, is my first. Every day we talk about food, about the dishes we want to attempt—hey, let's make our own ketchup this summer—and the mistakes that led us to a memorable meal. I still ask him questions about all the dishes I make because I love hearing how his mind works. Also, he knows more than me. Having a restaurant chef in the house has informed this book. We don't really repeat meals in our house. We're always playing, always trying new spices, always creating. The recipes you will find in this book might be simpler than the ones we made in our first cookbook, but they are still intended for people who like to cook.

My second great cooking teacher is our daughter, Lucy, whom we adore. She requires good food every few hours to fuel all the running and jumping she does. And she wants it now.

Lucy has been eating different meals every night, trying new ingredients as they grow in the garden, and sitting on the counter while we cook. She genuinely loves food. She eats everything we put in front of her, partly because she has been involved in every step of the process. (Also, we lucked out.)

Sometimes I'll read stories about what chefs' kids eat, or stories about amazing little gourmets. Always, they emphasize the unusual—"My kid loves uni!" And the expensive—"We feed her caviar." Lucy has eaten in some great restaurants, to be sure. But 95 percent of the time, she's eating good food, meals based on solid technique and fresh ingredients. This kid loves sautéed chard, especially when she pulls it out of the garden for us. It's more important to me that we eat a home-cooked meal together than it's fancy. The best meal is the one on the table.

The meals we make for her and for ourselves are much simpler now, and take far less time, than the meals we created for our first cookbook. If our first cookbook was about the first years of being a couple, this is a cookbook about family and friends. It's about community. This is a cookbook for busy families who still love to cook.

i don't need any gluten

GOING WITHOUT GLUTEN HAS OPENED MY EYES to food. When I found out I have celiac sprue, and thus have to avoid gluten for the rest of my life, I went through a small period of mourning. That's normal. But it didn't take me long to realize what a gift this was. I had been so sick that any cessation of it was relief. Even more than that, I decided to relax into reality instead of bracing myself against it. I said yes to what my body needed. I remembered that eating is an act of celebration. Instead of thinking about what I was missing with every bite, I opened myself to discovering foods I had never experienced before.

What a time these past seven years have been! Not only have I found a career as a food writer through giving up gluten—I never even dreamed that one—but I have eaten five hundred meals I could never have imagined. When I thought I could eat everything, I tended to make the same dozen or so meals, over and over again. Most of the time, I was eating food out of a package or jar.

There are, now, a huge number of packaged gluten-free foods on the market. A few of them are great. Some of them are perfect for when I'm in a transitional space—airports, train stations, or ferry boats—but not much else. Most of them are as overly sugary and filled with preservatives as gluten-filled packaged foods. For me, and for my family, that path isn't the way. Something out of a package never tastes as good as something I make for myself.

And so, I threw myself into cooking. Cooking my own meals was a way to ensure I could eat safely. But within a few weeks of cooking for myself every night, safety became the least of my reasons. Oh, there were a lot of mistakes and burned meals. But increasingly, I found such happiness in cooking, in the slowing down, in the sizzle, and the joy on friends' faces when I fed them. Cooking and me? We were stuck together.

Pretty quickly I decided to expand my food choices. Once I started looking at cuisines that weren't based in gluten—Thai, Mexican, Indian, Japanese, Latin American—I started to realize how myopic our common culture is when it comes to food. In the public spaces of the United States, it's hard to find something that doesn't come wrapped in dough or between two slices of bread.

That's why you'll find so many dishes here that are from other parts of the world than the Pacific Northwest. When I was a kid, my dad loved to play devil's advocate with me and my brother, asking us questions that were impossible to answer but made us think. One of his favorites was: "If you had to eat only one cuisine for the rest of your life, what would it be?" At first I was tempted to say Italian, because I loved the Italian restaurant in our town. Or Mexican, because I never grow tired of Mexican food. But then, I came up with my own clever answer: "I'd eat American food, because we have restaurants from every cuisine in this country!"

I still feel the same way. In Ethiopia, injera—the flatbread served with every meal—is made of teff flour. Tacos are best on corn tortillas. Sushi is meticulously prepared fish atop rice. By opening our kitchen to the spices and flavors of countries around the world, I have found foods that feed us well.

This is how we want to feed Lucy. It's important to us that our daughter experiences a variety of tastes in her life. That's not only because it makes meals more interesting but also because we want her to know with her tongue that people live differently around this world.

So, what you're holding in your hands is a cookbook full of food that intrigues us, food that makes us happy, food that our daughter has grown up on. We both really believe that cooking matters.

I certainly don't need gluten for any of that.

a little taste of our food

IF YOU COME INTO OUR KITCHEN, YOU'LL LIKELY find our daughter on the counter, cooking with us. As soon as she could stand, I stood her on a chair next to me, my hip up against her to make sure she didn't fall. Now, she sits on the counter with a cutting board and a nylon chef's knife we found for her. It cuts through carrots but isn't at all sharp, so she can help with dinner. She loves cutting mushrooms most of all but onions are also a big favorite. (She went through a phase of eating raw onions, when she was teething. We're glad she's out of that now.) She and I talk about what we are cooking or why a hot skillet makes a sizzling sound. I ask her to feel the dough when it's ready, to listen to the sound of the pasta water boiling, to see what the melted cheese looks like on the pizza. We talk with her often about listening to her body to know when something's right. Cooking is the same way.

When Danny's home, the two of them stand side by side, her in front of the stove, scrambling the eggs and Danny peering over her shoulder, beaming.

We want to involve our daughter in every part of cooking the food she eats. Hopefully, she'll appreciate food more than if we just sat her at the table and put food in front of her. Asking her to help us cook means significantly more flour on the floor than if I told her to play while I got dinner ready. It also takes more time and there's the occasional tantrum. Mostly, though, we just love having her there.

You won't find us rushing through the kitchen. Even though we're busy, and we know we have to feed our daughter by 5:15 before she turns hungry grumpy, we're not generally making meals with four ingredients that take less than twenty minutes. We love being in the kitchen. We're not trying to race through dinner to get somewhere else. This is where we feel at home.

However, we've usually planned ahead to make that time more spacious. I've made a big pot of brown rice and frozen it in two-cup portions. I'll pull one out to make a quick fried rice with bacon and bok choy. Or I roasted a chicken the night before and made a stock in the pressure cooker (set it for sixty minutes and walked away), so I can throw together an avgolemono soup in ten minutes. On the weekend, I made kale-walnut pesto, oven-dried tomatoes, and a big pot of beans. All I have to do is cook some pasta, toss in some pesto, tomatoes, and cannellini beans, and I have dinner. There are plenty of ways to make a meal in a leisurely fashion and still eat well.

Here are some the ingredients that show up in our kitchen, over and over again, depending on the season, and what might be in your dinner with us: leeks, fennel, plums, fresh sardines, limes, tarragon,

lobster mushrooms, English peas, spot prawns, radishes, fruity extra-virgin olive oil, arugula (especially from the garden), cucumbers, pistachios, lemon tahini dressing, cardamom, brown butter, polenta, spinach, savoy cabbage, corn on the cob, sunchokes, asparagus, prosciutto, strawberries, peaches, cherries, blood oranges, artichokes, goat cheese, eggs, apples, and sweet potatoes. And kale. We eat a lot of kale. Want some?

Danny and I both love big flavors, with layers of complexity in a dish. Danny can't really stand heat in a dish—too much spice actually causes him pain—so if you are like our friend Adam, you'll bring a bottle of hot sauce when you come to dinner. We won't mind. Sometimes we might have a big hunk of meat to eat, but it's rare. Many of the meals we serve at our table happen to be vegetarian. In the others, meat is merely one of the ingredients. We feel better about the meat we eat when we do it consciously. Mostly, the food

will be fresh, based on what is in season, and full of interesting tastes. And there will plenty for you to have.

Everybody's welcome, even at the last moment. Both Danny and I grew up wanting to have the kind of house someday where friends felt comfortable just stopping by. We set an extra place at the table. That's the kind of home we have. Spill something? No big deal.

So you see, this book isn't meant as an admonition of how we think you should eat or a lecture of what is the healthiest way to be. We all have to find our own way of eating that works for us now.

Instead, think of this book as an invitation. We've invited you into our kitchen. We hope you stay. We hope something inspires you. We hope you feel comfortable here.

Here's a peeler. I'm putting you to work. Can you peel apples? Let's make some pie.

Come Look in the Cupboards

"UNLIKE SOME
PEOPLE, WHO
LOVE TO GO OUT,
I LOVE TO STAY
HOME.... MY IDEA
OF A GOOD TIME
ABROAD IS TO
VISIT SOMEONE'S
HOUSE AND HANG
OUT, POKING INTO
THEIR CUPBOARDS
IF THEY WILL LET
ME."

—Laurie Colwin,
Home Cooking

I HATE MEAL PLANNING. I MEAN THE KIND OF MEAL PLANNING MY DEAR friend Tita does. She sits down with the circular from the grocery store, looking at specials that week, and makes a list of every single lunch and dinner she will make for the next seven days. Monday night is tuna noodle casserole. Thursday night is pot roast. Tita's great at it. She knows how to make a delicious meal and save a lot of money at the same time. I've tried to do it. I pulled it off for a few weeks. But here was the problem—I was utterly bored.

For me, and Danny, cooking is a creative act. We like to respond in the moment to what our tastes are saying. For years, that meant we were pretty dumb shoppers. We'd get a craving for something, or a wish to tackle a new kitchen project, and we'd run to the store. We'd come home with all the ingredients, plus an expensive French cheese because it looked good (and we were hungry). We couldn't remember if we were out of baking powder or baking chocolate, so we bought both. (Turns out they were both in the back of the cupboard.) Surely we need more garlic. Our daily shopping trip topped fifty dollars, regularly.

It doesn't matter that this is what we do, what our business is. That was just silly.

Luckily, I started paying more attention to the way Danny ran a restaurant kitchen. I changed my ways.

Restaurants would be utter chaos if they prepared for dinner service the way we did at home. Before 5 p.m., Danny and his crew spent a couple of hours braising short ribs, making polenta, and roasting off parsnips for the vegetarian special. More than that, each cook set up his mise en place, the gathering of prepped ingredients necessary for the dishes he would cook that night. Onions chopped, garlic sliced, meat cut into portions—these foods needed to be ready for the chaotic dance of a busy dinner service.

I learned this from Danny and put it into action soon after meeting him. Until I started writing recipes with him, I somehow didn't realize that the ingredient list was actually a prep list: "1 large onion, chopped. 2 garlic cloves, sliced. 1 tablespoon finely chopped fresh rosemary." Oh! I have to do each of those, and have them ready, before I ever turn on the stove. Cooking certainly grew easier once I started seeing this.

In the past couple of years, however, I have learned to run our kitchen like a restaurant kitchen in deeper ways. If I know all the ingredients we love the best, why don't I write an inventory? Danny's last restaurant job required him to take inventory of every single ingredient in the kitchen on a weekly basis. How many pounds of oranges did they have? How much stock? How many hamburger buns did they use that week? He began the week with a solid understanding of what he needed to order for service that week. Doing inventory is standard in a restaurant kitchen.

When I made us a list of all the ingredients we wanted in our pantry, and then checked it every week, I couldn't believe how much money we started saving. Instead of buying coconut milk because we might be out of it, I checked my inventory before I went to the store.

Here's my form of menu planning. We buy our meat for the week from a local butcher, one who gets his meat from sources we trust. Each week we choose two or three different cuts of meat we feel like cooking. We don't know what the meal will be yet. We just know the meat. We do the same with seafood, which is plentiful here. Generally, we have two or three dinners with some meat in it, two or three dinners with some seafood in it, and three dinners that are vegetarian.

For most of the year, we participate in a CSA with one of the farmers on Vashon, a woman we adore who grows incredible vegetables. If we run out of vegetables, or want more fruit, we buy more at a farm stand or the farmers' market on Saturday. (From October to March, we go to the grocery store for our produce.)

Mostly, we have our pantry stocked with whole grains, good oils, nuts and seeds, baking supplies, and noodles. It took us a few years to realize the ingredients we truly love, the ones we turn to again and again. Those are what we'll share with you here.

And then, each day, we figure out what we want to cook that night, based on what is fresh in the refrigerator and what is already in the cupboards. This way we keep to a budget, we know what is in the house, and we still get to make it up as we go along.

do you want to look in our cupboards?

In the Pantry

WHOLE GRAINS

We always make sure to have quinoa, millet, and brown rice in the house, since those are our favorite whole grains. We also love calrose medium-grain rice for stir-fry dishes, teff, oats, buckwheat groats, wild rice, black rice, and red rice.

OILS AND FATS

Danny and I both love to cook with extra-virgin olive oil for certain dishes. We save the good extra-virgin olive oil as a finishing oil or for dressings, since the good stuff is wasted as a cooking oil. I love coconut oil for anything like curries or dishes where the faint taste of coconut makes sense for the meal. Plus, it's the best oil for popcorn. We need peanut oil for stir-frying and grapeseed oil where we want an oil with a high smoke

point and neutral taste. Rice bran oil is also great for this purpose. We used to use canola all the time for this but we use less of it now. Our favorite savory fat is lard.

Okay, before you freak out about the word *LARD* here, let's take a breath. We're not talking about the kind of lard you find in the grocery store, which has been hydrogenated to keep it shelf stable. Do not buy this one. It's gross. But leaf lard, or rendered pork fat, is a completely different kind of fat. This was one of the most-used cooking fats in the United States before the 1950s and the invention of hydrogenated vegetable shortening. It's also recognized now as one of the healthiest fats available, right behind extra-virgin olive oil. We also love butter when we want that taste as part of the dish.

BEANS, PEAS, AND LENTILS

I really don't think we could live without beans. Although we occasionally use a can of beans at the last moment, we regularly soak and cook dry beans instead. It's not as time consuming as it sounds. Soaking happens without you being there. And the big pot of beans simmers on the back of the stove while we do other things.

We regularly keep cannellini beans, pinto beans, scarlet runner beans, chickpeas, midnight black beans, red beans, and flageolet beans, as well as adzuki beans, black-eyed peas, red lentils, green lentils, and edamame. (We're big fans of Rancho Gordo, which sells heirloom bean varieties.)

NUTS AND SEEDS

Pistachios. Walnuts. Almonds. Hazelnuts. Sunflower seeds. Peanuts. Pumpkin seeds. Cashews. These are always in our kitchen.

NOODLES AND PASTA

We particularly love a pasta made in Italy by a company called Jovial. They make spaghetti, capellini (Danny's favorite), penne, fusilli, and casarecce. Everyone who eats at our table loves this pasta. We also love quinoa pasta, as well as a pasta company called Tinkyada. (Everyone gluten-free knows them.) From those companies we find fettucine, shells, and macaroni. We also keep vermicelli rice noodles in our pantry.

VINEGARS

We love vinegar here. We always make sure to have champagne vinegar, red wine vinegar, apple cider vinegar, rice wine vinegar, sherry vinegar, and balsamic vinegar in the cupboard. We also usually have something a little more exotic like Banyuls vinegar and something made by our local farmer, usually blackberry vinegar from the summer.

SALT AND FRESHLY GROUND
BLACK PEPPER

Danny prefers kosher salt for cooking because it has a truly salty taste and pinches well between the fingers, so he can tell how much is going into a dish. I love a French sea salt, slightly gray and tasting of the sea. Danny teases me that I have a crush on a super-flaky salt we like to use for finishing dishes, and he's right. Pepper is a lot easier: we like to buy whole peppercorns and grind them ourselves.

CONDIMENTS

Oh, we could never run out of condiments we want to try. However, we always make sure we have Dijon mustard, gluten-free tamari, a good ketchup without any added sugar or high-fructose corn syrup, fish sauce, mirin, dry sherry, some kind of hot sauce, a chili sauce, red curry paste, prepared horseradish, and pomegranate molasses.

Smoked Paprika

Dukkah

Peppercorns

Coriander

Oregano

Berbere

Cinnamon

Fennel seeds

SPICES

This might be the most important part of our kitchen. Without fresh spices, our dishes would all start to taste the same. We buy spices from a local spice company where we watch them grind the spices in front of us. The difference in taste between those spices and the five-year-old ones in the cupboards I used to have is tremendous. We can't list all the spices we use in our kitchen here—you'll see them in the recipes—but the ones I simply couldn't live without are smoked paprika, dukkah, peppercorns, coriander, oregano, berbere, cinnamon, and fennel seeds.

FOOD WE DIDN'T MAKE

Honestly, we don't have much packaged food in our home. The more food I make from scratch, the more of a disappointment packaged foods are to our taste buds. However, a few foods we have in our cupboards: gluten-free cereal, usually some crunchy multigrain flakes, whole-grain crackers, and canned beans for an emergency. The one food we have no problem buying in cans is diced tomatoes and tomato paste.

Now I realize this list might look daunting. If you are just becoming confident in the kitchen, keep cooking. I don't want you to think you have to have all these ingredients to be a good cook. If you're going to choose a couple of vinegars, for example, buy champagne vinegar and a good rice wine vinegar. Over the course of the next few months, buy a bottle of vinegar that interests you. Over time, you'll build up your pantry and make your meals even more interesting.

"I DON'T WANT YOU TO THINK YOU HAVE TO HAVE ALL THESE INGREDIENTS TO BE A GOOD COOK."

In the Baking Pantry

GLUTEN-FREE FLOURS

There are more gluten-free flours in the world than there are gluten flours! So there are plenty for your choosing. Here are the ones we like to play with:

Almond flour

Buckwheat flour

Corn flour

Cornstarch

Garbanzo flour

Millet flour

Oat flour

Potato starch

Potato flour

Quinoa flour

Sorghum flour

Sweet rice flour

Teff flour

Now again, remember, we do this for a living. I never stop playing with the baked goods we make. You don't need to buy all these flours to eat well, gluten-free. See pages 31 and 32 to see how we combine some of these flours for a baking mix you could use for any of the baking recipes in this book.

SWEETENERS

We don't mind sugar in this house. When I'm making sugar cookies, I want that extra-fine baking sugar for a perfectly smooth texture. But I love playing with sweeteners as much as I like playing with flours. Some of the ones in our cupboards: muscovado sugar, whole cane sugar (known as sucanat or rapadura), honey, maple syrup, brown rice syrup, and Lyle's golden syrup.

MILKS

Danny is lactose intolerant, so traditional cow's milk and cream don't sit well with him. For that reason, I started playing with nontraditional milks. For a while we drank a lot of soy milk and rice milk, which are both good. Lately, I love making our own nut milks, such as hazelnut, almond, and cashew milk (see page 102 for that recipe).

BAKING SUPPLIES

We always have baking powder, baking soda, vanilla extract, some vanilla beans, chia seeds, psyllium husks, cocoa powder, yeast, and gelatin in the cupboards.

CHOCOLATE

Need I say more? We like good dark chocolate, preferably with a touch of sea salt, for some sweetness at the end of the evening. We also have semisweet and bittersweet baking chocolate in the cupboards for chocolate chip cookies. (The chocolate chips are okay but the cookies are better with chopped-up good chocolate.)

In the Refrigerator

There are going to be some interesting foods in our refrigerator, different every week. But what you will probably always find? Eggs, tofu, fresh chicken stock, several cheeses (sharp Cheddar, French feta, and soft chèvre, among others), some pickled vegetables and fermented things like sauerkraut, nut butters, and the various dips, sauces, and dressings for which you will find recipes in this book.

Coming into the House That Day

This will vary every single day, based on the season and what has caught our eye. It might be a dozen duck eggs from a farmer down the road. We might splurge on a little ahi tuna to celebrate something. Generally, it's going to be whatever vegetable or fruit is ripe at that moment. That's always the most exciting food in our home.

In the Drawers

POTS AND PANS

I love cast-iron skillets. They're hardy and dependable, take a beating, and keep going for years. They're also cheap. What other great cooking pans can you buy at the hardware store? We have a nine-inch and a twelve-inch cast-iron skillet that are in constant rotation on our stove. Danny prefers our twelve-inch stainless-steel pan. He also wants a nonstick egg pan in the cupboards. (Me? I could do everything with the cast-iron.)

I cannot imagine our kitchen without its blackened fourteen-inch flat-bottomed wok.

We love a Dutch oven, usually a big enamel-covered cast-iron pot that is great for everything from making soups and stews to baking crusty loaves of bread. We also need a big stockpot for making chicken stock each week. That's about it.

KNIVES

Chefs certainly love their knives. And it makes sense. If I have a good, sharp knife, I feel like I can chop anything like an expert. Danny and I both think that a chef's knife (ten or twelve inches long) will take care of most everything. I also like a paring knife for the small work and a utility knife, for anything else. Danny needs a boning knife for breaking down a chicken and any work with meat. Danny insists a serrated bread knife is necessary, and he's probably right. But that's it, no need for anything else.

SPATULAS AND SMALL TOOLS

When I found out I had to be gluten-free, I had to throw out all my old wooden spoons, rolling pins, and cutting boards. Wood is one of the few surfaces that traps gluten. (New wooden boards are fine, however.) I made the switch to rubber spatulas and I haven't regretted it. Perhaps my most-used kitchen tool is a metal fish spatula. Its thin flexibility makes it ideal for flipping food. I love a Microplane grater, for zesting citrus fruits and grating nutmeg. And a good pair of tongs takes care of nearly everything else.

BAKING TOOLS

Oh, this is one of my downfalls. A square Bundt pan at the thrift store? Of course I have to buy it! I wouldn't recommend that everyone owns this many baking pans, including the tiny fluted tart pans we still haven't used. In order to bake the recipes in this book, I'd recommend a nine-inch cake pan, a nine-inch pie pan, and a nine-inch springform pan. Our cupboards are filled with baking sheets (I like the rimmed ones), muffin tins, a one-pound bread loaf pan, and a nine by thirteen-inch casserole pan. Parchment paper or a Silpat makes life easier. And I think a small splurge on biscuit cutters is worth it for great buttermilk biscuits.

JARS AND STORAGE CONTAINERS

We need something to store all those flours, nuts, seeds, pastas, and grains in. After lots of fiddling and experimenting with sturdy plastic bins and fancy ones with pop tops, it turns out the storage containers we love the most are mason jars in pint, quart, and two-quart sizes.

APPLIANCES

We really aren't in the norm here. We have more appliances than the average cook and we just keep accruing them. Every time we prune down our kitchen to what is absolutely necessary, we realize we really want a juicer.

However, the appliances we use the most are a good blender (we have a Vitamix, which makes everything beautifully smooth in a matter of moments), a food processor, a spice grinder, a stand mixer (pretty much essential for gluten-free baking), a rice cooker, a pressure cooker, a waffle iron, a tortilla press, and a scale.

why you need a scale to bake out of this book

IF YOU LOOK AT THE BAKED-GOODS RECIPES IN this book such as the Apple Pie (page 309) or Chicken and Dumplings (page 77), you will notice that the recipes are written in grams. Before you panic, as some of you will, let me explain why.

* I want your baked goods to work. Baking by weight means the measurements will be accurate. Each gluten-free flour has a different weight. One cup of teff flour is far heavier than one cup of potato starch. If you bake by weight, you can replace the potato starch in the recipe with the accurate amount of teff flour, if you wanted a different taste or to use whole-grain flours instead. If you did this with cups, your cookies would not bake well.

* Since I want to give every one of you as much freedom as possible to play with the flavors and flours you have, a recipe that calls for 350 grams of a flour mix will work with your favorite combination of flour. A cup of a different gluten-free flour mix would have a different weight and the baked good would be too dense.

* Many people have other allergies besides gluten. If I use corn flour, but I put it in grams, someone who can't eat corn can still make the recipe successfully by replacing it with the same weight of sorghum or millet.

* People outside the U.S. bake by weight. In many places in the world, a cup holds more than a U.S. cup does. I want to make sure that everyone can make these recipes.

* A kitchen scale costs about thirty dollars. You would spend that much in flours making recipes that don't work.

* Measuring flours by weight means fewer dishes. Trust me—that alone makes this worth it.

* Every single person who has made the switch from cups to grams has written to tell me that she is thrilled she did. I have not heard from one person who bought a scale, tried to bake by weight, and then felt that it was worse than measuring by cups.

I know that baking by weight might be different for some of you, but believe me, it's worth the try. Eating gluten-free is new too, right? Might as well change it all in one fell swoop.

our flour mixes

FOR YEARS I SIFTED A LITTLE BIT OF EACH gluten-free flour I wanted to try into a bowl before I could begin baking. The mad scientist in me liked this just fine. But when our daughter arrived, I finally understood why so many of our readers asked if we could come up with mixes for our recipes. And so, we did.

Here's where gluten-free baking just grew easier for you. We have two mixes we use in our baking in this book, and each one will work for every recipe.

all-purpose gluten-free flour mix

I think of this as the transitional mix. We're all so used to white flour in our food that we kind of crave our gluten-free baked goods to be white as well. I understand. Try as I might, I could just never get behind a whole-grain pie crust. So I use this AP flour mix for pies, cakes, biscuits, and some cookies.

It's easy to make. All you have to do is mix up the following, based on the ratio of 40 percent whole-grain flour to 60 percent starches and white flours.

400 grams millet flour

300 grams sweet rice flour

300 grams potato starch

Dump them all in a large container (we like the large plastic containers restaurants use to store their food, which we buy at restaurant supply stores) and shake. Shake and shake and shake harder until all the flours have become one color. There. That's your flour. Whenever you want to bake, just reach for that container and measure out how many grams you need for that recipe.

Here's one of the main reasons I write my recipes in weight. What do you do with this mix if you can't do rice flour because of your rice allergy? Just substitute tapioca flour or arrowroot instead. You can't find millet? Try sorghum for your whole-grain flour, or buckwheat.

We don't think of this as OUR mix but *yours*. Make the mix that works for you, based on what flours you can eat, what you can find in your local store, or just what you have in the kitchen at the moment.

Think 40 percent whole-grain flour and 60 percent starches and white flours and you'll have flour in your kitchen for all your baking needs.

whole-grain gluten-free flour mix

More and more, I use this mix when I'm baking. Not only do I appreciate the health benefits of whole-grain baking over starchy flours, but I also love the flavors of whole-grain flours. Buckwheat has a gentle nutty taste. Teff has a faint taste of chocolate and molasses. Millet has a neutral taste, so it plays well with others. Amaranth is grassy. Quinoa is deeply savory, so it's great in quiches. Garbanzo flour tastes like. . . garbanzo beans. Oat flour tastes like oats.

When you mix whole-grain gluten-free flours, you can really build flavors with flours. This is brand new for baking. Most people aren't thinking about flours as a flavor builder. But when you taste the chocolate chunk cookies with teff flour and hazelnuts in this cookbook, you'll understand why.

300 grams teff flour

300 grams millet flour

300 grams buckwheat flour

Simply combine the flours in equal parts by weight.

Again, you can switch in the ones you want. I can tolerate gluten-free oats, so I use oat flour often, particularly in breads. Many celiacs cannot tolerate oats, however, which is why I don't recommend them in the basic recipe. I prefer the taste of raw buckwheat groats ground into a flour over toasted buckwheat flour. However, if you don't want to grind your own flour, skip the buckwheat and switch to sorghum instead.

And that's it. Again, mix them all up in a large container and keep it on your counter. Whenever you want to bake, simply pull the flour container toward you and pull out the scale.

Since we bake by weight instead of using cups, you can make these recipes if you are reading this book and can eat gluten. Simply substitute the same number of grams of traditional all-purpose gluten flour to make the biscuits and sausage gravy or millet waffles. Or, buy yourself a bag of buckwheat groats or quinoa flour. The flours we use in this book may be unfamiliar but they are great whole-grain flours with an interesting array of tastes. I think anyone interested in baking would like playing with these flours.

Finally, in some of the bready recipes, the doughs that rely more on gluten than muffins, cookies, or crumbles would, we use a teaspoon or two of psyllium husks. These husks are high in dietary fiber, have no real taste, and absorb water like you wouldn't believe. (They are the main ingredient in Metamucil, which warns on the side of the package that you must use enough water to mix these or beware of choking. That should tell you how much psyllium expands in water.) With these properties, a bit of psyllium husk can replicate some of the properties of gluten in doughs. Since I don't do well with xanthan or guar gum—they cause me digestive upset—and psyllium is widely available in every grocery store, we think these are a much better alternative for gluten-free baking than the expensive gums. (The whole husks are more effective in gluten-free baking, but the psyllium husk powder will do if that's the only kind you can find.)

Other than the psyllium, you will find that the baked goods in this book are free of any truly unfamiliar ingredients. In the end, gluten-free baking is simply baking. And baking is always good.

NOW, LET'S START COOKING.

breakfast for dinner

SOMETIMES THERE ARE NO MORE BEAUTIFUL WORDS THAN THESE: "HOW ABOUT BREAKFAST FOR dinner!" How excited my brother and I were when we were kids and heard those words. The day was turned upside down. Breakfast. For dinner. Fried eggs on top of waffles. At night. When I was little this concept was as surreal and intriguing as a David Lynch movie was in my twenties.

How little we knew—my mom had probably run out of steam on those occasional days. A long day, kids with clamoring demands, more left to do? Oh hell, let's just have waffles. That's easy.

That didn't take the magic away for me. We wanted to eat bacon and eggs, pancakes and maple syrup, at the dinner table, and not have to go to school afterward. That's all.

I'm still like that. All I need to make a simple dish feel like dinner is this: put an egg on top of it. I wilt dark greens fast in hot extra-virgin olive oil, with a few red pepper flakes, and a pinch of sea salt. Plop them on top of a bowl of warm polenta, perch a poached egg on top and I'm done.

Even though we are the parents now, Danny and I both love breakfast-for-dinner nights. We loved introducing our daughter to huevos rancheros, and we say yes every time she asks for it again (with a side of fresh avocado). In the fall, when we want to eat sweet potatoes every day, we make up a quick hash of sweet potatoes, soft onions, chorizo, and fried eggs. After making oatmeal for breakfast for months, I finally decided to stir some oats slowly, with chicken stock, adding in spinach and mushrooms at the end. We could eat this oat risotto every week.

Of course, sometimes a good breakfast seems to require something bready to sop up the gravy or absorb the honey to be satisfying. And so we played with gluten-free biscuits and sausage gravy, chicken and waffles, and lemon ricotta pancakes.

After Danny made bacon-tomato jam one summer day, we had to finally go on the quest for good gluten-free sandwich bread so we could make fried egg sandwiches with it.

A frittata with roasted potatoes and Irish Cheddar, baked eggs with collard greens, or grits with smoked salmon—these dishes satisfy us on the nights we want breakfast again. And of course—wink, wink—if you're stumped for breakfast ideas when you're gluten-free, there's no reason you couldn't eat these in the morning as well.

baked egg casserole with collard greens and bacon

We love our dark greens all year long but particularly when the sky outside is slate gray and spitting rain. At the end of a long morning like that, we love this dish of eggs puffed up around sautéed collard greens, goat cheese, and creamy cashew milk. And bacon, of course. The occasional bacon makes life much better. Think of a frittata but in casserole form, the frittata's much more casual cousin.

1 tablespoon neutral-tasting oil (such as canola) or butter

1 medium bunch collard greens

4 slices thick-cut bacon, diced into 1-inch pieces

$1/2$ red onion, peeled and chopped

6 ounces chèvre, crumbled

8 large eggs

$1/2$ cup cashew milk (see page 102) or $1/2$ cup heavy cream

Kosher salt and freshly ground black pepper

$1/2$ cup freshly grated Parmesan cheese

Preparing to bake. Preheat the oven to 375°F. Grease a 9 x 13-inch casserole dish with oil or butter, depending on your taste. (You could also use a square 8 x 8-inch pan here.)

Cutting the collard greens. With a sharp knife, cut the collard green leaves away from the stems. Pile 4 of the leaves on top of each other. Roll them up to make a shape like a cigar. Cut into the "cigar" at 1-inch intervals. This will leave you with ribbons of collard greens. (This technique is known as chiffonade.) Repeat with the remaining collard greens. Separate all the ribbons from each other and put them in a large bowl.

Cooking the bacon. Set a large skillet over medium-high heat. When the skillet is hot, add the bacon pieces. Cook, stirring occasionally, until the bacon has crisped and the fat has rendered into the pan, about 10 minutes. Remove the bacon and set aside.

Cooking the collard greens. Let the bacon fat grow hot for a moment, then add the ribbons of collard greens. Cook, stirring quickly, until the greens have wilted a bit but before they have shriveled, about 5 minutes. Remove the collard greens from the pan and arrange them in the greased dish.

Cooking the onion. If there is still plenty of fat remaining in the skillet, throw in the onions. If not, add a smidge of oil to the skillet before cooking the onions. Cook the onions, stirring occasionally, until they are soft and starting to brown, about 7 minutes. Put the onions and chèvre on top of the collard greens in the casserole. Scatter the bacon on top.

Finishing the casserole. When the greens, bacon, and onion have cooled, whisk together the eggs and cashew milk and season with salt and pepper. When the eggs are beaten well and fluffy, pour them over the other ingredients. Use a rubber spatula to push everything around gently until the eggs, vegetables, bacon, and onions are evenly distributed. Top with the grated Parmesan.

Baking the casserole. Bake the casserole until it has puffed up, the eggs feel set, and the top is beginning to brown, 20 to 30 minutes.

Serve it hot. It's also great the next day, cold.

Feeds 4 to 6

FEEL LIKE PLAYING?

You can easily make and assemble this the night before a big brunch gathering. Just wake up and slide it in the oven.

Any sturdy dark green will work here. We always love kale. Chard would be great too, as would spinach. Be aware that we grow northern collard greens here in the Pacific Northwest, which are more tender than the southern counterparts. If you have southern collard greens, you might want to blanch the leaves before cooking them.

If you can't have cashew milk, you can use regular cow's milk cream here. And I think cheeses like Gruyère or Havarti would be great too.

grits with smoked salmon and eggs over easy

Whenever I think of grits, I think of a scene from *My Cousin Vinny*. He walks into a diner for breakfast, a New Jersey tough guy in the Deep South for the first time, and says, "Just what is a grit?" Poor guy, not knowing about grits. Their creamy corny goodness makes breakfast or dinner a delight. Add in some smoked salmon and throw a fried egg on top? Done.

1 teaspoon kosher salt

1 cup stone-milled grits

4 tablespoons (½ stick) unsalted butter

4 large eggs

⅓ pound smoked salmon

COOKING THE GRITS. Set a large pot over high heat and add 3 cups water and the salt. Bring the water to a boil. Slowly, pour the grits into the boiling water, stirring all the time. Bring the water to a boil again, then turn the heat down to medium-low. Here's where you decide what kind of grits you want to eat. In a rush? Cook the grits, stirring frequently, until they are just cooked, about 7 minutes. They will be coarse and a little stiff but delicious. Have a little more time and want those grits creamier? Stir and stir. The more you stir and cook, the creamier the grits will be. After about 30 minutes, they should be pretty heavenly. If you want to be a purist, and experience more heaven, cook them even longer. When the grits are cooked to your liking, add 2 tablespoons of the butter and stir until the butter has fully combined with the grits. Take the pot off the heat and cover it while you fix the eggs.

FRYING THE EGGS. Set a large skillet over medium-high heat. Add the remaining 2 tablespoons butter. When the butter has melted crack the eggs into the skillet. Let them sit. Pinch a little salt onto the yolks. When the whites have turned white, and the edges a bit brown, flip the eggs. Cook them for 30 seconds then turn off the heat.

To serve, dollop grits into each bowl. Scatter the smoked salmon on top then put an egg on it.

Feeds 4

FEEL LIKE PLAYING?

Some might feel I need to apologize again for not putting cheese in these grits. I agree that cheese grits are a gift. When you're cooking the grits, put a handful of grated sharp Cheddar or dollops of soft goat cheese into the pot and stir.

lemon-ricotta pancakes

Whenever we have some leftover fresh ricotta—and darn, there's a problem—we make these lemon-ricotta pancakes. They're lovely and lemony, creamy with the ricotta and not too dense with flour. You might think that beating the egg whites is a bit fussy, but the lightness you'll find from this is worth the small amount of effort. Just try to make them last longer than 5 minutes.

$1^{1}/_{3}$ cups fresh ricotta (page 175)

4 large eggs, separated

3 tablespoons sugar

$1^{1}/_{2}$ tablespoons grated lemon zest

105 grams All-Purpose Gluten-Free
    Flour Mix (page 31)

$^{1}/_{2}$ teaspoon baking soda

$^{1}/_{2}$ teaspoon kosher salt

Pinch cream of tartar

Melted butter for oiling the pan

COMBINING THE WET INGREDIENTS. Whisk together the ricotta, egg yolks, sugar, and lemon zest in a large bowl. Set aside.

COMBINING THE DRY INGREDIENTS. Whisk together the flour, baking soda, and salt in a large bowl.

Scatter the dry ingredients over the wet ingredients and fold them together with a rubber spatula until just combined.

BEATING THE EGG WHITES. Put the egg whites in the bowl of a stand mixer (or you can use a bowl, a whisk, and your strong arms). Beat the egg whites with the cream of tartar until they form soft peaks, about 5 minutes. Fold the egg whites into the batter gently. Remember that you don't want to crush that lovely fresh ricotta or the structure of the egg whites.

MAKING THE PANCAKES. Set a cast-iron skillet over medium-high heat. Grease the pan liberally (and by liberally, I mean a lot) with butter. Pour the pancake batter into the buttered pan, about $^{1}/_{4}$ cup at a time. When bubbles have started to form and pop on top of the pancakes, flip them. Cook for about 1 minute more, and set aside on a plate. Continue until you have cooked all the pancakes.

Feeds 6

sweet potato–chorizo hash

I love sweet potatoes. Danny loves chorizo. He also makes a darned fine hash. With all this, we had no choice but to make this dish.

This hash is great in the fall, when the sweet potatoes are at their freshest and the starting-to-be-dreary skies demand some kind of color. We like a fried egg on top (see page 47).

2 large sweet potatoes, peeled and cut into large chunks

2 tablespoons kosher salt

2 links (about 6 ounces) fresh Mexican chorizo sausage

5 tablespoons extra-virgin olive oil

1 medium onion, peeled and sliced

2 cloves garlic, peeled and sliced

2 teaspoons chopped fresh sage or 1 teaspoon dried Kosher salt and freshly ground black pepper

4 fried eggs, for serving

COOKING THE SWEET POTATOES. Set a large pot over high heat. Put the sweet potatoes and enough cold water to cover them by 1 inch in the pot. Add the salt. Bring the water to a boil. Add the sausage links. Cook until you can run a knife through the sweet potato pieces easily, about 10 minutes. (The internal temperature of the sausages should be about 155°F.) Drain them.

BROWNING THE SAUSAGES. Slice the hot sausages. Put a large skillet over medium-high heat. Pour in 3 tablespoons of oil. When the oil is hot, add the sausage slices and cook until the slices are brown on the bottom, about 5 minutes. Flip them over and brown the other side, about 3 minutes. Remove from the pan. Keep all the fat and crispy bits in the pan.

COOKING THE POTATOES. Add the sweet potato chunks to the hot fat in the skillet. Cook the potatoes until they are brown on the bottom, about 3 minutes. Push the sweet potatoes off to the side of the skillet. Add the onion and garlic and cook, stirring frequently, until the onions are softened and beginning to brown, about 5 minutes. Add the sage and cook until the scent is released into the room, about 1 minute. Add back the sausage and cook the hash until everything is browned and mingling together well. Taste a bit and season with salt and pepper.

Put some of the hash onto a plate. Top with a fried egg. Apply salt and pepper at will.

Feeds 4

irish frittata

When Danny and I contemplated our honeymoon, we couldn't decide for a while: Ireland or Italy? Danny's pure Irish, an Ahern. He's never visited the home country. But then, there was all that incredible food in Italy to consider. We ended up in Umbria, high in the hills above Assisi, happy.

We frequently make frittatas, a crisp puffed-egg dish filled with roasted vegetables or sausages. Really, any good food will do. One morning I was talking to Danny about colcannon, the northern Irish dish of mashed potatoes, cabbage, and cream. He wanted some, right away. We had some roasted potatoes left over from dinner the night before, a bunch of Lacinato kale, and some Irish Cheddar. So we made an Irish frittata—our two honeymoon destinations in one dish.

2 large Yukon gold potatoes, peeled and chopped into 1-inch cubes

3 cloves garlic, peeled

1 sprig fresh rosemary

Kosher salt

$\frac{1}{4}$ cup extra-virgin olive oil

1 bunch Lacinato kale (you can also use green curly kale or Red Russian kale)

7 large eggs, at room temperature

$\frac{1}{2}$ cup grated Irish Cheddar cheese

Preparing to cook. Preheat the oven to 450°F.

Blanching the potatoes. Set a large pot three-quarters filled with cold water on high heat. Add the potatoes, garlic, and rosemary along with enough salt to make the water taste like the ocean. Cook the potatoes until tender to a knife, about 10 minutes. Drain the potatoes.

Roasting the potatoes. Pour the drained potatoes into a large cast-iron skillet. Pour a glug of oil (about 2 tablespoons) over them. Toss the potatoes around in the skillet to make sure they are completely coated in the oil. Put the potatoes in the oven and roast them, tossing them occasionally, until they are browned and crisp on all sides, 7 to 8 minutes. Take the potatoes out of the oven and allow them to cool to room temperature.

Cooking the kale. With a sharp knife, cut the kale leaves away from the stems. Pile 4 of the halves on top of each other. Roll them up to make a shape like a cigar. Cut into the "cigar" at 1-inch intervals.

This will leave you with ribbons of kale. (This technique is known as chiffonade.) Repeat with the remaining kale. Separate all the ribbons from each other.

Set the large skillet over medium-high heat. Pour in the remaining 2 tablespoons oil. When the oil is hot, add the kale. Cook, stirring frequently, until the kale is bright green and shrunken in size, about 3 minutes.

MAKING THE FRITTATA. Turn on the broiler. Add the roasted potatoes to the skillet with the kale and stir. Beat the eggs until they are frothy. Pour the beaten eggs into the pan. When it looks as though the eggs have started to set, gently lift up the edge closest to you from its place with a thin rubber spatula and allow the uncooked egg to run underneath. Lower the skillet onto the burner again and swirl it gently to distribute the eggs evenly. Cook the eggs until they are no longer runny, about 40 seconds. Sprinkle the Cheddar cheese over the top of the frittata. Slide it under the broiler and bake until the frittata is firm and the eggs puffed up and browning, 3 to 4 minutes. Take the frittata out of the oven.

Run a rubber spatula gently around the edges of the frittata to loosen it. You can now flip over the frittata onto a waiting plate for a lovely presentation. Or, you can take slices right out of the pan.

Feeds 8

FEEL LIKE PLAYING?

This is how you make any frittata you want to eat. Use this recipe as the template and play. Throw in some roasted vegetables left over from dinner. Try Italian sausage or chunks of ham. When it's asparagus season, we like roasted asparagus and not much else in our frittatas. If you have vegetarian friends coming over for dinner, try chanterelle mushrooms, leeks, and Asiago cheese. You can make a frittata every week of your life and not make the same one twice.

fried egg sandwiches with bacon-tomato jam

I love so many kinds of foods, but if you gave me my choice for breakfast every morning, it would probably be this dish. There's a good restaurant in Seattle called Skillet, which started as a food truck in a Silverstream trailer. They're famous for their bacon jam—delicious. However, Danny wanted to make his own rather than buying a jar. (Psst, I like this one better.) Pair it with a fried egg with a slightly runny yolk between a couple of pieces of crisp toasted bread? Heaven.

Bacon-tomato jam (makes 1 pint)

6 pounds (about 15) ripe plum tomatoes

3 tablespoons extra-virgin olive oil

1 teaspoon kosher salt

2 slices thick-cut bacon or 4 thin slices

2 medium shallots, peeled and chopped

2 cloves garlic, peeled and chopped

2 sprigs fresh basil, chopped

2 tablespoons sherry vinegar

$1/2$ small green apple, peeled and diced small

Freshly ground black pepper

Fried egg sandwich

Fat for frying

Eggs

Kosher salt and freshly ground black pepper

Gluten-Free Sandwich Bread (page 48)

ROASTING THE TOMATOES. Preheat the oven to 500°F. Lay a piece of parchment paper on a baking sheet. Put 5 spoons on a saucer in the freezer. You'll need them in a bit.

Cut the tomatoes in half lengthwise, then put them in a large bowl. Drizzle the tomatoes with 2 tablespoons of the oil. Sprinkle the tomatoes with the kosher salt and toss them in the bowl. Move them to the prepared baking sheet.

Roast the tomatoes in the oven at 500°F for 5 minutes, then turn down the oven to 350°F. Roast the tomatoes until they start to release their juices and shrivel a bit, about 1 hour. Remove from the oven.

continued . . .

COOKING THE BACON. Set a large skillet over medium-high heat. Pour in the remaining tablespoon of oil. Cut the bacon into 1-inch pieces. Spread out the bacon pieces in the hot pan and let them cook. This will render out the bacon fat, which you want. Cook the bacon, stirring occasionally, until the bacon pieces have browned, about 10 minutes. Remove the bacon from the pan to a paper towel–topped plate.

COOKING THE VEGETABLES. Turn down the heat under the skillet to medium. Wait a moment, then add the shallots and garlic to the hot bacon fat. Cook, stirring frequently, to avoid burning the garlic. (If you do burn the garlic, turn off the heat on the stove, throw away the garlic, and take a breath. Then, chop some more garlic and start over again.) Cook until the shallots and garlic are softened and browned, about 3 minutes. Toss in the basil and cook until it releases its fragrance, about 1 minute.

MAKING THE JAM. Add the vinegar to the skillet and let it reduce for 1 minute. Immediately add the apple pieces and roasted tomatoes. Cook, stirring frequently, until the tomatoes and apple have broken down and the sauce has begun to thicken, 30 to 45 minutes.

If the bottom of the jam feels like it is in danger of burning, turn down the heat. It's worth a little more time to make sure you don't have burned bacon-tomato jam.

Add a pinch each of salt and pepper. Taste the jam. If it needs more seasoning, add it here.

When the jam feels thickened, pull one of the cold spoons out of the oven. Drop some of the jam onto the cold spoon. Wait a moment then turn over the spoon. (Probably best to stand over the sink with this.) If the jam falls off the spoon, keep cooking it for a few more moments. Keep stirring the jam and checking it with a cold spoon every 5 minutes until the jam stays on the spoon. Turn off the heat and stir in the bacon pieces.

FEEL LIKE PLAYING?

As much as I love this bacon-tomato jam, I also love the Smoked Paprika–Chipotle Sauce (page 220), the Ginger-Scallion Sauce (page 248), or Ranchero Sauce (page 50) spread on bread for this sandwich.

MAKING THE FRIED EGG SANDWICH. Now that you have the bacon-tomato jam, all you have to do is fry up some eggs. That doesn't sound hard, right? But there are plenty of details to think about before you begin. How many eggs will you be frying? One for yourself? Use a small skillet, such as an 8-inch size. Trying to fry up eggs for everyone in the house? Use the largest skillet you own. (We have a 14-inch cast-iron skillet for that.) Or, if you're like my mom in the 1970s, you have a plug-in griddle, long and rectangular. You could make a lot of eggs on that.

What kind of skillet should you use? I like cast-iron skillets, but I like them for everything. Danny prefers the small nonstick pan we own. We call it the egg pan because we use it only for eggs. It holds heat well and cleans up easily. However, many folks have issues with nonstick pans, so you need to choose for yourself.

One thing is certain—you're going to have better fried eggs if you warm up the pan before you attempt to fry them. Put your chosen skillet on the burner and set it to medium-low heat. While it's warming up, pull out your eggs, find the fat of your choice, and get ready to fry.

Let's talk about the fat. Grapeseed oil is good. Extra-virgin olive oil is delicious for crispy edges. Bacon grease is a decadent pleasure. Still, in this house, nothing beats a couple of pats of good, creamy butter. You decide. Just do yourself a favor and don't skimp on the fat. Trying a tiny teaspoon will leave the eggs dry and the pan a horror to clean afterward.

Frying the eggs. Set a large skillet over medium-high heat. Add the fat of your choice into the pan. When it's sizzling, gently slide the egg from the shell into the skillet. Don't touch it. Let it cook for a bit.

Here's a point of difference between me and Danny. I like to muddle the yolk a bit by poking it with a fork. I like a scrim of cooked yolk in my fried egg, fully cooked. Danny likes his yolks jiggly and intact. Cook yours the way you prefer.

When the whites of the egg have grown fully white, and then a bit browned at the edges, you can pull the fried egg out of the pan. That's a sunny-side-up fried egg. (Danny loves this, with its runny yolk.) Or, you can carefully flip the egg and fry the other side too. That's eggs over easy. (This is what I prefer.) If you do this, cook the egg for only 30 seconds or so. Overdone eggs are so sad.

Sprinkle just a touch of salt and pepper over the eggs. Pull the skillet off the heat.

Grab two slices of bread. Spread each with some bacon-tomato jam. Gently, lay a fried egg on one slice of bread and cover with the other. Repeat until you have as many fried egg sandwiches with bacon-tomato jam as you want to serve.

Oh, and clean that egg pan now. It's worth the wait for the first bite, believe me. Eat.

Makes 4 sandwiches

gluten-free sandwich bread

Tell you the truth, I didn't care about sandwich bread for years after I went gluten-free. I maybe had six sandwiches in six years. Give me a warm corn tortilla or a buttermilk biscuit any day over a boring old sandwich. And then our daughter turned three and started preschool. I understood. I started working on sandwich bread.

For months I thought about flours, wondered about the right texture, and baked loaves. Some of them were as heavy as Sisyphus's rock. Some were good. Some of them were very good. But our favorite ones required a lot of fussy techniques and we didn't think you'd like that much.

And then I saw the light. For a gluten-free sandwich bread that's light and chewy, with a crunchy crust, you need a few things: the right mix of flours, baking powder, a few eggs. And to let go of the notion that the dough should look anything like bread dough. In fact, it's more like pancake batter when you pour it in the pan.

These days, I make at least one loaf of this bread a week. Lucy's happy with her sandwiches and so are we.

Baking spray or vegetable oil for greasing pan

100 grams whole-grain, high-protein flour (we use buckwheat or oat flour)

235 grams All-Purpose Gluten-Free Flour Mix (page 31)

15 grams whole psyllium husks (see page 33)

1 envelope (2¼ teaspoons) active dry yeast

2 teaspoons kosher salt

3 large eggs, at room temperature

1¼ cups hot water, about 110°F

4 tablespoons (½ stick) unsalted butter, melted and cooled

1 large egg, beaten

PREPARING TO BAKE. Grease a 9 x 5-inch loaf pan with baking spray or oil.

COMBINING THE DRY INGREDIENTS. In a medium bowl, combine the whole-grain flour, all-purpose flour mix, psyllium husks, yeast, and salt. Whisk together until they are one color. Set aside.

MIXING THE WET INGREDIENTS. In the bowl of a stand mixer, whip up the eggs with the paddle attachment on medium speed. Add the hot water and butter. Mix until the water has cooled to room temperature, about 5 minutes.

MAKING THE BATTER. With the mixer running on medium speed, pour in the dry ingredients, a bit at a time. Let the mixer continue to run to whip some air into the batter. The final dough will be like thick, yet pourable pancake batter. (If the dough is thicker than that, add a dribble of hot water at a time until your batter is the consistency of pancake batter.)

LETTING IT RISE. Pour the batter into the prepared pan. Allow the dough to rise until it is nearly at the top of the pan, about 1 hour.

BAKING THE BREAD. Heat the oven to 450°F. Brush some of the beaten egg onto the top of the bread dough. Slide the loaf pan into the oven, close the oven door, and bake the bread until the top is brown, the edges of the bread are pulling away from the pan, and the internal temperature registers 200°F on a thermometer, 30 to 45 minutes.

TAKE THE BREAD OUT OF THE OVEN. Let it cool in the pan for 20 minutes, then turn the bread out onto a wire rack. Do NOT slice until the bread has come to room temperature.

Makes 1 loaf of bread

FEEL LIKE PLAYING?

This bread recipe also makes great dinner rolls. Let the dough rise in a greased bowl, instead of the sandwich bread pan. When the dough's texture has tightened enough that you can knead it—about 2 hours—divide the dough into 6 pieces. Roll each one into a large ball. Let them proof on a parchment-covered baking sheet for another 30 minutes. Brush them with an egg wash. Bake the rolls until they have a brown crust and reach an internal temperature of at least 180°F, about 25 minutes.

huevos rancheros

One evening, Danny and I were at the Mexican restaurant on Vashon, Lucy jumping up and down in the booth. Since I was in the middle of working on this chapter, my ears perked up when I heard the waiter try to describe ranchero sauce to a customer: "It's the red sauce, not spicy. It goes great with eggs." My mouth started to water, thinking of huevos rancheros. We went home that night and started playing with this sauce.

Our friend Jorge runs a taco truck on the island. We gave him some of these huevos rancheros. He approves.

2 dried red chiles, seeds removed
(we like guajillos)

2 tablespoons neutral-tasting oil
(we like grapeseed)

$\frac{1}{2}$ medium onion, peeled and chopped

2 cloves garlic, peeled and sliced

$\frac{1}{2}$ teaspoon ground cumin

$\frac{1}{2}$ teaspoon chili powder

One 15-ounce can diced tomatoes, drained
(we like fire-roasted tomatoes)

$\frac{1}{4}$ small bunch fresh cilantro, chopped

Corn tortillas, for serving

Fried eggs, for serving

SOAKING THE CHILES. Set a small skillet over high heat. Add the chiles. Cover with water. Simmer the chiles until they are softened, about 30 minutes. (Check the water level. If you have the heat up too high, you might run out of water. Add more if it's getting low.) Remove the chiles from the skillet and set aside.

MAKING THE SAUCE. Set the skillet back on the stove, this time at medium-high heat. Add the oil to the skillet. When the oil is hot, add the onion and garlic. Cook, stirring occasionally, until the onion and garlic are soft and starting to brown, about 5 minutes. Add the cumin and chili powder and cook until the spices release their scent, about 1 minute. Add the softened chiles and the tomatoes. Simmer the mixture on low heat,

FEEL LIKE PLAYING?

If you want the flavors to be even more assertive, you can toast the chiles and some cumin seeds instead of using ground cumin.

It's tempting to make this super-spicy but the kids probably won't like it. And then it won't be ranchero sauce.

Honestly, if I have a warm corn tortilla, a slather of this sauce, and some grated Monterey Jack cheese, I'm happy with lunch.

stirring occasionally, until the tomatoes have broken down, about 20 minutes. Turn off the heat and allow the sauce to cool before proceeding.

FINISHING THE SAUCE. Transfer the sauce to a blender along with the cilantro. Puree the sauce until everything has become a single color. Put the sauce back in the skillet to heat. You want a thick sauce, not as thin as pasta sauce. If the sauce seems thicker than you would like, add some water and stir.

You can use the ranchero sauce immediately. However, like every other sauce or soup, it tastes better the next day.

To make the huevos rancheros, warm up a corn tortilla on the burner of your stove, taking care not to burn it. (Admittedly, this is easier with a gas stove.) Dollop a couple of tablespoons of the ranchero sauce on top of the warm tortilla. Top with a fried egg.

Eat.

Makes enough sauce for 6 huevos rancheros

chicken and waffles

It just sounds good, doesn't it? Chicken and waffles. This combination might seem strange at first, but think of this: fried chicken with a crackling crisp crust on top of soft buttermilk waffles, drizzled in honey. I'm getting hungry just typing this.

Fried chicken

1 quart buttermilk

¼ cup paprika

1 tablespoon plus 2 teaspoons garlic powder

1½ teaspoons each kosher salt and freshly ground black pepper

One 3½-pound fryer chicken, cut into 2 breasts, 2 legs, and 2 wings (save the rest for stock)

280 grams All-Purpose Gluten-Free Flour Mix (page 31)

1 tablespoon onion powder

1 gallon canola oil (we also like safflower or sunflower oil)

Waffles

240 grams All-Purpose Gluten-Free Flour Mix (page 31)

1 tablespoon baking powder

1 teaspoon kosher salt

6 tablespoons honey

1 cup buttermilk

2 large eggs, at room temperature

4 tablespoons (½ stick) unsalted butter, melted and cooled

Grapeseed, sunflower, or canola oil, for greasing the waffle iron

MARINATING THE CHICKEN. Mix the buttermilk, 1 tablespoon of the paprika, 2 teaspoons of the garlic powder, and 1 teaspoon each of the salt and pepper together. Marinate the chicken pieces in the buttermilk mixture for at least 4 to 6 hours.

COMBINING THE DRY INGREDIENTS FOR THE WAFFLES. Whisk together the flour, baking powder, and salt in a bowl. Sift them through a fine-mesh sieve into a large bowl. Set aside.

COMBINING THE LIQUIDS FOR THE WAFFLES. Stir together 3 tablespoons of the honey, the buttermilk, eggs, and melted butter in a large bowl.

MAKING THE WAFFLE BATTER. Make a well in the center of the flour mixture. Pour in the liquids. Stir them together with a rubber spatula until the batter is well combined.

WAITING. Allow the batter to sit for at least 30 minutes before you make the waffles. (If you have the time, make the batter the night before. The flavors really intensify.)

MAKING THE SPICED FLOUR MIX FOR THE CHICKEN. In a bowl, mix together the flour, the remaining 3 tablespoons of the paprika, the remaining tablespoon of garlic powder, the onion powder, and the remaining ½ teaspoon each salt and pepper. Set aside.

PREPARING TO BAKE. Preheat the oven to 450°F.

FEEL LIKE PLAYING?

Of course, if you don't feel like having waffles, this is just a good fried chicken recipe.

We like different herbs in our waffles: rosemary, tarragon, thyme. Try some of those.

If you can't do dairy, you can make "buttermilk" out of your favorite nondairy milk. Simply put 1 tablespoon of lemon juice or white vinegar at the bottom of a measuring cup and pour in 1 cup of your favorite milk. Stir and wait a few moments.

COATING THE CHICKEN. Set a large Dutch oven on medium-high heat. Pour in the oil. Heat the oil to 375°F. When the oil is fully heated, take each of the chicken breasts out of the buttermilk mixture and coat well in the flour mixture. Make sure every inch is coated and then shake the chicken breast to remove any excess flour. Repeat with the remaining pieces of chicken.

FRYING THE CHICKEN. Take a pair of tongs and put the 2 chicken breasts into the hot oil. Cook until the crust is golden brown, about 5 minutes. Remove the chicken breasts from the hot oil and put them in a casserole pan. Repeat with the legs and wings. (The legs and wings will take less time to brown, since they are smaller pieces and the oil will be hotter from all the cooking.)

FINISHING THE CHICKEN IN THE OVEN. Put the casserole dish into the oven and cook for 15 to 20 minutes, depending on the thickness of the breasts, or until the internal temperature of the chicken is 155°F in the thickest part of the breast.

PREPARING TO PUT IT ALL TOGETHER. Reduce the oven temperature to 250°F.

MAKING THE WAFFLES. While the chicken is in the oven, turn on the waffle iron. When it has come to heat, brush both surfaces of the waffle iron with oil. Pour about ⅓ cup of the waffle batter onto the bottom of the iron. Cook until the waffle is well browned, about 5 minutes. Put the waffle into the oven to keep warm. Repeat until you have made all the waffles and they are warming in the oven.

To serve, put a waffle on a plate, top it with 2 pieces of fried chicken, and drizzle with honey.

Feeds 4

savory oat risotto with mushrooms and spinach

It never occurred to me to use rolled oats for anything other than oatmeal until I went gluten-free. For years, I thought I wouldn't eat oatmeal again. Traditional oats are usually cross-contaminated with wheat from the way they are grown, transported, and manufactured. Luckily, in the last five years, several companies have started producing gluten-free oats. I was so happy to have them that I began playing with other dishes besides porridge and cookies.

A friend of ours talked one day about her favorite oats dish: curried oats. What? Once I heard that, I realized oats can be for dinner, not just for breakfast.

Now, I should say that some folks can't tolerate oats, even if the oats are grown in a dedicated gluten-free field and transported in a gluten-free truck and manufactured in a gluten-free plant. You should ask before you serve someone this risotto. However, you could serve it to me any time you feel like it.

1½ quarts chicken stock

2 tablespoons extra-virgin olive oil

1 leek, white part only, thinly sliced

2 cloves garlic, peeled and sliced

1 tablespoon chopped fresh thyme (you could also use 2 teaspoons of dried thyme)

1 cup caramelized onions (page 101)

2 cups gluten-free rolled oats

2 cups sliced wild mushrooms or cremini mushrooms

2 cups chopped fresh spinach, stems removed

PREPARING TO COOK. Set a large pot over medium-high heat. Pour in the chicken stock and cook until it comes to a boil. Turn down the heat to medium-low and let the chicken stock simmer while you start cooking the risotto.

COOKING THE AROMATICS. Set a deep, wide skillet over medium-high heat and pour in the oil. When the oil is hot, add the leek and garlic. Cook, stirring frequently, until the leek and garlic are softened and beginning to brown, about 3 minutes. Add the fresh thyme and cook until the scent releases into the room, about 1 minute. Add the caramelized onions and cook, stirring, until they are hot, about 3 minutes.

continued . . .

Cooking the oats. Pour the oats into the skillet and cook, stirring, until they are completely coated with the onions. Add ½ cup of the warm chicken stock and stir, stir, stir until the oats have absorbed the chicken stock, about 3 minutes. Repeat this process with the rest of the chicken stock until the oats are softened and porous with the chicken stock, about 20 minutes.

Turn off the heat under the chicken stock.

Finishing the risotto. Add the mushrooms to the oats and cook, stirring, until the mushrooms have shrunk into a certain softness, about 5 minutes. Add the spinach and stir until the spinach has begun to wilt and turn an even brighter green, about 2 minutes. Turn off the heat.

Feeds 4

FEEL LIKE PLAYING?

There are so many vegetables that would work well here, instead of the mushrooms and spinach. How about kale and carrots? Celery root and parsnips? Fava beans and baby peas? Zucchini and summer squash? You could play with a new version of this every season.

If you don't have caramelized onions on hand, you could caramelize 1 sliced onion before beginning the rest of the dish.

You don't have to use chicken stock here. We just like the flavor. However, if you have vegetarian or vegan friends, vegetable stock would work just fine. Even salted water would make a good substitute.

gluten-free biscuits and sausage gravy

For years, I looked at photos of perfect biscuits—flaky, with a rise like a skyscraper made of butter and flour—and despaired. How would I ever be able to do that without gluten? My friend Nancie McDermott, a great Southern food writer, put me at ease when she told me this: "You want to know why those biscuits always turned out perfect? Because those girls had to make them every morning for years." It's practice that makes great biscuits, not gluten.

This recipe reads long but don't be intimidated. I just wanted to share everything I have learned the past years so your first attempts are more successful than mine. There are only a few things you need to know: work with everything cold, don't twirl your biscuit cutter when you cut into the dough, and have fun with this. Even misshapen, lumpy biscuits sure taste good when smothered in sausage gravy.

280 grams All-Purpose Gluten-Free Flour Mix (page 31), plus extra for dusting

1 teaspoon whole or powdered psyllium husks (see page 33)

1 tablespoon baking powder

1½ teaspoons kosher salt

8 tablespoons (1 stick) cold unsalted butter, plus more for greasing pan

¾ cup buttermilk

¼ cup whole milk yogurt

2 tablespoons unsalted butter, melted

Sausage Gravy (recipe follows), for serving

COMBINING THE DRY INGREDIENTS. Whisk together the flour, psyllium husks, baking powder, and salt. (I like to put them in the food processor and let it run for a few minutes to aerate the flours. You can also use a whisk and bowl.) Put the dry ingredients in a large mixing bowl. Put the bowl in the freezer.

CUTTING THE BUTTER. Cut the cold butter into ½-inch cubes. Put the butter in the freezer too.

PREPARING TO BAKE. Preheat the oven to 425°F. Grease a 9-inch cast-iron pan or skillet (we use butter—you might like oil instead).

MIXING THE BUTTER AND FLOUR. When the oven is fully preheated and been at that temperature for 10 minutes, take the mixing bowl with the dry ingredients out of the freezer. Dump the butter cubes into the flour mixture. If you own a biscuit cutter, use it here to cut the butter into small chunks,

continued . . .

roughly the same size as lima beans, as you toss them with the flour. You can also use 2 knives to serve the same purpose. My favorite technique is to use my hands. Put your hands into the flour, palms up. Pick up some butter chunks and gently massage them into the flour, pushing your thumbs forward and your fingers toward your thumbs. Do this, picking up new pieces of butter, until all the butter is the size of lima beans. (If you want fluffier biscuits than flaky, keep going until the entire bowl is filled with coarse crumbs of butter and flour.)

If you're new at this, try the food processor. (And if you're going to do that, put the bowl of the food processor in the freezer instead of the mixing bowl.) Put the butter cubes into the bowl of the food processor. Pulse the ingredients together, about 7 times, until the butter chunks are about the size of lima beans. Move the flour mixture to a large bowl.

ADDING THE LIQUIDS. Make a well in the center of the ingredients. Mix together $^1/_3$ cup of the buttermilk and the yogurt in the well, then stir the liquids with a rubber spatula, moving in gentle circular motions, incorporating the flour as you go. The final dough should just hold together, with all the ingredients moist. If there is a bit of flour left on the sides of the bowl, add a dribble more of the buttermilk, then combine, then a dribble more if necessary. If the dough grows too wet, don't fret about it. Just add a bit more flour. You're looking for a shaggy dough, not a smooth round.

KNEADING THE BISCUITS. Sprinkle a little flour on a clean board. Turn out the dough on the board and sprinkle with just a touch more flour. Fold the dough in half, bringing the back part of the dough toward you. Pat the dough into an even round. Turn the dough 90 degrees, then fold the dough in half again and pat. This should make the dough fairly even. If not, you can fold the dough a third time. Pat out the dough to a $1^1/_2$-inch thickness.

Dip a $2^1/_2$-inch biscuit cutter into a bit of flour and push it straight down into the dough, starting from the outside edges. Do not twist the biscuit cutter. Cut out the remaining biscuits. Working quickly, pat any remaining scraps into another $1^1/_2$-inch-thick dough and cut the last biscuit.

Move the biscuits to the prepared cast-iron pan, nudging them up against each other. If you nestle the biscuits alongside each other, edges touching, you will have taller biscuits after baking. (They have nowhere to go but up!)

Slide the skillet into the oven and bake the biscuits for 6 minutes. Rotate the skillet 180 degrees and continue baking until the biscuits are firm and light golden brown, another 6 to 8 minutes. Remove the skillet from the oven and brush the tops of the biscuits with the melted butter. Let them rest for 10 minutes while you make the sausage gravy.

Feeds 4 to 6, depending on how many biscuits you want

sausage gravy

1 teaspoon unsalted butter (you can also use oil, if you prefer)

1/2 pound sausage (try the lamb sausage on page 201)

1 1/2 cups whole milk (you can try nondairy milks here)

1 1/2 to 2 1/2 tablespoons sweet rice flour

Kosher salt and freshly ground black pepper

COOKING THE SAUSAGE. Set a large skillet over medium heat and add the butter. When it's foamy, add the sausage, breaking it up with the spatula so it covers the bottom of the skillet. Cook the sausage, stirring occasionally, until entirely browned, about 10 minutes. Take the sausage out of the pan and put it on a plate. You'll need it in a moment. (If you're in a rush, you can also leave the sausage in the skillet and make the roux around it.)

HEATING THE MILK. Set a small pot on medium heat. Pour in the milk. Bring to a gentle simmer, then turn down the heat. Cover the milk to keep it warm.

MAKING THE ROUX. Take a moment to measure the amount of fat you have left in the pan. (After you've made this a few times, you'll know by sight.) You want a little more flour than fat, maybe by 1 teaspoon. So, if you have 2 tablespoons of fat, put in 2 1/2 tablespoons of sweet rice flour. And if you have more than 2 tablespoons of fat in the pan, take some out. Scatter the flour over the fat.

Whisk the flour and fat together. With gluten-free flour, you won't make a tight ball of roux, so don't overcook it trying to get it there. Simply stir and push the roux around the pan, cooking it to a blonde color.

MAKING THE GRAVY. Pour in 1/2 cup of the warm milk. The roux will now tighten up and form a ball. Don't worry, that's what gluten-free roux does. Keep stirring. Add another 1/2 cup of milk and stir, breaking up the ball of roux gently. Add the rest of the milk and whisk it vigorously to break up any lumps. Turn up the heat to medium-high and stir constantly until it comes to a boil. Turn down the heat to medium-low and let the gravy simmer, slowly, until it thickens, about 5 minutes.

FINISHING THE GRAVY. Add the sausage back into the gravy. Pour in 1/4 to 1/2 cup of water and stir. (If you only had a tablespoon of fat, use 1/4 cup.) Simmer the gravy slowly, allowing the water to blend fully with the gravy, 10 to 15 minutes. This will help to more fully cook the flour and let the taste of the sausage be the strongest. Add salt and pepper to taste. (We like a lot of pepper in our gravy.)

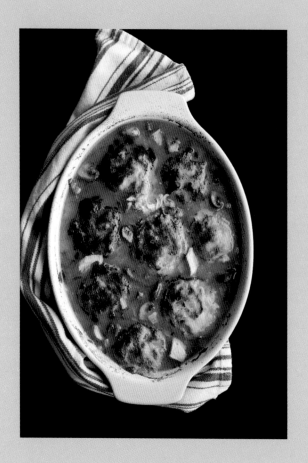

one-pot wonders

WHEN DANNY AND I FIRST FELL IN LOVE, WE SWOONED WITH EACH OTHER OVER FOOD. WE WERE deep in the throes of every moment together, never wanting it to end. And so, of course we'd happily spend all afternoon making a meal, using seven pots and pans, the food processor, and a sink full of dishes. Those first bites together made it all worth it.

Now, I love him even more fully than I did before. I relish every moment I can. But when he was gone most of the day in a restaurant kitchen, and our toddler daughter was tugging at my leg, wanting me to dance like a ballerina with her, right now? I learned to love one-pot dishes.

Most of my favorite dishes in the world are one-pot dishes: tortilla soup, seafood stew, chicken and dumplings, and sesame-pork congee. I don't have to dirty multiple dishes for the meal to be satisfying. Mostly, I want to be sure we make it to the table.

I love having Lucy sit on the counter while I cook, chopping mushrooms with her plastic knife. I adore that she's old enough to want to stir the onions in the pot while I add the stock. But I also love putting something to simmer on a back burner and playing a game of hide and seek with her before we eat dinner. (Later, when she's older, I'm sure she'll understand the concept of hiding instead of standing in the middle of her bedroom, grinning.)

Whatever I can do in advance to put a good dinner on the table makes me happy.

Everything that simmers in a pot tastes better the next day. I'll often make one of these dishes—like the chili with butternut squash and black beans or the stuffed cabbage—on a Sunday afternoon. Monday evening, when I have a hungry child clutching my leg, all I have to do is set the pot on the stove and wait for it to come to heat.

When I make a flatbread, like the injera we like to eat with the chicken doro wat, I'll make a double batch. When they're cool, I'll stack them with pieces of wax paper between them, put them in a resealable plastic bag, and freeze them for the next time we eat a stew.

The great thing about a one-pot dish is that the technique to make them is pretty much the same, no matter what the flavors. Once I figured out how to make a broccoli soup, I could imagine a caramelized four-onion soup. So I feel comfortable playing with slightly more exotic flavors like berbere or saffron when the rhythm of the dish is familiar.

In fact, I often make up a one-pot dish based on the leftovers of what's in the refrigerator that night. Here's the template I use to make one, suggested by our friends Tracy and Kim.

- Start with a flavor like sausage or bacon.

- Remove the meat and cook onions and garlic in that fat. (Vegetarian? Make caramelized onions.)

- Toss in a good spice or two. Wait until I can smell it.

- Add back the meat, some cooked beans, and whatever leftover cooked grains I have in the fridge.

- Pour in enough stock (or water) to cover it all and simmer it until it's all tender.

- Throw in some vegetables—preferably the ones hanging out in the refrigerator.

- End with an acid, like lemon juice, and something with a lot of flavor, like cheese.

- Serve.

Using whatever I have in the refrigerator, I can imagine a dish and have it on the table in less than an hour. How about a sausage and chicken stew with cannellini beans, millet, and lemony spinach, with a bit of Asiago cheese on top?

I think I might make that for dinner tonight.

popcorn with herbes de provence

Popcorn for dinner? Sometimes, when the three-year-old is having a meltdown because you can't find the doll's milk bottle, and she skipped her nap but is still refusing to go to sleep, and you have another five recipes to write that night before you can go to bed? Sometimes a big bowl of popcorn is the best you can do for dinner.

You might as well make it a good pot of popcorn. I've discovered that coconut oil is a mighty good oil for popping corn kernels. They all pop up white and plump, with nary a kernel left in the pot. I love the taste of herbes de Provence, an herb mix inspired by the flavors of the South of France. This and some good flaky salt? I'm ready for that break.

1 tablespoon dried rosemary

1 tablespoon dried thyme

1 tablespoon fennel seeds

1 teaspoon dried lavender buds

1 teaspoon dried tarragon

1 teaspoon dried marjoram

$^1/_2$ teaspoon dried oregano

$^1/_2$ teaspoon dried mint

2 tablespoons coconut oil

$^1/_3$ cup popcorn

1 teaspoon kosher salt

MAKING THE HERBES DE PROVENCE. Combine all the herbs and spices. Stir them up. Set aside.

MAKING THE POPCORN. Set a Dutch oven or large pot over medium-high heat. Add the oil. When it has fully melted, add a few kernels of the popcorn. When they have popped, after 2 or 3 minutes, move the pot off the burner. Add the rest of the popcorn, 2 teaspoons of the herbes de Provence mix, and the salt. Cover the Dutch oven almost entirely, leaving a crack open to let out the steam. Begin slowly moving the pot of popcorn over the burner, moving in a small circular motion. You're just shaking it up to avoid scorching the popcorn because burnt popcorn is sad. Keep moving the pot, faster and faster, as the popcorn pops more quickly. Listen. Is it still popping? Keep moving. Did it just go quiet in there? Turn off the heat.

Pour the popcorn into a large bowl. Mix it up with your hands. Taste. Maybe a bit more salt? Possibly.

Eat.

Feeds 4

broccoli soup with dukkah yogurt

Before I met Danny, I had only eaten cream of broccoli soup, in which the broccoli adds a certain greenness but not much flavor. But one day, Lucy and I went into lunch at the restaurant on the island where he was working at the time. He put a bowl of bright green soup in front of me. "Have some broccoli, girls!" he said, then went back to firing up something on the grill. Lucy and I shared spoonfuls, happy with the clear taste of broccoli and the smooth soup.

Because you blanch the broccoli just before pureeing the soup, this broccoli soup really tastes like broccoli. When we top it with a dollop of creamy dukkah yogurt, we're especially happy to be eating our greens.

2 tablespoons extra-virgin olive oil	2 large heads of broccoli
1 leek, white part only, sliced	2 cups chopped fresh spinach
1 medium carrot, peeled and chopped	2 teaspoons freshly grated lemon zest
2 stalks celery, chopped	1 cup cashew cream (page 102), strained
2 cloves garlic, peeled and chopped	2 tablespoons unsalted butter
1 tablespoon finely chopped fresh thyme	$1/2$ cup Greek yogurt
1 russet potato, peeled	$1/4$ cup finely chopped fresh Italian parsley
1 quart chicken or vegetable stock	2 tablespoons dukkah (page 252)

COOKING THE AROMATICS. Set a Dutch oven over medium-high heat. Pour in oil. When the oil is hot, add the leek, carrot, celery, and garlic and cook, stirring, until the carrot is softened, about 5 minutes. Stir in the thyme and cook until the scent is released, about 1 minute.

COOKING THE POTATO. Cut the potato into 1-inch cubes. Throw them into the Dutch oven and cover with the stock. Simmer until the potato is just tender to a knife, about 15 minutes.

ADDING THE BROCCOLI. While the potato is cooking, cut the broccoli into small florets. Cut off the tough bottom of the broccoli stalks and chop the rest into small pieces. When the potato is tender, throw in the broccoli. Cook until the broccoli is tender, about 3 minutes.

PUREEING THE SOUP. When the soup has cooled a bit, pour it in a blender, filling it no more than halfway. (Unless you have a large blender, you might have to do this in batches. You could also use an immersion blender here.) Add the spinach and 1 teaspoon of the lemon zest to the soup and puree until entirely smooth. Pour the soup back into the Dutch oven.

FINISHING THE SOUP. Bring the soup back to heat. Put in the cashew cream and butter. Stir until both are completely incorporated into the soup. Turn the heat down to medium-low and simmer slowly.

MAKING THE YOGURT TOPPING. Stir together the yogurt, the remaining lemon zest, parsley, and dukkah.

Ladle the broccoli soup into a bowl and top with a dollop of the dukkah yogurt.

Feeds 6

FEEL LIKE PLAYING?

You can use regular dairy cream or milk here instead of the cashew cream.

To make this vegan, use vegetable stock and a butter substitute. You won't be sacrificing flavor with this.

I love this dukkah yogurt with a number of foods: as a dip for fresh vegetables, on top of nearly any soup, and to top a bowl of warm beans.

chili with butternut squash, black beans, and kale

Some of our favorite dishes come from challenges. One week, Danny needed to make a vegan special at the restaurant where he worked on the island. When I suggested chili, he laughed out loud. And then he started thinking about it. What's chili but a big pot of flavor, with beans and tomatoes, spices and onions? When you start thinking about textures—the tenderness of butternut squash and the squiggly bend of Lacinato kale—instead of only flavor, you start throwing interesting foods into this pot. This dish is what he created that night.

We both love it. We make vegan chili all the time now.

1 butternut squash (aim for one without a big butt)

2 tablespoons extra-virgin olive oil

1 medium red onion, peeled and chopped

4 cloves garlic, peeled and chopped

2 teaspoons chili powder

1 teaspoon ground cumin

2 tablespoons tomato paste

One 28-ounce can diced tomatoes, drained

2 cups cooked black beans (see page 142 for Making a Big Pot of Beans)

1 bunch Lacinato kale (you could also use green curly or Red Russian kale), chopped

Kosher salt and freshly ground black pepper

Preparing the butternut squash. Peel the butternut squash with a vegetable peeler. (There might be some sticky ooze on your fingers. Don't fear, that's normal.) Cut the squash in half lengthwise. Scoop out all the seeds, then cut each piece in half lengthwise again. Cut the squash into 1-inch cubes.

Cooking the onions and squash. Set a Dutch oven over medium-high heat. Pour in the oil. When the oil is hot, add the onion, squash cubes, and garlic. Cook, stirring, until the onions and squash are softened, about 5 minutes.

FEEL LIKE PLAYING?

As with anything stewy, the taste of this chili is intensified by sitting in the refrigerator overnight.

You can use vegetable stock instead of water, if you wish.

If you would like more heat in this chili, try ¼ teaspoon of cayenne pepper with the rest of the spices and a couple of glugs of hot sauce at the end.

continued . . .

ADDING THE SPICES. Stir in the chili powder and cumin and cook until the scents are released, about 1 minute.

SIMMERING THE CHILI. Add the tomato paste and stir to coat all the vegetables with it. Add the tomatoes and beans and cook, stirring, until both are hot. Add 4 cups of water. When the water comes to a boil turn down the heat to medium-low. Simmer until the squash is knife tender, 30 to 45 minutes.

FINISHING THE CHILI. When the squash is tender, toss in the kale and cook just until it is wilted. Season with salt and pepper. Taste and season more, if you wish.

Feeds 4

FEEL LIKE PLAYING? > > > > >

If you can't find elephant garlic, you can use regular garlic. The soup will have a slightly more savory taste.

If you don't have sherry in your house, you can use a slightly fruity red wine instead.

caramelized four-onion soup

One dark day in January, Danny turned to me and said, "I'm going to make this four-onion soup I made at NECI." (That's the New England Culinary Institute, where he went to school.) I never complain when this mood strikes him, the mood to make a certain recipe that moment. I certainly didn't complain when we shared bowls of it for dinner later.

Deeply flavored with caramelized shallots, red and yellow onions, and the sweet heat of elephant garlic, this soup has the flavor of French onion soup. It's also creamy without any cream. It tastes like it takes a lot of time to make, but it doesn't. It also begs for grilled cheese sandwiches.

1 large yellow onion, peeled

1 large red onion, peeled

2 shallots, peeled

1 clove elephant garlic, peeled

2 tablespoons extra-virgin olive oil

$\frac{1}{2}$ cup dry sherry

1 large russet potato, peeled and diced

2 tablespoons unsalted butter

Kosher salt and freshly ground black pepper

PREPARING TO COOK. Cut the yellow onion, red onion, shallots, and elephant garlic into large pieces. Make sure they are about even in size, to prevent burning.

CARAMELIZING THE ONIONS AND GARLIC. Set a Dutch oven or large pot over medium-high heat. Pour in the oil. Add the yellow and red onions, shallots, and garlic and cook, stirring occasionally, until the onions are softened and browned, with particularly browned bits along the edges of the pot, 10 to 15 minutes. Pour in the sherry to deglaze the pan and stir.

FINISHING THE SOUP. Add the potato to the pot. Pour in enough water to cover everything by 1 inch. Cook, stirring occasionally, until the potato is tender to a knife, about 5 minutes. Take the pot off the heat and allow the soup to cool a bit.

Pour the soup into a blender, along with the butter, and puree until silky smooth. Return the soup to the pot. Season with salt and pepper. Taste. Season again.

Feeds 6

stuffed cabbage

One Sunday evening, Danny and I stood in the kitchen of one of our favorite farmers on Vashon, a robust woman named Leda. She had recently made friends with Anja, a Ukrainian woman who had lived in Cambodia for years before moving to the island. Leda had made us an Indian feast but while we waited for dinner to begin, we talked with Anja about stuffed cabbage rolls. Excited to share, she rattled off her recipe: a head of cabbage, a mix of pork and beef, onions and carrots and celery, some rice, tomato paste, and tomato juice. Nothing else.

We made it the next night. All three of us nibbled happily, sopping up the cabbage in the tomato juice. This is a plain recipe, not one filled with spices. We were tempted to jazz it up—some cayenne, a bit of smoked paprika, some cumin at least—but we resisted. Sometimes the best comfort food is plain and simple. We were satisfied that night.

1 large head savoy cabbage

2 tablespoons extra-virgin olive oil

1 medium onion, peeled and chopped

1 carrot, peeled and shredded

1 stalk celery, sliced thin

Kosher salt and freshly ground black pepper

$1/2$ cup basmati rice

$1/2$ pound ground beef

$1/2$ pound ground pork

2 tablespoons tomato paste

4 to 5 cups tomato juice

PREPARING THE CABBAGE. Remove the core from the cabbage with a sharp knife. Put the cabbage in a large bowl. Pour boiling water over the cabbage to cover and let it sit for 10 minutes to soften.

MAKING THE FILLING. Set a deep, wide skillet over medium-high heat and add the oil. Add the onion, carrot, and celery and cook, stirring, until softened, about 5 minutes. Season with salt and pepper. Add the rice and stir until the rice is coated with the onion mixture, about 1 minute. Take the pan off the heat and let the mixture cool.

Add the beef and pork to the onion mixture, along with the tomato paste. Mix it together with your hands until everything is well combined.

Making the stuffed cabbage. Take a large leaf of the softened cabbage and cut out the bottom third of the tough stem that runs up the middle of the leaf. Shape $1/4$ cup of the meat mixture into a small log. Place it, horizontally, where the stem of the cabbage now begins. Bring the two tail ends of the cabbage leaf up and over the meat mixture. Tuck the sides of the cabbage leaf over the top of the log of meat and roll up the cabbage. (Think burrito here.)

Put the stuffed cabbage into the same deep, wide skillet where you cooked the onions. Continue stuffing the cabbage leaves until you have run out of the meat mixture.

Cooking the stuffed cabbage. Set the skillet over medium-high heat. Pour the tomato juice over the rolls until they are just covered. Bring the tomato juice to a boil and then reduce the heat. Simmer the cabbage rolls until the meat reaches the temperature of 155°F, about 45 minutes.

Serve immediately.

Feeds 4

FEEL LIKE PLAYING?

Danny has always told me: make a recipe once as written and then you can change it the way you want. Well, I'd suggest you do the same here. I love this recipe as it is. Not everything has to be wildly spiced.

These freeze really well. We nestle them together in a glass container, top them with the tomato sauce, and stick them in the freezer for the next rainy day.

tortilla soup

Our daughter adores Pam Anderson. No, you don't have to worry, it's not that Pam Anderson. Our friend Pam is one of the most talented cooks and humble people we've ever had the pleasure to meet. Once the head editor of *Cook's Illustrated*, she knows how to make a great weeknight meal with plenty of flavor.

Lucy loves watching the videos on the website (ThreeManyCooks.com) Pam keeps with her daughters, Maggy and Sharon. We adore them too. For a solid week, Lucy insisted on watching Pam make tortilla soup, afterward walking around saying, "Mama, are we putting chipotles in adobo in the soup?" We had no choice. We had to come up with our own.

Oh am I glad we did. I've always loved ordering this soup at Mexican restaurants but it always seems a little bland. This is nothing like bland. With all the garnishes to nibble and drop on top of the soup, kids love this dish.

2 tablespoons chili powder

1 tablespoon smoked paprika

1 tablespoon oregano

Pinch red pepper flakes

1½ pounds chicken thighs, bone removed, skin on

Kosher salt and freshly ground black pepper

2 tablespoons peanut oil

2 quarts chicken stock

1 large onion, peeled and chopped

2 cloves garlic, peeled and sliced

2 canned gluten-free chipotle peppers in adobo sauce

6 corn tortillas

½ head savoy cabbage, sliced thin

½ cup chopped fresh cilantro

2 limes, cut open

1 cup grated Monterey Jack cheese

2 avocados, pitted, peeled, and sliced

½ cup sour cream

COOKING THE CHICKEN. Combine the chili powder, paprika, oregano, and red pepper flakes. Season the chicken thighs with salt and black pepper, then rub them with half the spice rub.

Set a Dutch oven over medium-high heat. Pour in 1 tablespoon of the oil. Lay the chicken thighs into the hot oil. (You might have to do this in batches.) Cook until the bottom of the chicken is browned, about 5 minutes. Flip the chicken and brown the other side, about 5 minutes. Remove the chicken to a plate.

SIMMERING THE STOCK. Set a pot over medium heat. Pour in the chicken stock and bring to a slow simmer.

COOKING THE AROMATICS. Pour the remaining tablespoon of oil into the Dutch oven. Add the onion and garlic and cook, stirring frequently, until the onion is softened, about 5 minutes. Add the remaining spice mixture and the chipotle peppers. Cook, stirring frequently, until the scent of the spices and peppers mingle together, about 2 minutes.

FINISHING THE CHICKEN. Shred up the chicken and put the pieces back in the pan. Pour in the hot chicken stock. Cook until the chicken is firm, about 10 minutes.

HEATING THE TORTILLAS. If you have a gas stove, put the flame on high. Toss a tortilla right on the flame. Let it heat until it is a bit charred at the edges, about 1 minute. Flip the tortilla with tongs and heat the other side for about a minute. Remove the tortilla to a plate. Repeat with the remaining tortillas. (If you don't have a gas stove, use a cast-iron skillet over high heat on the stove.)

When the tortillas have cooled to the touch, cut them into 1-inch strips.

FINISHING THE SOUP. Put the cabbage into the soup and stir. Cook until the cabbage is tender, about 5 minutes. Add the cilantro and stir for 1 minute. Remove the soup from the heat.

Put a handful of tortilla strips into a bowl and ladle the soup on top of it. Squirt some lime juice on top and dollop on some Jack cheese, avocado, and sour cream.

Feeds 4 to 6

FEEL LIKE PLAYING?

Some folks don't like cilantro. (And I'm so sorry to hear that.) If that's the case with anyone in your family, don't stir the cilantro into the soup. Use it as one of the toppings instead.

You might notice that this is the same spice rub we use in the chicken enchilada casserole. We use it in so many dishes that we make a big batch, using the same proportions, and keep it in our spice cupboard.

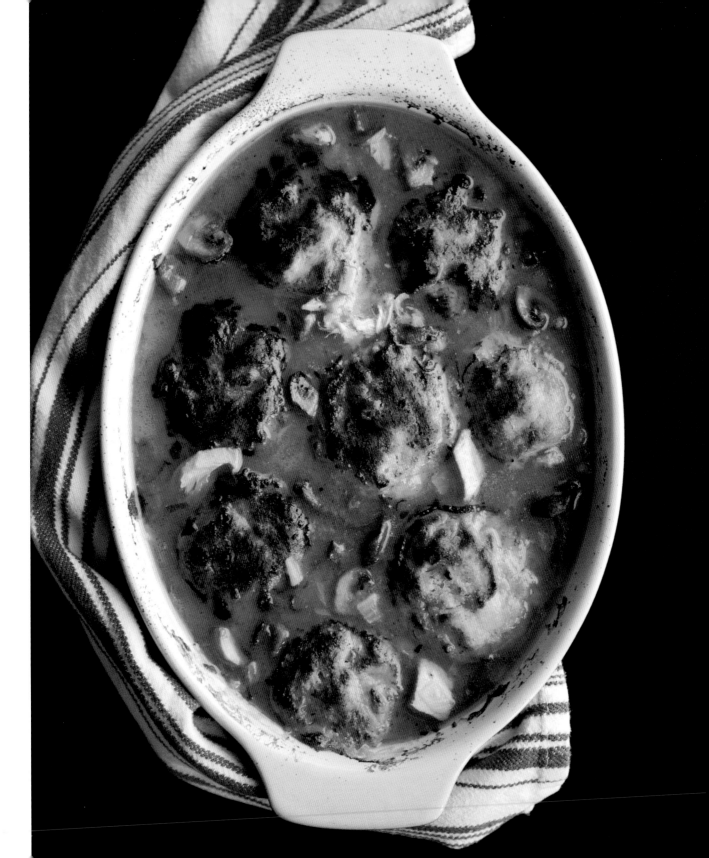

chicken and dumplings

My mom used a lot of packaged foods to feed us, like a lot of mothers in the 1970s. But she always made her chicken and dumplings from scratch. Maybe that's why I can still remember them so well today: those pillowy dumplings on top of a rich stew of chicken and softened vegetables. I could not get enough of those chicken and dumplings.

They're much easier to make gluten-free than you might think. You just need to make a chicken stew and plop biscuit dough on top, pop it in the oven, and let it all cook. It's the perfect casserole dish in this house.

2 tablespoons unsalted butter

2 large carrots, peeled, quartered, and chopped

2 cups white mushrooms, quartered and chopped

1 large onion, peeled and chopped

2 cloves garlic, peeled and chopped

1 tablespoon finely chopped fresh sage (you can use dried if you want to)

3 tablespoons All-Purpose Gluten-Free Flour Mix (page 31)

4 skinless, boneless chicken breasts, chopped

1 quart chicken stock

1 recipe Gluten-Free Biscuit dough (page 58)

COOKING THE VEGETABLES. Set a large Dutch oven over medium-high heat and add the butter. When it has melted, add the carrots and mushrooms. Cook, stirring, until the carrots are softened and the mushrooms are starting to brown, about 5 minutes.

Add the onion and garlic to the pot. Cook, stirring, until the onion has softened, about 5 minutes. Toss in the sage. Cook until it has released its scent, about 1 minute.

COATING THE VEGETABLES. Sprinkle the flour over the softened vegetables. Stir to coat. Cook, stirring, until the flour has cooked a bit, about 3 minutes.

FINISHING THE STEW. Add the chicken to the Dutch oven. Stir to coat it with all the vegetables. Pour in the chicken stock. Bring the liquid to a slight boil, then turn down the heat to medium-low. Simmer the stew until the chicken is tender and cooked through, 7 to 8 minutes.

continued . . .

ADDING THE DUMPLINGS. Using an ice-cream scoop, spoon out 8 equal balls of the biscuit dough. Plop them on the top of the chicken, distributing them evenly. Cover the Dutch oven with a lid and simmer the chicken and dumplings until the dumplings have steamed evenly, about 15 minutes.

FINISHING THE CHICKEN AND DUMPLINGS. Turn on the broiler. Put the chicken and dumplings under the hot broiler until the tops of the dumplings turn brown.

To serve, scoop some of the stew with 2 of the dumplings into a bowl.

Feeds 4

FEEL LIKE PLAYING?

Since these dumplings are meant to be fluffy in the stew instead of super flaky, you don't have to take quite so many precautions to keep the dough cold while you're making it as you do when you're making buttermilk biscuits. These are going to be more imperfect.

FEEL LIKE PLAYING?   > > > >

Since there is no one right way, you could cook the rice in chicken or vegetable stock, 4 cups or 6. You'll find your own way.

This is great with any number of toppings. I love fried shallots, a splash of fish sauce, thin garlic slices that you have slowly browned in sesame oil, or fresh scallions.

You could make this with tofu instead of pork. But I'd roast the tofu in that marinade. Pour any remaining marinade into the congee while it simmers and add the roasted tofu at the end.

sesame-ginger pork congee

Sometimes I let the worry of not making a dish the right way get in the way of making it at all. I'd heard about congee for years—a savory rice porridge with pork or garlic, topped with a splash of gluten-free tamari or fried garlic—and didn't feel qualified to make it. What if my dish wasn't authentic? Man, that was a mistake. I was missing out on what might now be my favorite comfort food.

Besides, what's the right way? One day I asked on Twitter for a simple liquid to rice ratio for congee from anyone who knew. There were answers from 4 to 1 to 8 to 1, with everyone insisting theirs was the ONLY way to do it. That's when I threw out the worries and moved into the kitchen instead. This is what emerged.

One 1-pound pork blade steak, bone-in

3 tablespoons sesame oil

1 tablespoon gluten-free tamari

1 clove garlic, peeled and sliced

One 1-inch piece fresh ginger, peeled and thinly sliced

1 tablespoon gluten-free fish sauce

1 cup calrose medium-grain rice

Marinating the pork. Cut the pork off the bone. Set aside the bone. Slice the meat into 1-inch pieces. Combine the oil, tamari, garlic, ginger, and fish sauce. Marinate the pork in this sauce while you cook the congee.

Preparing the rice. Rinse the rice in cold water in a colander, moving the rice around with your hands, for about 5 minutes. This will remove the starchiest part of the rice.

Set a Dutch oven or large pot over medium-high heat. Pour in the rinsed rice, the pork bone, and 8 cups of water. Bring the water to a boil and then turn down the heat to medium-low. Allow to simmer slowly until the rice is broken up and looks like porridge, 45 minutes to 1 hour.

Finishing the congee. Pull out the pork bone. Add the pork meat and marinade. Stir and return the congee to a simmer. Cook until the pork is firm to the touch, with just a touch of pink inside, about 7 minutes.

Feeds 4

ethiopian chicken stew

This dish is chicken stew with flavors that might be unfamiliar to you and your family. The cardamom, red onions, and berbere spice mix make this dish a call to your senses to wake up. Hey! You might just be eating dinner, but you're experiencing the world in a new way.

4 tablespoons clarified butter (see page 276)

2 medium red onions, peeled and chopped

2 cloves garlic, peeled and sliced

One 1½-inch piece fresh ginger, peeled and sliced

1 tablespoon berbere seasoning (page 229)

3 whole cloves

½ teaspoon kosher salt

¼ teaspoon ground cardamom

¼ teaspoon freshly ground black pepper

One 3-pound chicken, cut into breasts, legs, thighs, and wings

1 large potato (we like to use a purple potato here), peeled and chopped

1 carrot, peeled and chopped

¼ head savoy cabbage, sliced thin

3 cups chicken stock

1 lime, juiced

Injera bread (page 82)

Cooking the onions and garlic. Set a Dutch oven over medium-high heat. Add 2 tablespoons of the butter. When the butter is hot, add the red onions and garlic and cook, stirring frequently, until the onions have softened, about 5 minutes.

Adding the spices. Add the ginger, berbere seasoning, cloves, salt, cardamom, and pepper and cook, stirring frequently, until the smell of the spices fills the room, about 10 minutes.

Cooking the legs. Add the chicken legs, chicken thighs, potato, carrot, cabbage, and half the chicken stock to the Dutch oven. Cook at a slow simmer for 15 minutes.

Cooking the breasts. Add the chicken breasts, wings, and the remaining stock to the Dutch oven. Cook until the breasts have reached an internal temperature of 160°F, about 20 minutes more.

Finishing the stew. Add the remaining 2 tablespoons butter and lime juice to the stew and stir until it is fully incorporated. Serve with injera bread.

Feeds 4

FEEL LIKE PLAYING?

This goes great over rice. Teff porridge might be more authentic but it's an acquired taste. Mostly, you just want a bowl of this with a couple of pieces of injera bread to sop up the juices at the bottom of the bowl.

You could make a vegetarian version of this pretty easily. Simply cook the stew without any chicken—you might want to add some sweet potatoes in its place—and vegetable stock instead of chicken stock. Again, it won't be the same dish but it will be good.

injera (ethiopian flatbread)

True injera is a work of art. In Ethiopia, women spend years making injera every day: pounding the teff grains into flour, letting the batter ferment for three days to get that sour taste, making an enormous thin pancake and lifting it off a special round grill at just the right time to make it thin and crisp at the edges and bubbly soft in the middle.

I tried making it the traditional way, letting the batter sit and sour, but it didn't work in this house. I've been told that the teff grown in the United States is different than the teff grown in Ethiopia, as is the water.

But I love the softness of injera against the lips after being dipped in Ethiopian chicken stew. I wasn't going to give up. This recipe, inspired by one from the great Marcus Samuelsson, works like a teff crepe. The baking powder helps them to rise a bit and the yogurt lends a slight tang. Once you get the hang of making them, you might be making injera for other dinners pretty often.

140 grams teff flour

70 grams Whole-Grain Gluten-Free
    Flour Mix (page 32)

1 teaspoon baking powder

$^1/_2$ teaspoon psyllium husks (see page 33)

$^1/_2$ teaspoon kosher salt

$^1/_4$ cup whole milk yogurt

$1^1/_2$ cups club soda

Clarified butter (see page 276)

MAKING THE BATTER. Whisk together the teff flour, whole-grain flour, baking powder, psyllium husks, and salt. Put the flour mixture in a blender. Add the yogurt and club soda. Blend until the batter is smooth and thin, like a crepe batter. (If the batter is too thick, add more water.) Strain through a fine-mesh sieve into a large bowl.

WAITING TO MAKE THE INJERA. Let the batter sit in the refrigerator for at least 1 hour. It's best if you let it sit overnight, giving the flavors a chance to deepen and mingle.

MAKING THE FLATBREAD. Pull the batter out of the refrigerator. If it has thickened up too much, add a splash of club soda and stir.

Set a large skillet over medium-high heat. When the skillet is hot, add a couple of tablespoons of clarified butter. Swirl the butter around the pan, then pour about $1/3$ cup of the batter into the center of the skillet, spiraling outward. Stop when there is about 1 inch of skillet left bare. Cook the injera for about 30 seconds. Cover the skillet and cook for another 20 seconds. Lift up the cover. If the edges are crisp and the top of the injera is dotted with bubbles, use a rubber spatula to lift the edges. Grab the injera with your fingers and put it onto a plate. Cover it with a towel.

Repeat with the remaining injera batter.

Makes 6 injeras

FEEL LIKE PLAYING?

If you need a quick injera fix—and I understand—then make these on the spot before dinner. However, making a batch of the batter the night before really does help the taste of this flatbread enormously.

If you don't have clarified butter, use oil instead. Regular butter might burn too fast.

I love this flatbread with everything: broccoli soup, chicken stew, and as wraps for chicken salad.

pacific northwest seafood stew

This is a celebration dish. It calls for a little splurge on saffron, a trip to the seafood store for fresh clams, mussels, prawns, and scallops. And if it's really a special occasion, a Dungeness crab claw for everyone. Perhaps the best celebration is that it's really not hard to make.

¼ cup extra-virgin olive oil	16 fresh clams
1 medium onion, peeled and chopped	16 fresh mussels, debearded
1 bulb fennel, chopped	8 extra-large shrimp
3 stalks celery, chopped	8 large scallops
1 clove garlic, peeled and chopped	½ pound salmon fillet, chopped
1 teaspoon saffron threads	1 tablespoon unsalted butter
1 quart clam juice	4 cooked Dungeness crab claws (optional)

COOKING THE VEGETABLES. Set a Dutch oven over medium heat. Pour in the oil. When the oil is hot, add the onion, fennel, celery, and garlic and cook, stirring, until the vegetables are softened. Add the saffron threads and gently cook, stirring, until the vegetables are colored that vivid yellow orange, 3 to 4 minutes.

FINISHING THE STEW. Pour in the clam juice, all the seafood, and the butter. Bring to a gentle boil, then reduce the heat to medium-low. Cover with the lid and cook until the clams and mussels open, about 3 minutes. Keep cooking. When the shrimp are a bright pink and scallops and salmon are firm, 3 to 4 minutes more, turn off the heat. Discard any mussels or clams that do not open.

To serve, scoop some of the stew, plus 4 clams, 4 mussels, 2 shrimp, and 2 scallops, into each bowl. Top with the Dungeness crab claws, if using.

Feeds 4

FEEL LIKE PLAYING?

Again, we know not everyone has the same access to good seafood that we do here in the Pacific Northwest. However, this dish is worth seeking it out. If you have to use frozen clams, mussels, scallops, and shrimp, that's much better than skipping this dish.

a big pot of whole grains

I EAT FAR MORE WHOLE GRAINS NOW THAN I EVER DID WHEN I THOUGHT I COULD EAT GLUTEN. For breakfast we eat warm quinoa with kale and poached eggs or teff porridge with poached pears and hazelnuts. I've come to prefer brown rice, especially basmati, over white rice in most cases. I toss handfuls of cooked millet into savory breads or waffles and use the leftovers to make little fritters with golden raisins and feta.

Once I started making a big pot of whole grains at the beginning of the week and keeping them in the refrigerator or freezer, instead of making only the portion I needed for that night's dinner? We all started eating whole grains in meals that made us happy.

In this chapter, we're sharing some of the recipes we love that use quinoa, brown rice, and millet. There are many other gluten-free grains we cook with in our kitchen, often: amaranth, teff, sorghum, gluten-free oats, and buckwheat groats. Did you know there are more gluten-free grains in the world than there are gluten grains? Most of the grains without gluten are merely unfamiliar. (And also, delicious.) We hope you'll want to explore some of those grains too.

However, quinoa, brown rice, and millet are fairly ubiquitous in this culture now. If I can find these grains in our local store on a quick shopping trip, I'm far more likely to make dishes with them than the ones that need an online order. And they're good. Good for you too.

We cook all our grains in the rice cooker. You can cook them on the stove, of course (see next page for How to Cook Whole Grains), but I promise you—if you make a big pot, you're going to eat more of them.

If I know I'm going to be making something with brown rice the next night too, I'll just keep the leftover brown rice in the refrigerator, in an airtight container. Most of the time, however, I like to freeze one or two cups of rice, quinoa, or millet in a resealable plastic bag. They lie flat, meaning I can fit more of them into our already crowded freezer. And when it's time for dinner, I just take out a bag of quinoa and start cooking. (In fact, I've discovered that fried rice, like the Fried Rice with Chicken, Bok Choy, and Pickled Ginger on page 92, is much better when you start with cold, dry rice.)

When I first met Danny, he wanted potatoes or white rice at nearly every meal. Now, however, I think it's possible he likes quinoa more than I do. (And that's saying something.) I've fed him enough of these whole-grain dishes that he likes them now. Keep cooking them and you could fall in love with whole grains too.

how to cook
WHOLE GRAINS

You might have eaten a pile of dry grains (or soggy grains) before and felt horrified. Why would anyone eat this stuff? Don't worry. Those were poorly cooked grains. A new experience awaits you.

The template for how to cook whole grains is the same for any of the three grains we feature in this chapter. Bring a pot of water to boil, add salt and a bit of fat (butter or olive oil) and pour in the grain. Use 2 cups of water for every 1 cup of grain. Let the water boil for a moment, then reduce the heat to a low simmer. Cover the pot and let the grain cook until all the water has been absorbed and the grain is fluffy. Done.

We cook all our whole grains in the rice cooker. It's easy—toss in the ingredients and hit start. Not only does the rice cooker do all the simmering without any fear of burning but most models have a "keep warm" setting. This way, we can set up a big pot of brown rice in the morning and simply scoop some out for dinner when we're ready to eat. We highly recommend a good rice cooker if you are trying to eat more whole grains.

However, the stove works well too. Here are some guidelines for how to cook quinoa, millet, or brown rice on the stove. We've given you proportions for enough grains for three days' worth of meals.

quinoa

6 cups water

2 tablespoons butter (extra-virgin olive oil
or any oil you prefer are good too)

1 teaspoon kosher salt

3 cups quinoa

Bring the water to a boil. Add the butter and salt.
When the butter has melted, add the quinoa.
Bring the water back to a boil. Turn down the heat
to medium-low. Cover the pot. Let the quinoa
simmer for 12 minutes. Shove the pot to the back
of the stove and allow the quinoa to steam for 20
to 40 minutes. Eat.

Makes 6 cups

brown rice

6 cups water

2 tablespoons butter (extra-virgin olive oil
or any oil you prefer are good too)

1 teaspoon kosher salt

3 cups brown rice

Bring the water to a boil. Add the butter and salt.
When the butter has melted, add the brown rice.
Bring the water back to a boil. Turn down the heat
to medium-low. Cover the pot. Let the rice cook
for 45 to 55 minutes without stirring. After 45
minutes, lift the lid and tilt the pot to the side a
bit. If any water runs out, keep simmering. When
all the water is absorbed, and the rice is fluffy,
you're done.

Makes 6 cups

millet

6 cups water

2 tablespoons butter (extra-virgin olive oil
or any oil you prefer are good too)

1 teaspoon kosher salt

3 cups millet

Bring the water to a boil. Add the butter and salt.
When the butter has melted, add the millet. Bring
the water back to a boil. Turn down the heat to
medium-low. Cover the pot. Let the millet cook
for 30 to 40 minutes, without stirring. After 30
minutes, lift the lid and tilt the pot to the side a
bit. If any water runs out, keep simmering. When
all the water is absorbed, and the millet is fluffy,
you're done.

Makes 6 cups

*Note: If you want the millet to be creamy, instead of
fluffy, use 3 cups of water for every 1 cup of millet.*

chickpea vegetable stew with brown basmati rice

This isn't the kind of stew that needs to be braised for many hours or simmered for a couple of hours. This quick cooking suits the summer—you don't want the stove on for long—and keeps all the flavors fresh. If you grow these vegetables in your garden, this will be a particularly vibrant dinner. Serve this with pita bread (page 281).

3 tablespoons coconut oil

1 large onion, peeled and sliced

2 cloves garlic, peeled and chopped

1 tablespoon yellow curry paste

1 zucchini, sliced lengthwise, cut in half, and chopped

1 yellow squash, sliced lengthwise, cut in half, and chopped

1 small eggplant, peeled and chopped

One 14-ounce can chickpeas, drained (or cooked from dried if you want)

Two 14-ounce cans full-fat coconut milk

1 pint grape tomatoes, cut in half

$\frac{1}{2}$ large bunch fresh cilantro, finely chopped

2 tablespoons finely chopped fresh mint

2 tablespoons fresh lemon juice

Kosher salt and freshly ground black pepper

2 cups cooked brown basmati rice

Cooking the aromatics. Set a Dutch oven over medium-high heat. Add the oil. When it has melted, add the onion and garlic and cook, stirring, until the onion is softened, about 5 minutes. Add the curry paste and stir vigorously until the onion and garlic are coated, about 1 minute.

Cooking the vegetables. Add the zucchini, yellow squash, and eggplant to the Dutch oven and cook, stirring occasionally, until the vegetables start to soften, about 5 minutes.

Simmering the ragout. Add the chickpeas and coconut milk and bring to a gentle boil. Turn down the heat to medium-low and simmer until the vegetables are tender without being mushy and the coconut milk has reduced a bit, 7 to 8 minutes.

Finishing the ragout. Add the tomatoes, cilantro, and mint to the stew. Cook for a minute or two until the cilantro and mint start to wilt. Pour in the lemon juice. Season with salt and pepper. Taste and season more if necessary. Turn off the heat. Serve over the brown rice.

Feeds 4

fried rice with chicken, bok choy, and pickled ginger

Fried rice is a great way to use up leftovers. You have some brown rice in the freezer? Some vegetables just on the edge of wilting? A bit of leftover roasted chicken. Throw them together for dinner in 10 minutes.

2 tablespoons peanut oil

1 slice thick-cut bacon, cut into 1-inch pieces

1 large shallot, peeled and finely chopped

4 scallions, sliced thin

2 cloves garlic, peeled and sliced

2 tablespoons chopped pickled ginger

2 cups shredded roasted chicken

3 bunches baby bok choy, stems and leaves chopped separately

2 large eggs, beaten

2 cups cooked brown rice (make sure it's cold)

1 tablespoon gluten-free tamari

1 tablespoon rice wine vinegar

Kosher salt and freshly ground black pepper

PREPARING TO COOK. Set a 14-inch flat-bottomed wok over high heat. When the wok is screeching hot, add 1 tablespoon of the oil. Immediately add the bacon. Let the bacon cook for a moment, then move it around in the wok. Cook until it is starting to brown and crisp, about 3 minutes. Remove the bacon and drain it on a plate.

COOKING THE VEGETABLES. Add the shallot, scallions, and garlic to the wok and cook, stirring frequently, until the shallots begin to soften, about 3 minutes. Add the pickled ginger and cook until the kitchen begins to smell of ginger, about 1 minute.

Quickly, add the chicken and cook for about 1 minute. Add the bok choy stems and cook, stirring frequently, for 1 minute. Add the chopped bok choy leaves and cook, turning the mixture in the wok frequently, for 1 minute.

ADDING THE EGGS. Push everything to the sides of the wok, making a well in the center. Pour in the eggs. Scramble the eggs until they cease being runny, then mix the chicken and vegetables in with the eggs until they are all jumbled together.

Frying the rice. Add the cold rice and cook, tossing frequently, until the rice is hot and coated with all the other ingredients. Add back the crisp bacon. Stir together the tamari, vinegar, and the remaining 1 tablespoon oil, then drizzle it over the fried rice. Stir thoroughly.

Turn off the heat. Taste the fried rice. Season with salt and pepper to taste.

Feeds 4

FEEL LIKE PLAYING?

Since this is a dish meant to showcase the leftovers, think of this as a template. Do you have some roasted cauliflower in the refrigerator? Throw that in there. A few cubes of wasabi-roasted tofu? That would be good in there. Play.

brown rice quiche with chicken, kale, and preserved lemons

I never thought of using brown rice as a crust until Danny and I ate the first meal of our honeymoon in Rome. We'd saved up for months and months to go there. We stepped off the plane exhausted and excited. That first meal didn't disappoint. Danny had a dish of veal cheeks with stuffed squash blossoms. It was the first time in our life that he curled his arm around the plate and prevented me from having a bite. (The recipe is in our first cookbook because I wanted him to make it for me!) I wasn't suffering, however. The waiter lay down a sunny-yellow quiche with brown rice as the crust.

I love my gluten-free pie dough recipe, which doubles as a quiche crust, but sometimes a quick brown rice quiche is really satisfying. When we're cleaning out the refrigerator, and I find a couple of bags of cooked rice, I'm making this. With a quiche batter based on Thomas Keller's method and the bright taste of preserved lemons, this is one of my favorite quiches.

Neutral-tasting oil for greasing the pan

4 cups cooked brown rice, at room temperature

8 large eggs

Kosher salt and freshly ground black pepper

2 cups milk (nondairy milk works fine here too)

2 cups cashew cream (page 102) or 1½ cups heavy cream

Several scrapings fresh nutmeg

1 cup shredded roasted chicken

½ bunch Lacinato kale, finely chopped (you can use any kind of kale you want)

¼ cup Preserved Lemons (recipe follows)

¾ cup grated Gruyère

PREPARING TO BAKE. Preheat the oven to 375°F. Line a baking sheet with parchment paper. Lightly grease the inside of a 9-inch springform pan.

MAKING THE BROWN RICE CRUST. Combine the rice and 2 of the eggs in a large bowl. Using your hands, smoosh them all together until you have a slightly wet pile of rice. Season with salt and pepper.

WET YOUR HANDS. Press the rice mixture into the springform pan. Your hands will be sticky with it and the rice will cling to itself at times—don't worry. Keep working, patiently, until the rice mixture has evenly covered the bottom and halfway up the sides of the springform pan.

Put the pan on the baking sheet and slide it in the oven. Bake until the crust is set and just starting to brown, 20 to 30 minutes. Remove the crust from the oven and let it cool to room temperature.

MAKING THE BATTER. Pour 1 cup of the milk, 1 cup of the cashew cream, 3 of the remaining eggs, $1/2$ tablespoon of salt, and a couple of pinches of fresh nutmeg in a blender. Blend on low speed for 10 seconds. Turn up the speed to high and blend until the mixture is frothy, about 30 seconds. Pour this into the cooled quiche crust.

LAYERING THE INGREDIENTS FOR THE QUICHE. Scatter the chicken, kale, preserved lemons, and $1/2$ cup of the Gruyère evenly over the bottom of the quiche crust.

FINISHING THE QUICHE. Blend the remaining ingredients for the batter in the same manner as instructed above. Pour this into the quiche shell, taking care to cover all the ingredients. Scatter the rest of the Gruyère on top.

BAKING THE QUICHE. Bake the quiche until the eggs are firmly set and the top is browned, 1 to $1 1/2$ hours. Remove the quiche from the oven and let it cool completely to room temperature before serving.

Feeds 8

FEEL LIKE PLAYING?

To be honest, this quiche (like all quiches) gets better every day that it is in the refrigerator. It's worth making the day before.

If you want to serve the quiche hot, preheat the oven to 375°F. Slice the quiche into 8 pieces. Put them on a baking sheet and into the oven until they are hot, about 15 minutes.

preserved lemons

Traditional preserved lemons are a thing of beauty but they also take months to be fully cured. This quick preserved lemon recipe will give you the bright flavors without the wait. If you're really in a rush, you can use these lemons in a recipe only 3 hours after making them. However, give them a day or two and they'll really pack a wallop.

4 large lemons (organic is best, since you will be eating the peel)

1 tablespoon kosher salt

2 tablespoons sugar

$\frac{1}{4}$ teaspoon cinnamon, toasted

$\frac{1}{2}$ teaspoon ground coriander, toasted

1 small bay leaf

PREPARING THE LEMONS. Scrub the lemons with water. Take the ends off. Slice the lemons lengthwise, in thirds. Take out the seeds. Cut up the lemons into 1-inch pieces.

COMBINING THE INGREDIENTS. Toss together the salt, sugar, toasted cinnamon, toasted coriander, and the bay leaf. Add the lemons, making sure to include the juice, and mix up everything together.

Put the lemon mixture into an airtight container. Let them sit for at least 3 hours before using.

Makes about 2 cups

millet fritters with feta, spinach, and golden raisins

These little millet fritters are something special. We were inspired by our friend, Heidi Swanson, and the recipe for her quinoa fritters in her wonderful cookbook, *Super Natural Every Day*. I loved the idea of repurposing some leftover cooked grains into something that shimmered. Millet is wonderful since it has such a neutral taste. It takes on the flavors of sage, golden raisins, fresh spinach, and French feta. Okay, I want some right now!

2 cups cooked millet (page 89)

3 large eggs

1 yellow onion, peeled and chopped

2 cloves garlic, peeled and chopped

1 teaspoon finely chopped fresh sage
(use $^1\!/_2$ teaspoon dried if you want to)

$^1\!/_2$ teaspoon kosher salt

2 cups chopped fresh spinach

$^1\!/_2$ cup golden raisins

$^1\!/_3$ cup French feta cheese

1 cup gluten-free breadcrumbs

2 tablespoons extra-virgin olive oil

MAKING THE FRITTER DOUGH. Combine the millet, eggs, onion, garlic, sage, and salt in a large bowl. Toss together with a rubber spatula (or, really, your hands). When fully combined, add the spinach, raisins, and feta and toss together. Add half of the breadcrumbs and combine together. Let the mixture sit for a few moments to give the breadcrumbs a chance to absorb some of the moisture.

If you can form the mixture into a small patty, easily, you're done. If the fritters still feel wet, add more of the breadcrumbs, a bit at a time. You should be able to pinch together a bit of the mixture and have it stick together without oozing.

FRYING THE FRITTERS. Set a large skillet over medium heat. Add the oil. When it has heated, add 6 or 7 fritters to the skillet, taking care not to overcrowd. Cover the skillet and cook the fritters until the bottoms have browned, 5 to 10 minutes. Flip the fritters and cook until the second side has turned a golden brown, about 5 minutes more. Put the cooked fritters onto a wire rack and cook the remaining fritters.

Feeds 4 to 6

millet skillet bread with caramelized onions and mushrooms

Think of a crisp-at-the-edges cornbread but with the milder taste of millet. Think warm millet bread stuffed with caramelized onions and soft mushrooms. Think of the basil, the cashew milk, the fresh mozzarella. Think of how many times you are going to make this to go with a good pot of soup or stew.

1 tablespoon extra-virgin olive oil

1 tablespoon unsalted butter

2 cups sliced cremini mushrooms

115 grams Whole-Grain Gluten-Free Flour Mix (page 32)

115 grams coarse cornmeal

1 teaspoon baking powder

$^1/_2$ teaspoon baking soda

$^3/_4$ teaspoon kosher salt

2 large eggs

2 cups cashew milk (page 102)

150 grams cooked millet (page 89)

$^1/_2$ cup Caramelized Onions (recipe follows)

3 large sprigs fresh basil, leaves torn (optional)

1 large ball (4 ounces) fresh mozzarella

Preparing to bake. Preheat the oven to 350°F.

Cooking the mushrooms. Set a large cast-iron skillet over medium-high heat. (We use a 10-inch skillet, one with high walls.) Add the oil and butter. When the butter has melted and the oil moves easily around the pan, add the mushrooms. Cook, stirring occasionally, until the mushrooms have browned and shriveled in size, 5 to 7 minutes. Remove the pan from the heat.

Combining the dry ingredients. Whisk together the flour, cornmeal, baking powder, baking soda, and salt and mix until the mixture is one color. Set aside.

Finishing the batter. Pour the eggs and cashew milk into a large blender. (If you have a small blender, you might want to do this in a food processor instead.) Turn on the blender and let it run on low until the eggs and cashew milk are light and frothy. Add the cooked millet. When it is entirely combined in the liquid, add the dry ingredients. Turn up the blender to high and let it run until the batter is silky smooth.

continued...

BAKING THE BREAD. Remove the mushrooms from the pan. There should still be oil on the bottom of the pan. Brush some of it on the sides of the skillet to make sure it is well greased. Pour half of the batter into the pan. Add the mushrooms, caramelized onions, and basil onto the batter. Pour the remaining batter on top. Tear the ball of mozzarella into small shreds and scatter it over the top of the batter.

Transfer the bread to the oven and bake until the top is firm to the touch and golden brown, 45 to 60 minutes. If you want to brown the top further, turn on the broiler and let the bread sit under that heat for 3 minutes.

Remove the skillet bread and allow it to cool until it's barely warm to the touch.

Feeds 8

FEEL LIKE PLAYING?

You can do this with any cooked grain you happen to have. I love it with brown rice and Asian flavors as well.

If you can have cream, you can use that here instead of the cashew milk. But I think the cashews really add a depth here you don't want to miss.

FEEL LIKE PLAYING?   > > > > >

I love making a giant pot of caramelized onions, using a handful in a dish that night, and saving the rest. If I know I'm going to use them that week—and that's highly likely—I'll leave them in a covered container in the refrigerator. If it's an especially large pot, or I don't plan on using them that week, I put them in the freezer. Sometimes I freeze single portions (about ½ cup) in freezer bags. Sometimes I freeze them all in an airtight container and chip off onions when I need them. Believe me, you'll be happy if you do this.

caramelized onions

This is more of a technique than a recipe. Pay attention and keep stirring. The reward will be a rich sweetness, an onion taste without any of the raw heat, and the easiest way to add flavor to a dish that you will ever find.

4 large white onions, peeled

3 tablespoons extra-virgin olive oil

2 tablespoons unsalted butter

1 teaspoon sugar (optional)

$^1/_2$ teaspoon kosher salt

CUTTING THE ONIONS. Cut the onions in half lengthwise, and then take off the ends, where the last of the peel is probably clinging a bit. Cut each half in half. Slowly, slice the onions. Try to make the slices as even in size as possible.

STARTING TO COOK. Set a Dutch oven or large, wide pot over medium-high heat. When the air above the pot feels hot to your touch, pour in the oil. Add the butter. When the butter has melted and the oil shimmers in the pot, add the sliced onions. Toss them to coat with the oil and butter.

ADDING THE SUGAR AND SALT. After 10 minutes, pinch the sugar (if using) and salt over the top of the onions and stir well to coat. Cook the onions, stirring every 10 minutes or so, until they soften and then begin to reduce in volume. After about 30 minutes, the onions shrink into themselves, browning. Stir the onions, scraping the bottom of the pot with a metal spatula, to catch all that brown caramelized goodness.

PAYING ATTENTION. Don't let the onions burn! One bit of burn and the entire pot of caramelized onions will taste nasty, furrowing the brow of anyone who eats them. You don't want that.

STILL PAYING ATTENTION. Turn down the heat to medium. Cook the onions, stirring and scraping the bottom of the pot about every 2 or 3 minutes, to make sure they don't burn. If you wish, you can add a tablespoon of water to the pot to deglaze the pot and make sure you don't miss any of the browned bits. This is where you have to be attentive.

After 45 minutes, the onions will be lovely. After 60 minutes, the onions will be dark brown, wafting a slight sweetness. The longer you cook them, the darker and sweeter the onions will grow.

Makes 2 cups caramelized onions

cashew milk

I remember how weird it felt to make cashew milk the first time. The cashews that I had soaked overnight felt sort of floppy soft. It didn't make much sense to me how these, water, and salt could make milk. Then, I turned on the blender. Within a moment, the cashews and water had become. . . milk. A delicious nut milk. I strained it a few times for the errant bits of cashew. After a few hours, it was cold milk with the faintest taste of cashews. Magic.

Now, I make at least a pint of this a week, usually a quart. Since Danny's lactose intolerant, he can't digest cream without discomfort later. We use cashew milk for many recipes in this book. And I bet, like us, you'll find yourself making this over and over again.

2 cups raw whole cashews	1 tablespoon fresh lemon juice (optional)
1 teaspoon kosher salt	1 tablespoon honey (optional)

SOAKING THE CASHEWS. Put the cashews in a large bowl. Cover them with cold water. Set aside to sit overnight.

ADDING THE OTHER INGREDIENTS. In the morning, drain the cashews, which should be plumped up and softened. Put them in a blender. If you are making a savory cashew milk, add the salt and lemon juice. If you will be using the cashew milk for sweeter treats, add the honey. Cover the cashews with enough fresh water to cover them by 1 inch.

BLENDING THE CASHEW MILK. Blend the cashews and water until the milk is smooth, 3 to 5 minutes. Add more water, 1 tablespoon at a time, if the blender is working too hard. If you have a high-quality blender, the cashew milk will be ready to use at this point. If your blender needs a little help, strain the cashew milk through a fine-mesh sieve to set apart the remaining cashew bits.

Refrigerate the cashew milk for at least 2 hours before using. It will thicken and the flavors will settle.

Makes 1 quart cashew milk

FEEL LIKE PLAYING?

To make a thicker cashew cream, use only enough water to barely cover the cashews in the blender. The longer you keep this in the refrigerator, the more it will thicken. We usually make recipes that need cashew milk the first few days and cashew cream the rest of the week.

Use cashew cream with chocolate to create a thick, creamy nondairy dessert.

millet waffles with smoked salmon, crème fraîche, and capers

Every once in a while in our house when I was a kid, my mother said the magic words: "How about waffles for dinner?" My brother and I jumped up and down a bit, anticipating the sweet waffles draped in maple syrup, the bacon drenched a bit in it too. For dessert, we always had chocolate waffles. Now that was decadence.

There's nothing wrong with chocolate waffles sometimes, of course, but I feel better about eating waffles for dinner if they're filled with whole grains and savory instead. These have some of our favorite flavors: smoked salmon, crème fraîche, and capers. (I swear that our daughter would eat half a jar of capers on her own, if we let her.) The idea of having these for dinner makes me jump and down a bit now.

170 grams Whole-Grain Gluten-Free Flour Mix (page 32)

55 grams cooked millet (page 89)

1 tablespoon baking powder

1 teaspoon kosher salt

1 cup buttermilk

2 large eggs, at room temperature

4 tablespoons ($^1/_2$ stick) unsalted butter, melted and cooled

Neutral-tasting oil (such as canola), for greasing the waffle iron

$^1/_2$ cup crème fraîche

$^1/_4$ cup drained capers

$^1/_2$ pound smoked salmon

Combining the dry ingredients. Whisk together the flour, millet, baking powder, and salt in a bowl. Sift them through a fine-mesh sieve into a large bowl. Set aside.

Combining the liquids. Stir together the buttermilk, eggs, and melted butter in a large bowl.

Making the batter. Make a well in the center of the flour mixture. Pour in the liquids and stir together with a rubber spatula until the batter is well combined.

Waiting. Allow the batter to sit for at least 30 minutes before you make the waffles. (If you have the time, make the batter the night before. The flavors really intensify.)

continued...

MAKING THE WAFFLES. Turn on the waffle iron. When it has come to heat, brush both surfaces of the waffle iron with the oil. Pour about ¹⁄₂ cup of the waffle batter onto the bottom of the iron. Cook until the waffle is well browned, about 5 minutes. Put the waffle into a 250°F oven to keep warm while you make the rest of the waffles.

To serve, dollop the top of each waffle with a bit of crème fraîche, a scattering of capers, and shreds of smoked salmon.

Feeds 4

FEEL LIKE PLAYING?

Put together your waffle batter in the morning, before you go to work. Dinner will be easy when you return home.

Smoked trout or mackerel would be tremendous here.

Instead of crème fraîche, you could try thick Greek yogurt. I also love the idea of thin slivers of pickled vegetables on top.

quinoa-stuffed peppers

My mom made stuffed peppers when I was a kid. She stuffed green bell peppers with a meat and rice mixture like the one we made in the stuffed cabbage (on page 72). No offense, Mom, but I can't stand green bell peppers. And as much as Danny and I love meat, we love that so much food without meat can be great, like this dish.

6 tablespoons olive oil

2 cloves garlic, peeled and chopped

$^1/_2$ cup caramelized onions (page 101)

1 teaspoon ground cumin

2 cups cooked quinoa (page 89)

$^1/_2$ cup golden raisins

1 bunch Lacinato kale (or any type of kale), stems removed and leaves chopped

8 red bell peppers, cut in half and seeds removed

PREPARING TO BAKE. Preheat the oven to 425°F. Line a baking sheet with parchment paper.

MAKING THE STUFFING. Set a large skillet over medium heat. Pour in 2 tablespoons of the olive oil. Add the garlic and cook, stirring, until it is softened, about 2 minutes. (Take care to not burn the garlic.) Add the caramelized onions and cook, stirring, until they are heated. Stir in the cumin and cook until it releases its scent, about 1 minute.

Toss in the quinoa and raisins. Stir until everything is heated. Add the chopped kale and cook until it is just wilted. Turn off the heat.

STUFFING THE PEPPERS. Coat each of the peppers with the remaining oil. Spoon the quinoa stuffing into the peppers.

Put the peppers onto the prepared baking sheet. Roast in the oven until the edges of the peppers are a little crisp and the stuffing hot, about 25 minutes.

Feeds 4

FEEL LIKE PLAYING?

You could use cooked brown rice or millet here too. Use whatever is ready to go!

If you don't like the golden raisins, try dried cranberries or dried sour cherries. Some walnuts or pine nuts would be great too.

quinoa-sweet potato-peanut stew

We really love quinoa in this house. Even Danny, who was reluctant when he first met me to eat anything whole grain, loves to eat it three or four times a week. Its soft nutty flavor works well with so many foods, but particularly the foods that also came from South America. That's why we worked out this stew, with quinoa, sweet potatoes, and black beans. Sure, it's healthy and all that, but it's mostly harmonious. It all just works together. It's not deeply spiced. We wanted these ingredients to shine on their own.

I love this stew in the late winter, when nothing much else is growing. We're waiting for the first greens of spring but they're still a full month away. On those days, this is such a satisfying dish.

3 tablespoons peanut oil

1 large onion, peeled and chopped

2 cloves garlic, peeled and sliced

1 teaspoon ground cumin

$\frac{1}{2}$ teaspoon cinnamon

2 tablespoons salted natural creamy peanut butter

1 large sweet potato, peeled and diced into 1-inch cubes

One 14-ounce can diced tomatoes, drained

Two 14-ounce cans black beans, drained and rinsed

4 cups chicken or vegetable stock

Kosher salt and freshly ground black pepper

2 cups cooked quinoa (page 89)

$\frac{1}{2}$ cup chopped fresh cilantro

1 lime, zested and juiced

BUILDING THE FLAVORS. Set a Dutch oven or large pot over medium-high heat. Add the oil. When the oil shimmers and moves around the pot easily, add the onion and garlic and cook, stirring frequently, until softened and starting to brown, about 5 minutes. Stir in the cumin and cinnamon and cook until the scent of the cinnamon fills your nose, about 1 minute. Add the peanut butter and stir it into the onions well.

FEEL LIKE PLAYING?

If you can't do peanuts, then almond butter or hazelnut butter would work well here. If you can't eat nuts at all, you can leave them out here.

Play with the spices if you want. We like the earthy flavor of cumin with the surprise of cinnamon and peanut butter here. But you might want more heat.

SIMMERING IT INTO STEW. Add the sweet potato and stir to coat it with the fragrant onions. Cook, stirring frequently, until the sweet potato has begun to soften, about 5 minutes. Stir in the tomatoes and beans. Pour in the stock and bring to a boil. Reduce the heat to medium and simmer the stew until you can pierce a piece of sweet potato with a sharp knife, about 20 minutes. Taste the stew. Lightly season with salt and pepper, then stir the stew and let it simmer for 5 more minutes. Taste it again. Season more, if required.

SERVING THE STEW. Put $1/2$ cup quinoa at the bottom of each bowl. Pour some of the stew over it. Top with chopped cilantro, lime zest, and a squeeze of lime juice.

Feeds 4

black bean–quinoa burgers

Danny came up with these for the restaurant where he worked. The veggie burgers they had been serving make the same mistake so many others make—they tried so hard to replicate meat that they fell short. These burgers instead rely on oats and quinoa flakes—like rolled oats, but made of quinoa—for the fiber, and lots of fresh vegetables for a fresh taste. A little tahini for taste and these are good. I know they worked when Danny said he wanted some for dinner.

1 cup quinoa flakes

½ cup gluten-free rolled oats

One 14-ounce can black beans, drained and rinsed

6 tablespoons extra-virgin olive oil

1 large onion, peeled and chopped

4 cloves garlic, peeled and sliced

1 large carrot, peeled and grated

2 cups shredded green cabbage

1 tablespoon chopped fresh Italian parsley

1 teaspoon chopped fresh thyme

1 cup cooked quinoa (page 89)

30 grams Whole-Grain Gluten-Free Flour Mix (page 32)

2 tablespoons tahini

Kosher salt and freshly ground black pepper

Toasting the quinoa flakes. Set a large skillet over medium-high heat. Add the quinoa flakes to the hot pan. Toast, stirring frequently, until the flakes are starting to brown and smell toasty, 5 to 7 minutes.

Breaking up the oats. Put the oats in a food processor. Pulse until the oats are broken up, ragged, without going so far as to make oat flour. Put the oats in a bowl and set aside.

Pureeing the beans. Put the beans into the food processor. Pulse until the beans are mostly pureed with some beans in pieces.

Cooking the vegetables. Set the skillet back over medium-high heat. Add 2 tablespoons of the oil. Add the onion and garlic and cook, stirring frequently, until

FEEL LIKE PLAYING?

Of course, you can play with different vegetables here. I'd use the ones that are in season where you live on the week you want to eat them!

If you can't eat oats, even if they are gluten-free, try doubling up on the quinoa flakes instead.

starting to soften, about 5 minutes. Add the carrot and cook, stirring occasionally, until it starts to soften, about 2 minutes. Add the cabbage and cook, stirring, until it starts to wilt, about 1 minute. Add the parsley and thyme and cook until the scent of the herbs releases into the room, about 1 minute. Take the skillet off the heat.

MAKING THE BURGERS. In a large bowl, combine the quinoa, pureed beans, toasted quinoa flakes, oats, and the cooked vegetables together. Add the flour, tahini, and salt and pepper and mix it all up with your hands.

If you can form the mixture into a small patty, easily, you're done. If the fritters still feel wet, add more flour, a bit at a time. You should be able to pinch together a bit of the mixture and have it stick together without oozing.

MAKING A TASTER. Set the skillet back on medium heat and add a bit of oil. Make a small patty. Cook until the bottom of the patty has browned, about 5 minutes. Flip and cook on the other side as well. When the patty has cooled, taste it for seasoning. More salt? More herbs? You decide.

Let the mixture sit for an hour in the refrigerator to give the grains a chance to absorb some of the moisture.

COOKING THE BURGERS. Preheat the oven to 250°. Line a baking sheet with parchment paper.

Set a large skillet over medium heat. Pour in 1 tablespoon oil.

Form patties about 3 inches across, using your hands to even out the sides into smooth discs. Put 3 burgers into the skillet. Cook until the bottoms are browned and crisp, 4 to 5 minutes. Flip the burgers and cook until the other sides are browned, 4 to 5 minutes.

Put that batch onto the baking sheet in the warm oven. Add more oil to the skillet. Repeat until all the burgers are cooked. Remove the burgers from the oven and serve.

Makes 12 burgers

stir-fries

FOR YEARS I MADE TERRIBLE STIR-FRIES. WHEN I WAS IN MY TWENTIES, MY EAGER VEGETARIAN days, I made a stir-fry dish a few nights a week. I crowded a pound of vegetables into a skillet on moderate heat, stirring them together until they were all hot. After a few moments, I tumbled all those vegetables, slightly soggy and dripping with too much soy sauce, onto a bowl of damp rice. I called it a stir-fry and ate it dutifully.

Now, when it comes to cooking, I'm still asking my husband questions about the best technique for most dishes we make. He's the chef, and I'm the home cook. But when it's time for stir-fry, he steps back. I get that blackened wok blazing hot and start making vegetables fly. Every time we eat a stir-fry dinner, Danny looks at me in equal parts of gratitude and bewilderment. How is this so good?

I owe my love for (and decent skill at) stir-fry to two factors: (1) the inimitable Grace Young and (2) a lot of practice.

Grace Young's books on the mysteries of authentic stir-fry, *The Breath of a Wok* and *Stir-Frying to the Sky's Edge*, are the clearest instruction manuals for stir-frying I have ever read. Gentle in her wise instruction and meticulous in her preparation, Grace Young is an incredible teacher. She has such passion: she wants you to eat great stir-fry.

Why? It's the same reason I'm so happy to be sharing these recipes with you. Once you have a good wok and confidence with the process, you will probably find stir-frying to be the easiest, healthiest, and quickest way to get dinner on your table. There is no other way to make a dish with this many big, vibrant flavors without much work. And once you know the rules for stir-frying, you'll be inventing dishes left and right. I have been.

Here are a few general rules I have learned from several seasons of stir-frying our dinners in less than thirty minutes.

* **Get a wok.** They don't cost much, especially if you factor in how much you will use it over the next few years. Ours cost about thirty dollars. We have a fourteen-inch flat-bottomed, carbon-steel wok, at Grace Young's suggestion. (She was kind enough to talk me through this chapter of the book before I began it.) The flat bottom means it will be easier to use on American stoves. The carbon steel means that the wok, once it is seasoned, will be virtually nonstick. Easier to clean and less oil needed—those are enough for me.

* **Can you use a skillet instead of a wok?** Can I be honest? If you must, yes. But seriously, it's not going to be as good. If you like stir-frying, you want a wok.

* **Season your wok before you use it.** Most woks arrive to stores shiny and coated with oil from the factory. Scrub the wok with hot soapy water and a sponge. Set it on low heat and let it gather heat until there are no water droplets left on it. Finally, get it scorching hot, swirl in a little peanut oil, and cook some scallions and ginger, tossing them around the wok and pressing them over every inch of its surface, for about fifteen minutes. This should season your wok for its first use.

* **There's no question that stir-frying is easier on a gas stove.** If your electric stove runs hot, you'll be fine. If your stove is sort of paltry, you might look at thrift stores for electric woks. (I always see them there.)

* **Before you start stir-frying, make sure you have all your ingredients peeled, sliced, and ready to go.** Stir-frying goes fast, so you don't want to be chopping garlic while the wok is smoking.

* **Make sure all your ingredients are dry.** Any water will make the food steam instead of stir-fry.

* **Get that wok HOT.** Turn on the exhaust fan if you're worried. When the wok just starts to smoke, you're ready for stir-frying.

* **Swirl some oil into the wok.** Don't dump it directly, but let it circle around the sides of the wok. Be sure to use an oil with a high smoke point because you're working with a lot of heat here. We prefer peanut oil to any other oil for stir-frying. Depending on the flavors of the dish, I also like coconut oil. Rice bran oil has one of the highest smoke points of any oil and has a clean, neutral taste. If you use an oil with a low smoke point, like extra-virgin olive oil or sesame oil, your stir-fry will probably have a slightly bitter, unpleasant taste.

* **Listen for the sizzle.** If the ingredients are sizzling when you stir-fry them, then the dish will taste like a true marriage of many flavors. If the oil isn't hot enough, the dish is going to taste like a failed relationship. You don't want that.

* **Use restraint.** When I first began making stir-fry dishes, I thought complexity was the goal. I used six different vegetables, several spices, and sauces with too many ingredients. Now, I know a great stir-fry dish can come from ginger, garlic, salmon, chard, and a sauce of gluten-free tamari, rice wine vinegar, and sesame oil.

* **There's a structure to stir-frying.** Once you know the structure—which you'll see in each of these recipes—you'll know how to make your own. Get the wok hot. Swirl in oil. Cook aromatics like ginger or garlic quickly. Push them to the side of the wok. Add the protein and sear. Remove it from the wok. Stir-fry the vegetables. Push the aromatics back into the wok and toss the protein back into the vegetables. Swirl in the sauce. Stir-fry. Done.

AND THAT'S ABOUT IT. SEE WHAT I MEAN? ONCE YOU LEARN THIS NEW TASK, YOU'LL BE MAKING A LIFELONG HABIT.

When we did the photo shoot for this book, I put some of the process shots up on Twitter as it happened. After I shared the shot for the chile-lime shrimp stir-fry, Grace Young wrote back that my wok had a beautiful patina and the stir-fry looked fantastic. I nearly fainted. Oh, if that girl in her twenties with the soggy stir-fry dishes only knew what awaited her.

how to cook rice

If you grew up on Uncle Ben's rice, you may not have any idea how to make steamy, fluffy, tender rice. It's easier than you think. In general, more water means softer rice, while less water means firmer rice. If you know this, and choose the method here that works best for your kitchen, you're bound to have good rice for dinner tonight.

FIRST, RINSE IT.

If your rice turns out a little clumpy after cooking, it's probably because you forgot to rinse it.

The outside of rice grains holds a lot of excess starch. Rinsing the rice will help you to find the fluffy rice of your dreams. (It also means you're rinsing the rice of any little stones or bugs that might be in that bag.)

Of course, if you want rice to hold together, like sushi rice, skip this step.

All you have to do is put the rice in a colander and run cold water over it. Move your hand through the rice, making sure every grain gets water. Drain the water completely. Repeat three times. That's it.

YOU COULD COOK IT ON THE STOVETOP.

For every 1 cup of rice, use 1¾ cups water. (Or, if you want to go by feel, add the rice and add enough water that it is at the level of your first knuckle of your pointer finger.) Add some salt, a pat of butter, and any spices or herbs you want for your dish.

Set the pot over medium-high heat. Bring the water to a boil. When the water is bubbling up through the top surface of the rice, turn down the heat to medium-low. Cover the pot. Cook for 15 to 20 minutes for white rice, 45 to 50 minutes for brown rice. When there is no more steam escaping from the space between the pot and lid, turn off the heat and let the rice sit covered for 15 minutes. This allows the moisture in the pot to be distributed evenly through the rice. Serve.

YOU COULD BAKE IT IN THE OVEN.

I didn't know I could bake rice until a few years ago, when my friend Luisa wrote about our friend Francis Lam's method on her blog. It's a pretty great way to get dinner started and forget about the rice.

Preheat the oven to 375°F. Set a large pot with a tight-fitting lid on medium-high heat. Add 1 tablespoon of oil or butter. Add 2 cups long-grain rice and stir until it's entirely coated. Cook until the rice smells toasty. Add 1 teaspoon kosher salt and 3 cups of water. When the water boils, stir up the rice a final time, and put the pot in the oven. Bake white rice for 20 minutes and brown rice for 60 minutes. Pull the pot out of the oven and let the rice rest with the cover on for another 15 minutes. Fluff it up and serve.

YOU COULD COOK IT LIKE PASTA.

This one never occurred to me until I heard Lynne Rossetto Kasper talk about it on *The Splendid Table.* Instead of worrying about getting the proportion of water to rice exactly right and timing the cooking to the moment, how about treating rice like pasta?

Boil up 3 quarts of salted water. Throw in 1 cup of rice. Cook until the rice is slightly tender, 8 to 10 minutes. (Think of this as cooking pasta al dente—tender but still with a bit of a bite.) Drain the rice and return it to the pot. Cover the pot and let the rice sit for 10 to 15 minutes to absorb the water fully.

YOU COULD MAKE IT EASY ON YOURSELF AND BUY A RICE COOKER.

A friend of mine who is of Japanese-Filipina descent told us once, laughing, "It was only when I got married that I had to learn how to make rice on the stovetop. Before that, I just threw rice in the rice cooker and turned it on."

To be honest, that's how we make all our rice as well. If you know that you love rice—and you intend to make a lot of stir-fries—and you love whole grains such as quinoa, millet, and oats, buy yourself a good rice cooker. Whatever investment we made in the beginning has more than paid for itself with all the pots of perfectly cooked rice we have made.

You can also cook up a batch of rice and keep it warm all day and into the next day as well. Start rice in the morning and you're halfway to dinner before you leave the door.

how to make stir-fry sauces

Even if you overcome your fear of the hot burner and a blackened wok, you might wonder, "How am I going to make these taste good?" Here's the good news: it's easy.

I learned quite a bit intuitively about how to make stir-fries that have an interesting depth of flavor from following some of Grace Young's recipes. But I felt relaxed enough to play when our friend Matthew Amster-Burton broke down the component parts of stir-fry sauces in a piece for Culinate. He guided this outline of ingredients for you here. Laura Russell's book, *The Gluten-Free Asian Kitchen*, was also really helpful in understanding these ingredients.

Start simply. Think about flavor. Play.

SIMPLE, MINIMAL SAUCES

You can make these with what's already in your kitchen. These are especially good for quick stir-fried vegetables like bok choy or cabbage. Grate some ginger, finely chop up some garlic, splash in some chicken stock, some sesame oil, a bit of lemon juice, and pinch in some salt. Add a bit of cornstarch and stir it up. Pour this into the wok as your vegetables are nearly cooked. Let it boil and take the wok off the heat.

That's about all you need. Don't worry about proportions. Add what feels right to you. If the dish is overly garlic in nature, use less next time. You'll know.

* Chicken stock
* Cornstarch
* Garlic
* Ginger
* Lemon or lime juice
* Kosher salt
* Sesame oil
* Sugar

THESE MIGHT REQUIRE A TRIP TO THE GROCERY STORE

If you want a bit more depth of flavor, stop in the Asian aisle of your grocery store. (Danny and I both hate that it's called "the Asian aisle." Or worse yet, some stores call it "the ethnic aisle.")

* Dry sherry adds a pleasant dry fruitiness to sauces.

* Peanut oil is great for Thai stir-fries.

* Rice wine vinegar is a very mild acid. Be sure to look for unseasoned rice wine vinegar, as the seasoned one often has high-fructose corn syrup. You want to control the sweetness of your stir-fry.

* Toasted sesame oil adds a darker taste than plain sesame oil.

* Gluten-free tamari is like soy sauce, except more subtle in its flavoring. It adds saltiness and a certain inexplicable depth to sauces.

THESE MIGHT REQUIRE A TRIP TO AN ASIAN GROCERY STORE OR MAKING SOMETHING FROM SCRATCH

Depending on where you live, you might have to go to an Asian grocery store or order these online. They're worth the effort, however.

* **Chili-garlic sauce** is a potent mixture of chiles, garlic, salt, and vinegar. Think Sriracha or Mae Ploy. (We have a recipe to make your own in this chapter on page 133.)

* **Fish sauce** is heavenly. You wouldn't think so, since it's a fermented liquid of anchovies, but it adds a depth of flavor to everything it touches. Be sure to find a gluten-free brand.

* **Hoisin sauce** is sweet and thick, which means you don't need to add cornstarch or sugar when you use it.

* **Mirin** is a slightly sweet, syrupy cooking wine made from sweet rice. It adds sweetness to stir-fries.

* **Ponzu** is the Japanese equivalent of vinaigrette. Its citrus notes make it a great addition to chicken, shrimp, or tofu stir-fry (see recipe on page 124).

* **Oyster sauce** works a bit like fish sauce, except it's made from oysters. It's also thicker than fish sauce, more syrupy.

HOW TO PUT THEM TOGETHER

Now, how do you work with all these ingredients? Think about the kinds of flavors you want for the stir-fry you are making, and start splashing some into a bowl. Play mad scientist.

* You want some kind of acid: lemon or lime juice, rice wine vinegar, or chili-garlic sauce.

* You want something salty: salt, gluten-free tamari, fish sauce, or oyster sauce.

* You might want something slightly sweet: sugar, hoisin sauce, or mirin.

* You want a little oil or liquid for volume: chicken stock, sesame oil, toasted sesame oil, or peanut oil.

* You want some aromatics: garlic, ginger, or dry sherry.

NOW, COMBINE THEM

Here's a sauce as an example. This would work with nearly anything you wanted to throw in the wok.

2 tablespoons gluten-free tamari

2 tablespoons rice wine vinegar

2 teaspoons dry sherry

1 teaspoon toasted sesame oil

$^1\!/_2$ teaspoon cornstarch

THAT'S IT! Once you gather all the ingredients in your kitchen, you can start balancing flavors and tasting how these foods work with your favorite vegetables and proteins. In other words, make a lot of stir-fry dishes.

FEEL LIKE PLAYING?

If you are feeding this to kiddos, strain the marinade before you swirl it back in the pan to remove the chiles.

Any mushrooms will do but the texture of chanterelles here really makes them worth the wait.

Other greens that would work: napa cabbage, kale.

If you want to make this suitable for your pescetarian friends, use vegetable stock instead.

chile-lime shrimp stir-fry

Shrimp and chanterelle mushrooms have a similar texture—a bounce on the teeth when you chew them. A little crisp napa cabbage and bok choy and you're set.

1/3 cup chicken stock	3 tablespoons peanut oil
1 tablespoon gluten-free tamari	2 cloves garlic, peeled and sliced
1 tablespoon rice wine vinegar	One 1-inch piece fresh ginger, peeled and sliced
1 red Thai chile, seeded and finely chopped	1/2 pound chanterelle mushrooms, chopped
1 large lime, zested and juiced	1 pound bok choy, stems and leaves chopped
1 pound large shrimp, peeled and deveined	

MARINATING THE SHRIMP. Whisk together the chicken stock, tamari, vinegar, chile, and lime zest and juice. Add the shrimp and marinate for at least 30 minutes.

STIR-FRYING THE AROMATICS. Set a 14-inch flat-bottomed wok over high heat. When the wok starts to smoke, swirl in 1 tablespoon of the oil. Add the garlic and ginger and stir-fry until they release their scent, about 30 seconds. Push the garlic and ginger to the side of the wok.

SEARING THE SHRIMP. Remove the shrimp from the marinade, reserving the marinade for later. Lay them flat on the bottom of the wok. Cook without touching them for 1 minute. Flip over the shrimp and stir-fry until all the shrimp have color, about 30 seconds. Remove the shrimp to a plate.

STIR-FRYING THE VEGETABLES. Swirl in the remaining 2 tablespoons oil. Add the mushrooms and stir-fry for 1 minute. Add the bok choy and push the garlic and ginger back into the wok. Stir-fry for 30 seconds.

FINISHING THE STIR-FRY. Add back in the shrimp and stir-fry for 30 seconds. Swirl in the remaining marinade and stir-fry until the shrimp are fully cooked and the sauce is bubbly and reduced, about 2 minutes.

Serve immediately.

Feeds 4

chicken and baby bok choy stir-fry with ponzu sauce

I have found that if I make up a batch of ponzu sauce on a Sunday afternoon, I have a delicious salty-citrus-flavored sauce for any stir-fry I want to make that week. Here, chicken thighs add meaty flavor and baby bok choy crisps up the texture. The only ingredient that might not be familiar is kombu, which is a kind of kelp. It's sold in Asian markets, and online, mostly dried. It's also widely available in health food stores and big markets like Whole Foods. A relatively small piece of it adds a mineral depth of flavor to this sauce. All you have to do is throw it in the mix and let the sauce sit. Again, stir-fry doesn't have to be complicated to be delicious.

Ponzu sauce

1 cup gluten-free tamari

$^2/_3$ cup fresh orange juice

$^1/_3$ cup fresh lemon juice

2 tablespoons gluten-free fish sauce

2 tablespoons mirin

One 3-inch piece kombu

Stir-fry

1 teaspoon cornstarch

1 pound chicken thighs, skin and bones removed, cut into bite-size pieces

3 bunches baby bok choy

2 tablespoons peanut oil

1 medium onion, peeled and thinly sliced

MAKING THE PONZU SAUCE. Combine the tamari, orange juice, lemon juice, fish sauce, mirin, and kombu in a large bowl. Let them sit together for at least 2 hours and preferably overnight. Strain the sauce.

MARINATING THE CHICKEN. In a medium bowl, combine $^1/_3$ cup of the ponzu sauce with the cornstarch and then combine with the chicken. Let the chicken marinate for 30 minutes.

FEEL LIKE PLAYING?

Once you make ponzu sauce, you'll start using it all through the week. It's an instant marinade for meat on the grill. I like it as a dressing for a cabbage slaw. Ponzu is great on rice with vegetables as well.

Certainly you could do tofu instead of the chicken here too.

CHOPPING THE BOK CHOY. Cut off the tough base of the baby bok choy. Cut the white stems into 2-inch pieces. Chop the leaves separately into 1-inch pieces.

MAKING THE STIR-FRY. Set a 14-inch flat-bottomed wok over high heat. When a drop of water immediately vaporizes on contact with the wok, swirl in 1 tablespoon of the oil. Remove the chicken from the marinade and add the chicken to the wok, carefully arranging it so that each piece touches the bottom of the wok. Cook for 1 minute without touching the chicken. With a metal spatula, stir-fry the chicken until all sides are evenly browned. Remove the chicken to a plate.

Swirl in the remaining tablespoon of oil to the wok. Add the onion slices and stir-fry until they begin to brown, about 1 minute. Add the stems of the bok choy and stir-fry until they begin to soften, about 1 minute. Add the bok choy leaves and stir-fry until they begin to wilt, about 1 minute more.

Add back the chicken and its juices to the wok. Pour in the remaining ponzu sauce and stir-fry until the chicken is cooked through and the sauce is bubbling, 1 to 2 minutes.

Feeds 4

pork, apple, and spinach stir-fry

This isn't a traditional stir-fry at all, but once I got the hang of the technique, I just started playing. Pork and apple are best friends. Why not pair them together in a stir-fry? Tossing the spinach at the last moment means it will be wilted but not totally mush.

½ cup apple cider

3 tablespoons gluten-free tamari

2 tablespoons sesame oil

1 fresh Fresno chile, seeded and thinly sliced

One 1-inch piece fresh ginger, peeled and finely chopped

12 ounces pork loin, cut into ½-inch pieces

3 tablespoons peanut oil

1 medium onion, peeled and chopped

2 cloves garlic, peeled and chopped

1 medium green apple, peeled and julienned

2 cups chopped spinach

MARINATING THE PORK. Whisk together the apple cider, tamari, sesame oil, chile, and ginger in a bowl. Put the pork into the liquid and let it marinate for 30 minutes.

STIR-FRYING THE VEGETABLES. Set a 14-inch, flat-bottomed wok on high heat. Swirl in the peanut oil. Add the onion and garlic and stir-fry until they release their scent, about 30 seconds. Push the onion and garlic to the side of the wok.

FEEL LIKE PLAYING?

Of course, other vegetables would go great in here. Bok choy, napa cabbage, kale, and chard would complement the pork and apples well. Bok choy and napa cabbage should go in with the pork. Kale and chard can go in at the last moment, like the spinach.

SEARING THE PORK. Lay the pork pieces down on the bottom of the wok. Cook them for 1 minute, allowing the bottom of the pieces to sear. Stir-fry until the meat is evenly browned, about 1 minute.

FINISHING THE STIR-FRY. Move the onion and garlic back into the wok. Add the apple and stir-fry for 1 minute. Swirl in the remaining marinade and stir-fry until the pork is fully cooked and the sauce is bubbly, 2 to 3 minutes. Toss in the spinach and stir-fry until it wilts.

Feeds 4

chicken teriyaki with kale and sweet potato

When you feel comfortable with the form, you can start playing. I love the taste of teriyaki sauce with its complexity of flavors—dark, slightly sweet, a tiny bit bitter, a little acidic—but most bottled teriyaki sauces contain gluten. Here's another good reason to make this sauce from scratch.

Teriyaki sauce

$\frac{1}{4}$ cup gluten-free tamari

2 tablespoons finely chopped fresh ginger

2 tablespoons maple syrup

1 tablespoon sesame oil

1 large lime, zested and juiced

1 clove garlic, peeled and finely chopped

1 teaspoon sherry vinegar

Stir-fry

2 boneless chicken thighs, cut into 1-inch cubes

2 tablespoons peanut oil

1 large shallot, peeled and finely chopped

1 tablespoon cornstarch

1 small sweet potato, peeled and cut into 1-inch cubes

1 small bunch Lacinato kale (or use any kale you like), stems removed and leaves chopped

MAKING THE TERIYAKI SAUCE. Add the tamari, ginger, maple syrup, sesame oil, lime juice and zest, garlic, and vinegar to a blender. Blend until the sauce is smooth, about 3 minutes.

MARINATING THE CHICKEN. Put the chicken pieces in a large bowl. Cover with the teriyaki sauce. Let the chicken marinate for 30 minutes.

COOKING THE AROMATICS. Set a 14-inch, flat-bottomed wok over high heat until it begins to smoke. Add the peanut oil. When the oil is hot, add the shallot. It should sizzle immediately. Cook, moving the shallot around in the wok, until it is softened, about 1 minute. Move the shallot and ginger to the side of the wok.

COOKING THE CHICKEN. Add the chicken pieces to the wok. Let them remain in the wok, searing, for at least 1 minute. (While this is happening, add the cornstarch to the remaining teriyaki sauce and stir.) Move the chicken around to cook the other side, then remove the chicken to a plate.

COOKING THE SWEET POTATO AND KALE.
Let the wok heat up again for 1 minute, then add the sweet potato to the wok. (You should still have plenty of oil left but if you need more, add a drizzle of peanut oil here.) Cook, stirring, until the sweet potato starts to soften, about 2 minutes. Add the kale and cook until it begins to turn a brighter green and wilt, about 1 minute.

FINISHING THE STIR-FRY. Add back the chicken to the wok. Stir everything, which should still be sizzling, until the chicken is fully cooked, about 2 minutes. Add the teriyaki sauce. Stir until the sauce is reduced by half its volume, about 2 minutes. Serve.

Feeds 4

FEEL LIKE PLAYING?

Make a triple batch of this teriyaki sauce ahead of time. It's good on everything. Try it on roasted chicken or grilled fish or as a dipping sauce.

Try any dark green here. Sweet potatoes can be replaced with parsnips or another root vegetable. Just make sure you use very small pieces so they have a chance to cook.

stir-fried salmon with chard

As much as I love fish, I won't stir-fry most varieties. Tender fish fillets fall apart in the vigorous cooking in the wok. A few types of fish work in the wok, however. Halibut is meaty enough. Sardines are great. Mackerel works too. But here in Seattle, the ubiquitous fish is salmon. If you treat the salmon gently, this will work. Here in Seattle, chard is available through the year. With its rainbow-colored stems and wonderful dark green leaves, chard lends a wonderful color and texture to the salmon. Grace Young learned to stir-fry salmon from a chef friend. That recipe taught us how to make this one.

One 1-pound salmon fillet, skin on

3 tablespoons peanut oil

1 clove garlic, peeled and finely chopped

1 tablespoon dry sherry

2 teaspoons sesame oil

1 teaspoon gluten-free tamari

2 teaspoons cornstarch

3 scallions, chopped

One 1-inch piece fresh ginger, peeled and finely sliced

$\frac{1}{4}$ cup chicken stock

1 bunch rainbow chard, stems and leaves chopped separately

PREPARING THE SALMON. Run your hand over the top of the salmon flesh. If you feel any pinbones, gently pull them out with a pair of tweezers. Cut the salmon fillet in half lengthwise, then slice it into $\frac{1}{2}$-inch-thick pieces.

In a large bowl, combine 1 tablespoon of the peanut oil, the garlic, sherry, sesame oil, and tamari. Add in the cornstarch and whisk until there are no clumps. Toss the salmon pieces in this marinade.

MAKING THE STIR-FRY. Set a 14-inch flat-bottomed wok on high heat. When a drop of water dissolves immediately on contact with the wok, swirl in 1 tablespoon of the peanut oil. Add the scallions and ginger and use a metal spatula to stir-fry them until they release their scent, about 10 seconds. Push the scallions and ginger to the side of the wok. Gently lay the salmon pieces on the bottom of the wok. Cook without touching them for 30 seconds. Gently loosen the salmon from the bottom of the wok.

Swirl in 2 tablespoons of the chicken stock, incorporating the scallions and ginger, and cook the salmon for another 2 minutes, loosening the pieces once in a while but not stir-frying yet. When the pan gets dry, gently flip over the salmon.

Swirl in the remaining tablespoon of peanut oil. Add the chard stems. Put a cover on the wok and cook for 1 minute. Uncover and add the chard leaves. Cover the wok again and cook for 1 minute more. Uncover, swirl in the remaining marinade, and gently stir-fry everything together for a few moments to combine it all well. Turn off the heat and serve.

Feeds 4

FEEL LIKE PLAYING?

You could try this same dish with halibut when it's in season.

If you haven't tired of kale in this book, then throw that in here instead of the chard.

chicken stir-fry with homemade chili sauce

Coconut milk, chili sauce, a bit of brown sugar for sweetness, lemongrass, ginger, a twirled stack of vermicelli noodles, and the crunch of napa cabbage—I can't get enough of this combination.

$^{2}/_{3}$ cup full-fat coconut milk

3 tablespoons Sriracha sauce (or try your own Homemade Chili Sauce, recipe follows)

1 tablespoon gluten-free fish sauce

1 tablespoon dark brown sugar

2 teaspoons finely chopped Thai basil (traditional basil will work fine as well)

12 ounces boneless chicken thighs, cut into $^{1}/_{2}$-inch pieces

4 ounces rice vermicelli noodles

3 tablespoons peanut oil

2 cloves garlic, peeled and chopped

2 tablespoons grated fresh ginger

One 1-inch stalk lemongrass, bashed

2 cups thinly sliced napa cabbage

MAKING THE MARINADE. In a large bowl, whisk together the coconut milk, Sriracha, fish sauce, brown sugar, and basil. Add the chicken. Let them sit together for a few moments.

SOFTENING THE NOODLES. In a bowl, pour boiling water over the rice noodles. Let them sit until they are softened, 3 to 5 minutes. Drain the noodles and set aside.

COOKING THE AROMATICS. Set a 14-inch flat-bottomed wok on high heat. When the wok just begins to smoke, swirl in 2 tablespoons of the oil. Add the garlic, ginger, and lemongrass. Quickly stir-fry them until their fragrances are released, about 10 seconds. Push the garlic, ginger, and lemongrass to the side of the wok.

SEARING THE CHICKEN. Lay the chicken pieces on the bottom of the wok (reserving the marinade), taking care to not crowd the pieces. Cook without touching them for 1 minute. Stir-fry until the chicken begins to brown evenly, about 30 seconds. Move the chicken to a plate.

COOKING THE CABBAGE. Swirl the remaining tablespoon of peanut oil into the wok. Add the cabbage and incorporate the garlic, ginger, and lemongrass. Stir-fry until the cabbage begins to wilt, about 1 minute.

FINISHING THE STIR-FRY. Add the chicken back into the pan, followed by the soaked noodles.

Stir-fry for 1 minute. Swirl in the remaining marinade and stir-fry until the chicken is cooked through and the sauce is bubbling and reduced a bit.

Feeds 4

homemade chili sauce

Surely you have heard of Sriracha, right? Some of you might have eaten gallons of it by now. That spicy red sauce has become popular in this country. (I'm thrilled that spicy sauces now beat out ketchup for most popular red stuff on the table.) I love it too. However, it contains xanthan gum, which gives my digestive system fits. Many folks who are gluten intolerant or have celiac report the same. And since every other dip or sauce I have ever made from scratch has turned out better than the bottle, I thought I'd give this one a try.

Turns out this recipe, based on one from the wonderful Food52 community, is fresher and sharper in taste than the bottled any day.

8 ounces chopped red Fresno chiles

1 cup white vinegar

6 cloves garlic, peeled

1 tablespoon gluten-free fish sauce

1 teaspoon kosher salt

2 tablespoons turbinado sugar

BRINING THE PEPPERS. Add the chiles, vinegar, garlic, fish sauce, and salt to a large bowl. Let it sit overnight. This will soften some of the intense heat of the chiles.

SIMMERING THE SAUCE. Set a pot over high heat. Add the chiles and their brine to the pot. Add the sugar and stir. When the liquid comes to a boil, turn down the heat to medium-low and simmer until the sauce has reduced and started to thicken, about 20 minutes. Turn off the heat and allow the sauce to cool to room temperature.

BLENDING THE SAUCE. Pour the sauce into a blender. Blend until the sauce becomes smooth, with a texture a little like ketchup, about 5 minutes. Push the sauce through a fine-mesh sieve.

REFRIGERATING THE SAUCE. Let the sauce sit in the refrigerator overnight. Use at will. Store for up to a month (but it will disappear before that).

Makes 1½ cups sauce

wasabi-roasted tofu with mushrooms and napa cabbage

Most stir-fry dishes are really one-pot dinners. Know the order of when to cook foods in a dish and you have dinner in just a few minutes. This one has a slight exception. Roasted tofu has my favorite texture of any tofu dish. In this meal, I like to roast the tofu with a wasabi-ginger marinade, then throw it into the wok at the last moment to blend with the mushrooms, bok choy, and napa cabbage.

1 pound firm tofu

6 tablespoons sesame oil

$\frac{1}{4}$ cup canola oil

$\frac{1}{4}$ cup rice wine vinegar

One 1-inch nub fresh ginger, peeled and grated

2 tablespoons gluten-free tamari

$\frac{1}{2}$ to 1 teaspoon wasabi powder (depending on the heat you want)

1 tablespoon cornstarch

2 cloves garlic, peeled and sliced

1 cup chopped maitake (hen of the woods) mushrooms (or whatever type you can find)

$\frac{1}{2}$ bunch bok choy, stems and leaves chopped separately

$\frac{1}{2}$ big bunch napa cabbage, outer leaves only, chopped

MARINATING THE TOFU. Cut the tofu into 1-inch cubes and add them to a large bowl. In a small bowl, whisk together 4 tablespoons of the sesame oil, the canola oil, vinegar, ginger, tamari, and wasabi powder. Pour over the tofu and gently toss the tofu cubes in the sauce. Let sit for 1 hour to build flavor.

ROASTING THE TOFU. Preheat the oven to 450°F. Line a baking sheet with parchment paper. Put the tofu cubes on the baking sheet, allowing space between the cubes, reserving the marinade. Roast until the bottoms are dark-golden brown, about 15 minutes. Flip the tofu and roast until the second side is dark-golden brown and the cubes have puffed up, about 10 minutes. Take the tofu out of the oven.

While the tofu is roasting, add the cornstarch to the remaining marinade and stir. Set aside.

continued . . .

MAKING THE STIR-FRY. Set the wok over high heat. When the wok is starting to smoke, add the remaining 2 tablespoons of sesame oil. When the oil is hot, add the garlic. It should sizzle immediately. Stir-fry until the garlic begins to brown. Push the garlic up the side of the wok to take it off the heat. (If you are using a skillet, remove the garlic from the pan at this point.)

Add the mushrooms and bok choy stems to the hot wok. Stir-fry until they have begun to wilt a bit, about 2 minutes. Add the bok choy leaves and napa cabbage. Stir-fry until the leaves begin to wilt, about 1 minute. Add the roasted tofu and stir. Pour in the sauce. Watch the steam billow up, then stir-fry quickly for 1 minute. Turn off the heat. Serve immediately.

Feeds 4

FEEL LIKE PLAYING?

If you don't want to take the extra step of roasting the tofu, you can stir-fry it in the typical way: in the wok, after the onions and garlic and before the mushrooms.

I love roasted tofu as a snack. Roast the tofu and use this marinade or the Ponzu Sauce on page 124 as a dipping sauce.

lemongrass-beef stir-fry

I love the therapy of bashing a lemongrass stalk. That stalk is too tough to chop with a knife, even the biggest chef's knife you have, so you have to beat the heck out of it to release the fragrance and flavor into what you're cooking. Turn that chef's knife upside down and carefully smack the stalk with the back of the knife. Your stress will break up with each whack and the scent of lemongrass is bound to melt your tensions. On top of that, dinner will taste great.

Lemongrass and beef go together well and marinating flank steak makes it tender. So, add lemongrass to the marinade for beef, let it sit for a while, and then stir-fry it all up in the wok? That's a darned fine meal.

1 pound flank steak

One 2-inch piece lemongrass stalk, bashed

One 3-inch white part of leek, thinly sliced

$\frac{1}{4}$ cup gluten-free tamari

1 orange, zested and juiced

2 cloves garlic, peeled and finely chopped

3 tablespoons sesame oil

2 to 3 tablespoons peanut oil

One 1-inch piece fresh ginger, peeled and thinly sliced

1 medium onion, peeled and thinly sliced

$\frac{1}{2}$ pound sliced porcini mushrooms (or whatever mushroom is available)

CUTTING THE BEEF. Make a long slice down the length of the steak, with the grain of the meat. Put one of the strips on the cutting board and slice $\frac{1}{4}$-inch-thick slices against the grain of the beef. Repeat with the other strip.

MARINATING THE BEEF. In a large bowl, combine the lemongrass, leek, tamari, orange juice and zest, garlic, and sesame oil. Put the beef slices in this mixture. Marinate for at least 1 hour and preferably 6 to 8 hours.

MAKING THE STIR-FRY. Set a 14-inch flat-bottomed wok on high heat. When a drop of water dissolves immediately on contact with the wok, swirl in 1 tablespoon of the peanut oil. Add the ginger. Cook until the scent is released, about 30 seconds. Push the ginger to the side of the wok. Add the onion and stir-fry with a metal spatula until softened, about 2 minutes. Move the onion to the side of the wok.

continued . . .

If the wok is dry, swirl in another tablespoon of the peanut oil. Spread the pieces of beef evenly on the bottom of the wok and let them cook undisturbed for 1 minute. Flip over the beef and stir-fry with a metal spatula until it is a little brown but not done cooking, about 1 minute. Remove the beef to a plate.

Swirl in the rest of the peanut oil. Add the porcini mushrooms and incorporate the ginger and onions. Stir-fry for 1 minute, then add back the beef and its juices. Swirl the remaining marinade into the wok and stir-fry until the beef is fully cooked and the marinade has reduced and thickened, about 1 minute.

Feeds 4

rice and beans

WHENEVER FRIENDS ARE SHORT ON MONEY AT THE END OF THE MONTH, THEY ALL SAY THE SAME thing: "We're eating a lot of rice and beans."

We say it too, particularly after retesting all the recipes for this book in one month. Instead of being able to make up dishes, spontaneously, based on what was in our pantry, we needed to buy every ingredient in this book at once. After that, we were relieved to be eating rice and beans again.

Rice and beans are the food of the working class, the folks trying to make it, those of us not lucky enough to have cars made within the last decade. Maybe that's why so many people disdain rice and beans—they don't want to remember their hard-scrabbling years.

Me? I love rice and beans. It doesn't matter how much or little is in our bank account—I'm always going to be happy putting some beans to soak in the morning, come home and combine them with onions and garlic, a hit of spice, and put on some rice. There's something deeply satisfying about this kind of dish.

Since people are scrabbling all over the world, hoping that the bank account will surprise them with fullness the next week, we wanted to play with world flavors here. Sure, there are Cuban beans and rice, pinto beans to refry the next day, and Louis Armstrong's favorite: red beans and rice.

But I love edamame and sticky rice together. Adzuki beans and calrose medium-grain rice. African yellow rice with black-eyed peas. If you're going to have a simple comfort food, with relatively uncomplicated technique, why not play with flavors?

That way you never have to get tired of rice and beans.

When I'm tired of rice and beans, I'll know I'm tired of life.

making a big pot of beans

It's Sunday afternoon. We spent the morning in the garden or reading books with Lucy or dancing to The Beatles while making breakfast. Sunday is the day for making a new batch of ponzu sauce, now that the jar is empty, so we can have a quick stir-fry this week. I set up a batch of bread dough to rise while Danny breaks down a chicken for that evening's roast. And slowly, I'm simmering a pot of beans for the week.

Making a pot of beans is one of the humblest acts of our cooking life. For years, I bought cans of already cooked beans and lined them up on my pantry shelves. And if the choice is between no beans and canned beans, there's a clear choice. Beans are full of fiber and protein. But when they're cooked well, they're so full of flavor that they can make a meal on their own.

For some reason, I worried for years that making beans from scratch would be difficult. When I lifted a spoon of warm, creamy beans to my lips, drinking in the heady fragrance of the liquid they were cooked in, I was convinced.

Dried beans are cheaper than canned beans, by far. When you cook your own beans, you can create the taste you want—a bit of onion cooked in a smidge of olive oil with cumin and chili powder before you pour in the dried beans and add water—instead of having to doctor up a flat-tasting can of beans. And with growing concerns about the amount of the chemical BPA (Bisphenol-A) in canned goods, we just prefer to make our own beans.

Maybe you would like to try it too.

THE KEY TO MAKING A GOOD POT OF BEANS IS to start with good beans. Not all beans come out equal. Some of the dried beans in plastic packages you'll find at the grocery store might have been sitting in that bag for years. We buy heirloom beans, more recently picked and dried, from local farmers' markets or Rancho Gordo, our favorite bean company. Choosing a good bean means you'll have great flavor later.

I like to soak my beans. I cover them with water in the morning and let them sit for 2 to 6 hours before I cook them. Soaking beans means the cooked beans are plump and evenly cooked. I think it's worth the utter lack of effort.

Danny thinks I'm silly. He pulls beans out of the pantry and cooks them on the spot, without soaking. Apparently, almost all cooks in Mexico agree with him. Frankly, the difference in the final beans is pretty small. I think the only determining factor is if you planned ahead to soak the beans in the morning or you remembered the beans just before you started making dinner.

And by the way, soaking or not soaking does not affect the famous propensities of beans. There's nothing inherent in beans that will give you gas. Instead, their huge fiber content can overwhelm a system that hasn't been eating that much fiber. Introduce beans into your diet slowly and you'll work up a tolerance.

Grab a Dutch oven or big pot. Pour in some olive oil (or lard, if you're going with that flavor). Add some finely diced carrots, onions, and celery. Depending on what you will be making with the beans, you might play with spices or fresh herbs here as well. Pour the beans—soaking liquid too, if you have soaked them—into the pot. Cover the beans with more water, if they are not entirely covered by at least 1 inch of water.

Bring the water to a boil and let it boil rapidly for 5 minutes. Turn the heat down to low until the beans are at a gentle simmer, with just the occasional bubble breaking the surface of the liquid. Leave the lid off. Cook the beans until they are soft and plump. This could be 1 hour. It could be 4 hours. It depends on the age of your beans. (Another reason to buy newer beans!)

When the beans are soft to the bite and ready to go, add some salt. You can start with about 2 teaspoons for the pot. Stir. Taste. Add some more, if you need. Simmer the beans until every little nibble of the beans is evenly seasoned, 10 to 15 minutes.

And that's it. Beans.

You could also cook beans in the oven, in that same large pot. Preheat the oven to 350°F. Cook the onions, carrots, and celery in oil. Throw in the beans. Add twice as much water as beans. Bring the liquid to a simmer, then cover the pot and put it in the oven. The beans should be done in an hour or two. Salt them about halfway through. You're done.

And if you want cooked beans available later for a quick dinner, freeze 2 cups of the cooked beans, along with their cooking liquid, in a plastic bag or airtight container. Any time you want to cook beans, just pull them out of the freezer. Simmer them in a pot, drain away the liquid, and you're ready to go.

Set a big pot of beans to simmer on a Sunday afternoon and you'll be amazed by how good your home smells by the evening. You might make it a weekly ritual too.

new orleans red beans and rice

I love all the rice and beans recipes in this chapter, and we eat them all on a regular basis. But when I think of rice and beans, I think of red beans and rice from New Orleans. Folks in New Orleans eat red beans and rice every Monday—think of what those streets smell like after a full day of simmering in every kitchen. Louis Armstrong loved red beans and rice so much that he used to sign his autograph, "Red beans and ricely yours." That's good enough for me.

Traditionally, the trinity of New Orleans cooking is onions, celery, and green onions. Please forgive my transgressions, New Orleans, but we just can't stand green bell peppers in this house. They taste so. . . underripe. So we use red bell pepper here. Other than that, folks from New Orleans have told me that this is pretty darned good.

¼ cup nonhydrogenated lard (use extra-virgin olive oil if you can't find this kind of lard)

1 large onion, peeled and chopped

1 red bell pepper, chopped

3 stalks celery, chopped

5 cloves garlic, peeled and chopped

1 teaspoon chopped fresh thyme

1 pound dried kidney beans, soaked in water to cover for at least 4 hours and drained

½ pound smoked ham hock or one ½-pound piece of ham

1 bay leaf

Kosher salt and freshly ground black pepper

½ pound Andouille sausage, sliced

2 cups cooked white long-grain rice (page 117)

Tabasco or other hot sauce, to taste

PREPARING TO MAKE THE DISH. Preheat the oven to 400°F.

COOKING THE BEANS. Set a Dutch oven over medium-high heat. Add 2 tablespoons of the lard. When the lard has melted, add the onion, red pepper, celery, and garlic and cook, stirring, until the onions and pepper have softened, about 5 minutes. Add the thyme and cook until the scent is released, about 1 minute.

Add the beans and stir to coat them with the fragrant vegetables. Add the ham hock and bay leaf. Pour in 4 cups of water, stir, and put the lid on the Dutch oven.

Put the dutch oven in the oven. Every 30 minutes, take the Dutch oven out of the oven, remove the lid, and stir it all up. Repeat this until the beans are creamy, which will take at least 2 hours. Three hours is even better.

When the beans are creamy, add salt and black pepper. Start with at least a teaspoon of each. Stir the beans and taste them. Season with more salt and pepper to taste.

Cooking the sausage. Just before the beans are done, set a large skillet over medium-high heat. Add the remaining 2 tablespoons lard. When the lard has melted, add the sausage slices. Cook until the bottoms have browned, about 3 minutes. Flip the sausages over and brown the other sides. Turn off the heat and set aside.

Finishing the dish. Remove the pot from the oven. Take the ham hocks out of the beans. Pull the meat off the bones, shred it up, return the meat to the beans and stir to combine. Remove the bay leaf. Plop some rice in a bowl, add some of the beans, toss in some of the sausage, and top with splashes of Tabasco or other hot sauce. Stir it all up.

Serve.

Feeds 4 to 6

FEEL LIKE PLAYING?

As you can imagine, this tastes so much better the second day that it's sort of ridiculous. If I were you, I would cook the beans one evening, after making dinner, then reheat it and brown the sausage just before serving.

If you wanted to make this vegetarian, it won't be the same taste at all. However, it would still be good. Use extra-virgin olive oil instead of the lard, and perhaps some smoked tofu to build the flavor.

cuban black beans and rice

Across the street from where I used to live in Manhattan was one of the funniest and best little restaurants in that part of town. Flor de Mayo had two halves to the menu: one Chinese and the other Cuban. At first this seemed entirely random until I understood that all the cooks were of Chinese descent who had grown up in Cuba and then immigrated to New York. Their Chinese food was pretty mediocre. The Cuban food? Some of the best comfort food I've ever eaten. At least once a week I walked down there to get a rotisserie chicken and black beans.

Long gone from New York, I tried to make those black beans at home. Sure, they were spiced well and tender, but they just weren't the same. What was I missing? It wasn't until I started asking around and researching that I realized the secret ingredient: pork fat. Remember, lard isn't bad for you, if it's the right lard.

When I made this the first time, Danny sat on the couch late at night, eating. He sighed: "This is my favorite kind of dinner, honey."

1 pound dried black beans

$1\frac{1}{2}$ medium white onions, peeled

1 bay leaf

$\frac{1}{3}$ cup pork fat (preferably leaf lard)

$\frac{1}{4}$ cup extra-virgin olive oil (if needed)

6 cloves garlic, peeled

1 teaspoon cumin seeds

1 teaspoon kosher salt and cracked black pepper

1 cup sour cream

1 lime, zested and juiced

2 cups cooked white basmati rice (page 117)

SOAKING THE BEANS. Cover the beans in enough water to cover them by 3 inches. Add $\frac{1}{2}$ onion to the beans. Soak for at least 4 hours, if not overnight. (I start soaking them in the morning for dinner that night.)

COOKING THE BEANS. Set a Dutch oven or large pot over medium-high heat. Pour the beans, onions, and the water in which you have been soaking the beans into the pot. Add the bay leaf. Cook the beans until the water is boiling vigorously, about 5 minutes. Turn down the heat until the water is doing a gentle, slow simmer (that's medium on our stove, but it might be low on yours). Cook the beans until you can easily run a fork through them, $1\frac{1}{2}$ to 3 hours, depending on how old your beans are. Don't worry if the beans run low on water—add more. (You could also use chicken or vegetable stock, if you want.)

Cooking the onions. About 45 minutes before the beans are done, dice the remaining onion. Set a large skillet over medium-high heat. Add the pork fat. When it has melted and begun to simmer, add the diced onion. The ideal is to have the onion submerged in the pork fat, burbling away. If the onion is not completely covered, add more pork fat or extra-virgin olive oil—your choice. Cook the onions, stirring occasionally, until they are softened, about 7 minutes. Add the onions to the pot of beans.

Finishing the beans. After you have added the onions to the beans, stir vigorously and simmer for 5 minutes. Meanwhile, add the garlic, cumin seeds, and salt into a mortar. Using a pestle, bash away until the garlic has become a paste. (If you don't have a mortar and pestle, you can do this with a sharp knife on a cutting board with a lot of patience.) Add the garlic paste to the beans. Cook the beans until they are entirely tender. Add more salt and the pepper. Taste. Season more, if necessary. Cook for at least 10 minutes more to allow the beans to absorb the salt. (Be sure to remove the bay leaf from the beans before serving.)

Making the lime sour cream. While the beans are finishing their final simmer, in a bowl, combine the sour cream with the lime zest and juice and mix well. Put it in the refrigerator until it's time to eat.

To serve, put ½ cup of the rice at the bottom of a bowl, spoon over the beans, and add a dollop of the lime sour cream.

Feeds 6

FEEL LIKE PLAYING?

Of course, if you're a vegetarian, you can make these with extra-virgin olive oil or peanut oil, and they'll still be pretty darned good.
I love this lime sour cream for tacos as well.

pinto beans with mexican rice

We have a just-above-mediocre Mexican restaurant on our island. About once a month, thinking it's going to be better suddenly, we pile Lucy in the car and go. After years of cooking at a restaurant, Danny can actually sit and enjoy the experience. (But he's always thinking about what they're doing in the kitchen.) I can't resist hot corn chips and house-made salsa. Lucy gets excited about tacos, but really, all she wants? Rice and refried beans.

Now that our friend Jorge has a taco truck on the island, we buy our rice and beans there when we leave the house. But, since I learned how to make them at home, knowing what is going into them, I'm happy to say that these are Lucy's favorite Mexican rice and beans.

For the beans

2 tablespoons nonhydrogenated lard
(or you can use extra-virgin olive oil)

1 large onion, peeled and chopped

2 cloves garlic, peeled and chopped

1 tablespoon ground cumin

1 teaspoon dried Mexican oregano

1 cup dried pinto beans, soaked in water to cover for at least 2 hours and drained

3 cups chicken stock

For the rice

1 tablespoon unsalted butter

1 large onion, peeled and chopped

2 cloves garlic, peeled and chopped

1 teaspoon chili powder

1 teaspoon ground cumin

2 tablespoons tomato paste

One 14-ounce can diced tomatoes, drained

1 cup long-grain white rice

3 cups chicken stock

1 tablespoon lime juice

$1/2$ cup chopped fresh cilantro

2 avocados, pitted, peeled, and sliced

For serving

Salsa (optional)

Grated cheese (optional)
(We like Monterey Jack)

Sour cream (optional)

COOKING THE PINTO BEANS. Set a large pot over medium-high heat. Add the lard. When it has melted, add the onion and the garlic. Cook, stirring frequently, until the onion has softened, about 5 minutes. Add the cumin and oregano and cook until their scents are released, about 1 minute. Add the beans and stir until they are entirely coated in the onion mixture. Add the chicken stock. When it has come to a boil, turn down the heat to medium-low and simmer until the beans are tender but not mushy, 60 to 90 minutes. Take the pot off the stove and set aside.

MAKING THE RICE. Set a Dutch oven over medium-high heat. Add the butter. When it has melted, add the onion and garlic and cook, stirring, until the onion has softened, about 5 minutes. Add the chili powder and cumin. Cook until their scents are released, about 1 minute. Add the tomato paste and stir it into the mixture thoroughly. Pour in the tomatoes and cook until they have softened, about 3 minutes. Add the rice and stir until it is entirely coated with the mixture. Pour in the chicken stock. Bring it to a boil, then turn down the heat to medium-low. Put on the lid of the Dutch oven. Simmer until the rice has absorbed the chicken stock, 15 to 20 minutes. Turn off the heat and let the beans sit for an additional 15 minutes. Fluff up the rice.

To serve, dollop some rice on a plate, top with the beans, and squeeze on some of the lime juice. Top with cilantro and avocado. (Of course, a little salsa, cheese, and sour cream never hurt either.)

Feeds 4

edamame and sweet rice salad with salty seeds

One of our favorite restaurants in Seattle was in a tiny space in the middle of a strip mall on a busy street. Nettletown, run by Christina Choi, was a place dedicated to food made in the moment, based on what was growing that week, and especially what could be foraged. Every meal we ate there was a satisfying surprise. Everything seemed simple, the ingredients unadorned, the preparations fairly humble. But the taste of this food? Fantastic. The freshness made each bite alive.

One of our favorite dishes was the simplest: a bowl of brown sticky rice, drizzled with toasted sesame oil, and an utterly interesting mix of toasted salty seeds. Those seeds. We needed them. We started playing at home and came up with this mix for ourselves. We like mixing up whatever is freshest from the farm stands near us with rice and these seeds. But in the middle of winter, when nothing is growing, we use frozen edamame and sticky rice, drizzle them with miso-maple-ginger dressing, and top them with these seeds.

Christina died last year, of a sudden brain aneurysm, at thirty-four years old. We're still in shock. We raise our forks to her here.

2 cups sticky rice

3 tablespoons pumpkin seeds

3 tablespoons sunflower seeds

2 tablespoons sesame seeds

2 tablespoons chia seeds

1 teaspoon cumin seeds

1 teaspoon coriander seeds

1 teaspoon fennel seeds

$^1/_2$ teaspoon kosher salt

1 cup cooked shelled edamame

$^1/_4$ cup Miso-Maple-Ginger Dressing (recipe follows)

SOAKING THE RICE. Rinse the rice in a colander, moving your hand through the rice with the water running. Drain the water completely. Repeat this three times. In a bowl, soak the rice in cold water for at least 1 hour.

ROASTING THE SALTY SEEDS. Set a large skillet over high heat. When the pan is hot, add the pumpkin seeds and sunflower seeds. Roast, moving the pan around to prevent burning, for 3 minutes. Add the sesame and chia seeds. Roast in the same manner for 2 minutes. Add the cumin, coriander, and fennel seeds. Roast in the pan, shaking it about, for another 2 minutes. Turn off the heat. Add the salt, toss the seeds together, and set aside.

COOKING THE RICE. Drain the rice and put the rice in a microwave-safe bowl. Add enough water to be on the same level with the rice (usually about 1½ cups). Heat in the microwave for 2 minutes, then stop, and stir the rice. Cook the rice in 2-minute increments until it is soft and fluffy.

If you don't have a microwave (as we did not, for years), then you can steam the rice. Fill a large pot with hot water, leaving 3 inches of space before the top of the pot. Put a bamboo steamer, or the metal insert that comes with pasta pots, into the pot. Put the rice in the steamer. Cover with a lid. Steam until the rice is soft and fluffy, about 10 minutes.

HEATING THE EDAMAME. Heat the edamame to piping hot by either putting it in the microwave, or plopping it in a pot of boiling hot water for a couple of minutes and then draining.

To serve, combine some of the sticky rice and edamame. Toss with the dressing. Top with the salty seeds.

Feeds 4

FEEL LIKE PLAYING?

If you have a good rice cooker with a sweet rice setting, making this dish is ridiculously easy. Have some salty seeds in the house, because you're going to want to put them on everything. Make the sweet rice in the morning. For dinner, you just heat up the edamame, spoon in some rice, and top with the salty seeds. Dinner in 3 minutes.

miso-maple-ginger dressing

This tangy, complex dressing goes well with the edamame salad, but it's also great for any number of foods you might want to make. I like it drizzled on warm brown rice, tossed in a salad of dark greens and sunflower seeds, or atop roasted chicken. The umeboshi plum vinegar adds a slightly sour, salty taste here, which keeps the taste mysteriously interesting. If you can't find umeboshi plum vinegar, however, try rice wine vinegar instead.

$\frac{1}{2}$ cup apple cider vinegar

2 tablespoons umeboshi plum vinegar (you can use rice wine vinegar instead)

2 tablespoons maple syrup

1 tablespoon brown rice miso

1 large shallot, peeled and finely chopped

One $\frac{1}{2}$-inch piece fresh ginger, peeled and chopped

1 tablespoon white sesame seeds

1 teaspoon sea salt

6 tablespoons extra-virgin olive oil

$\frac{1}{4}$ cup sesame oil

MAKING THE DRESSING. Add the vinegars, maple syrup, miso, shallot, and ginger in a blender. Turn on the blender and mix until frothy. Add the sesame seeds and salt and blend for 1 minute more.

In a small bowl, combine the olive oil and sesame oil. With the blender running, slowly pour in the combined oils. Turn off the blender and taste the dressing. Do you want a little more acid? Add some more umeboshi plum vinegar. A bit smoother taste? Try some more sesame oil.

Makes $1\frac{1}{2}$ cups

italian fried rice with artichoke hearts and mozzarella

I was having so much fun with the wok after researching and cooking for the stir-fry chapter in this book that I started playing with other flavors than Asian. This is a completely nontraditional dish. But the flavors will feel familiar to you. And let me tell you, it's delicious.

3 tablespoons extra-virgin olive oil

1 medium onion, peeled and chopped

2 cloves garlic, peeled and chopped

1/2 cup marinated artichoke hearts, 3 tablespoons of the liquid reserved

1/2 cup sun-dried tomatoes (not oil-packed), soaked for 30 minutes and drained

2 cups cooked Arborio rice (page 117; make sure it's cold)

One 14-ounce can cannellini beans, drained and rinsed

2 tablespoons balsamic vinegar

4 ounces fresh mozzarella, torn into shreds

1 tablespoon finely chopped fresh basil

PREPARING TO COOK. Set a 14-inch flat-bottomed wok on high heat. When the wok is just starting to smoke, swirl in 2 tablespoons of the oil. Immediately add the onion and garlic and stir-fry until they are starting to soften, about 1 minute. Push the onion and garlic to the side of the wok.

COOKING THE VEGETABLES. Add the artichoke hearts and sun-dried tomatoes to the wok. Stir-fry until they are heated, about 1 minute.

COOKING THE BEANS AND RICE. Swirl in the remaining tablespoon of oil. Add the rice and beans. Stir-fry until they are fully heated, about 2 minutes.

ADDING THE SAUCE. In a small bowl, stir together the vinegar and reserved liquid from the artichoke hearts. Swirl this sauce into the wok. Stir-fry until the sauce is bubbly, about 1 minute.

FINISHING THE STIR-FRY. Toss in the shreds of mozzarella and basil. Stir-fry until the mozzarella begins to melt, about 30 seconds. Turn off the heat.

Feeds 4

wild rice salad with flageolet beans

Flageolet beans are tiny and narrow, not very impressive in their dry state. However, they turn creamy when cooked. Throw a little butter in the pot to intensify this and you have a pretty decadent pot of beans.

We love the soft bite of wild rice. This, plus creamy beans, and the crunch of pistachios makes for a more varied texture than most rice and bean dishes have. You might like this salad as it is, but we love kale so much that we have to throw it into everything.

2 tablespoons extra-virgin olive oil

1 large onion, peeled and chopped

2 cloves garlic, peeled and chopped

2 tablespoons chopped fresh tarragon

1 cup dried flageolet beans, soaked in water to cover for at least 2 hours and drained

2 tablespoons unsalted butter

1 teaspoon kosher salt

2$^1\!/_4$ cups chicken stock

1 cup wild rice

$^1\!/_2$ cup unsalted pistachios

1 bunch Lacinato kale (optional, or use any kind of kale you like), cut into ribbons

2 tablespoons champagne vinegar

1 teaspoon Dijon mustard

6 tablespoons extra-virgin olive oil

4 ounces chèvre

Cooking the beans. Set a pot over medium-high heat and add the oil. When the oil is hot, add the onion and garlic and cook, stirring, until the onion is softened, about 5 minutes. Add the tarragon and cook until its scent is released, about 1 minute. Add the beans and stir to coat. Pour in 4 cups of water. Bring the water to a boil, then turn down the heat to medium-low. Simmer the beans until they are tender to the teeth, about 90 minutes. Add 1 tablespoon of the butter and the salt. Cook, stirring, until the butter is fully incorporated and the beans are seasoned. Taste. Add more salt if necessary. Drain the beans and set aside.

Cooking the wild rice. Meanwhile, set another pot over medium-high heat. Add the chicken stock, the remaining tablespoon of butter, and salt. When the stock has come to a boil, add the rice.

continued . . .

Turn down the heat and simmer, with the lid on, until the rice is tender and the water has evaporated, 50 to 60 minutes.

MAKING THE WARM SALAD. Combine the beans and wild rice. Sprinkle the pistachios into the salad. Toss in the kale, if you are using it.

MAKING THE VINAIGRETTE. Add the vinegar, mustard, and a pinch of salt into a small jar. Stir them up. Add the oil and shake the jar until the dressing has come together. Drizzle the dressing over the salad (you might not use all of it). Toss with your hands. Crumble up the chèvre on top and serve.

Feeds 4

FEEL LIKE PLAYING?

This vinaigrette is our standard for salads. Look how easy it is! And the flavors are so much sharper than bottled dressings could offer.

We have a recipe on our website for wild rice salad with chanterelles, dried cherries, and cashew cream. We made it for Thanksgiving one year and everyone approved of the vegan dish. (Speaking of, if you wanted to make this dish vegan, you could use vegetable stock and nondairy butter.)

green-curried red lentils

The closest I ever had to a fight with Danny over this cookbook happened because of this dish. He called me from the grocery store and said, "Okay, I'm picking up some galangal and fresh turmeric." I had to stop him there and tell him we couldn't use those ingredients in this cookbook. Don't tell a chef he can't use ingredients to make the best dish he can. He's not happy. However, he forgets that we are pretty blessed in the Pacific Northwest with easy access to Asian ingredients. I know from my friends in other places that even lemongrass is a stretch. We want you to be able to make these dishes. I convinced Danny to put down the galangal.

This dish doesn't suffer for that absence, however. This green curry is so wonderfully comforting, and with soft lentils simmering in it, this is going to be a good dinner. You'll never remember that it's vegan.

And hey! If you happen to have access to galangal and fresh turmeric, try those too.

2 stalks lemongrass

1 cup chopped fresh cilantro

1 medium onion, peeled and chopped

One 2-inch nub fresh ginger

1 serrano chile, seeded

3 cloves garlic, peeled and smashed

2 kaffir lime leaves (optional)

1 tablespoon ground cumin

2 sprigs fresh basil, chopped

2 sprigs fresh mint, chopped

2 tablespoons peanut oil

One 14-ounce can full-fat coconut milk

1 tablespoon gluten-free tamari

1 cup red lentils, rinsed

Cooked rice or rice noodles, for serving

1 jalapeño pepper, seeded and thinly sliced (optional)

BASHING THE LEMONGRASS. Cut off the root end and top stalks of the lemongrass. Bash the remaining stalk with the back of a chef's knife to release the scent. Chop the stalk into 4 pieces.

MAKING THE CURRY PASTE. Put the chopped lemongrass, cilantro, half the onion, the ginger, serrano chile, 2 garlic cloves, lime leaves (if using), cumin, basil, and mint into the bowl of a food processor. Run the food processor until each ingredient is evenly chopped into a fine paste, about 5 minutes.

continued . . .

Cooking the curry. Set a large skillet over medium-high heat. Add 1 tablespoon of the oil to the skillet. When the oil is hot, add the curry paste. Cook the paste, stirring frequently, until the scent of the curry wafts into your face, enticing, about 3 minutes. Add the coconut milk and tamari. Stir, then turn down the heat to medium and simmer, stirring occasionally, until the curry has turned a light green and is evenly heated, about 15 minutes.

FEEL LIKE PLAYING?

This curry is good for so many meals. It makes a great curry for chicken, shrimp, or halibut.
If you can't find lemongrass at your store, double up on the ginger here.

Cooking the lentils. Meanwhile, set a pot over medium-high heat. Add the remaining tablespoon of oil. When the oil is hot, add the remaining onion and clove of garlic. Cook, stirring occasionally, until the onion has softened, about 5 minutes. Add the lentils and 3 cups of water. Allow the water to come to a boil, then turn the heat down to medium-low and simmer until the lentils are soft, about 20 minutes.

Finishing the dish. Strain the curry and return the liquid to the same skillet. Add the lentils and stir. Simmer for a few moments to allow the flavors to mingle.

Serve over rice or rice noodles. Top with jalapeño slices for those who need more heat.

Feeds 4

adzuki beans and rice

I always associated adzuki beans (also known as aduki and azuki) with health food stores. It seemed that only hippies ate them in the 1970s. Of course, that's only in the U.S. These little maroon-red beans with a white stripe on one side are eaten all over Asia but are most popular in Japan. They're easy to cook and quite creamy and tender. And, because most people in the U.S. still don't eat them, they are one of the least expensive beans available.

Typically, they're used for Asian sweet foods, in the form of red bean paste. However, I like them best in this dish. Based on a dish called *sekihan*, meant for special celebrations in Japan, this dish is wonderfully easy because you throw cooked beans in with the rice while it's cooking. Typically the dish is made with sweet rice, but we like calrose here. Soft rice studded with plump beans, flavored with ginger and scallions? That's a weeknight celebration here.

1 cup calrose medium-grain rice (or sticky rice, depending on your taste)

1 cup dried adzuki beans

1 piece kombu (optional)

Kosher salt

2 tablespoons sesame oil

One 1-inch nub fresh ginger, peeled and grated

1 tablespoon umeboshi plum vinegar (you could use rice wine vinegar)

1 tablespoon gluten-free tamari

$1/2$ cup finely chopped scallions

SOAKING THE RICE. Rinse the rice in a colander several times until the rice runs clear. Soak the rice in cold water while you are cooking and preparing the beans.

COOKING THE BEANS. Set a large pot of water over high heat. Add the beans and kombu, if using, and bring the beans to a boil. Let them boil for 5 minutes, then turn the heat down to medium-low and allow the beans to simmer until they are tender to a fork, 30 minutes to 2 hours, depending on how old your beans are. Add a good pinch of salt. Cook the beans for 5 more minutes, then taste them again. Season to taste. Drain the beans.

SAUTÉING THE BEANS. Set a large skillet over medium-high heat. Add the oil. When the oil is hot, add the ginger, vinegar, and tamari. Cook, stirring, until the liquids begin to simmer and the ginger smell wafts to your nose, about 2 minutes. Add the beans and coat them in the liquids. Turn off the heat.

Cooking the rice and beans. Add the rice and beans into the pot in which you sautéed the beans and set it over high heat. (You could also use your rice cooker here, which is what we do.) Add 2 ½ cups of water. Bring the water to a boil, then turn the heat down until the water simmers. Cook, covered, until the water is completely absorbed into the tender rice, about 15 minutes. (Feel free to lift the lid after about 12 minutes to check—just put the lid back on quickly!)

Take the pot off the burner and let it sit, with the lid on, for at least 5 minutes. This allows the moisture in the rice to settle into every part of the dish.

Put the rice and beans into a bowl and top with the scallions.

Feeds 4

FEEL LIKE PLAYING?

I love this dish drizzled with the Ginger-Scallion Sauce (see page 248).

If you would prefer to eat this with sweet rice, use the method described in the Edamame and Sweet Rice Salad with Salty Seeds on page 151.

chana masala

One of the reasons I love cooking rice and bean dishes is that they're usually so darned simple to make. It's the different blend of spices that makes one dish different from another. This intoxicating mix of ginger, jalapeño, cumin, coriander, and cardamom will make your kitchen smell incredible while the chickpeas are cooking. And this may be a vegetarian dish but the taste is so hearty here that you'll never miss the meat.

Chickpeas are one of my favorite beans in the world. Any way I eat them, I'm happy. But this is probably my favorite.

2 tablespoons clarified butter (see page 276)
   (or extra-virgin olive oil)

1 large onion, peeled and chopped

2 cloves garlic, peeled and chopped

1 jalapeño pepper, seeded and thinly sliced

2 tablespoons grated fresh ginger

2 teaspoons ground cumin

2 teaspoons ground coriander

1 teaspoon garam masala

$\frac{1}{2}$ teaspoon ground cardamom

Pinch cayenne pepper

One 28-ounce can diced tomatoes

Two 14-ounce cans chickpeas,
   drained and rinsed

Kosher salt

$\frac{1}{4}$ cup chopped fresh cilantro

$\frac{1}{2}$ cup whole milk yogurt

1 large lemon, juiced

Cooked basmati or jasmine rice,
   for serving

COOKING THE AROMATICS. Set a Dutch oven over medium heat. Add the butter. When it has melted, add the onion and cook, stirring frequently, until the onion has started to brown, about 10 minutes. Keep cooking and stirring until the onion is caramelized, about 5 minutes more.

Add the garlic and cook until it has softened, about 3 minutes. Add the jalapeño, ginger, cumin, coriander, garam masala, cardamom, and cayenne pepper. (Go easy on that last one!) Cook and stir until the kitchen smells incredible with all these spices, about 3 minutes.

continued . . .

Simmering the masala. Stir in the tomatoes, mashing them up a bit as you do. Scrape up any spices or onions that might have stuck to the bottom of the pan. Cook until the tomatoes start to soften, about 3 minutes. Add the chickpeas. Bring the liquids to a gentle boil, then turn the heat down to medium-low and simmer until the chickpeas are tender-soft, about 10 minutes. If it feels like there aren't enough liquids, add $\frac{1}{4}$ cup hot water and stir until you have the consistency you want. Add the salt and taste. Season again if necessary.

Add the cilantro and cook until it has started to wilt. Turn off the heat and stir in the yogurt and lemon juice.

Serve with basmati or jasmine rice.

Feeds 4

FEEL LIKE PLAYING?

Sure, you can use canned tomatoes (and we do, if it's not tomato season) and canned chickpeas. I have, at times. But the difference between canned chickpeas and ones you have cooked yourself is like watching videos of swimming and then diving into that warm water for the first time.

african yellow rice with black-eyed peas

Danny cooked this as one of the weekly vegetarian specials at the restaurant on the island where he worked. He piled soft black-eyed peas on top of bright yellow rice, with a hint of ginger, a bit of bite. Immediately I asked him to show me how to make it.

He was inspired by a South African dish called bobotie, which is a casserole made with beef or lamb, a medley of spices, raisins, and eggs. It's often accompanied by bright yellow rice. Since he was making a vegetarian special, he left the casserole alone and played with the black-eyed peas instead. Black-eyed peas are cheap and easy to cook. They take far less time to cook than most other beans. The color of this dish alone makes it worthy of attention at the dinner table.

For the black-eyed peas

2 cups dried black-eyed peas, soaked in water to cover for at least 4 hours

4 cups chicken stock

1 medium onion, peeled and quartered

1 carrot, peeled

2 cloves garlic, peeled and smashed

1 bay leaf

Pinch red pepper flakes

One 1-inch piece fresh ginger, peeled and cut in half

Kosher salt and freshly ground black pepper

For the yellow rice

2 cups basmati rice

2 teaspoons ground turmeric

1 shallot, peeled and thinly sliced

1 tablespoon unsalted butter

1 teaspoon kosher salt

COOKING THE BEANS. Put all the ingredients for the black-eyed peas except for the salt and pepper into a large pot. Set the pot over medium-high heat. Bring to a gentle boil, then turn the heat down to medium-low. Simmer until the beans are tender and have absorbed most of the liquid, about 20 minutes. Season with salt and pepper. Turn off the heat. Remove the bay leaf.

continued . . .

Rinsing the rice. Meanwhile, put the rice in a colander and run cold water over it. Move your hand through the rice, making sure every grain gets wet. Drain the water completely. Repeat three times.

Cooking the rice. Add the rinsed rice, 3½ cups water, the turmeric, shallot, butter, and salt to a large pot. Set it over medium-high heat. When the water is bubbling up through the top surface of the rice, turn down the heat to medium-low. Cover the pot and cook for 15 to 20 minutes. When there is no more steam escaping from the space between the pot and lid, turn off the heat and let the rice sit, covered, for 15 minutes.

To serve, scoop some of the rice into a bowl and top with the black-eyed peas.

Feeds 4

FEEL LIKE PLAYING?

Those of you with rice cookers could set up this dish for dinner in no time flat. Set up the yellow rice in the rice cooker before you leave for work. It will keep warm all day. All you have to do when you return home is cook up the black-eyed peas.

If you have access to plantains where you live, make a side of fried plantain chips to go with this dish. Cut the plantains into long lengthwise strips. Heat a few inches of oil in a deep skillet to 350°F. Fry the plantains, without crowding them, until they turn a golden color. Remove and sprinkle with salt.

a big bowl of pasta

LUCY ATE EVERY SINGLE DISH IN THIS COOKBOOK FOR DINNER AT SOME POINT IN HER LIFE.
Plus, there are always new meals, based on what is coming up in the garden or what we found at the store.
Pan-seared sturgeon, lentils with preserved lemons and a radicchio slaw? She gobbles it up while we talk.

But if we give her the choice for dinner, what does she choose? "Pasta please!"

So we give her pasta a few times a week. Heck, we love it too. A big bowl full of slippery noodles, coated in red sauce or extra-virgin olive oil or pesto? A few scrapes of aged cheese, a handful of hazelnuts, a bite of chili? A creamy sauce made from cashews? Lemongrass-sesame sauce on rice vermicelli noodles? She'll eat them all, happily.

What we've realized is that as long as noodles are the base—even when they are noodles made out of zucchini—she's happy with anything we put on them. Wilted dark greens, roasted sweet potato, or lemon-parsley butter—they're all slurped up.

And of course, sometimes you just need spaghetti and meatballs.

Does the fact that our house is gluten-free affect her love for pasta? Not one bit. There are now a plethora of gluten-free packaged pastas on the market. We eat Jovial pasta from Italy exclusively in our house.

Most of the brands of gluten-free pasta seem to ask you to cook the pasta far longer than you should. Don't pay attention to how many minutes those packages say. Put the pasta in a big pot of boiling, salted water. For the first minute the pasta is in the water, give it a gentle stir. This will help separate the noodles from each other. Let the pasta cook for eight to nine minutes, then start testing it. Take out a strand. Bite into it. When the first part of the bite has a soft yield but the rest still snaps against your teeth, the pasta is done. Drain it immediately.

For the best pasta dish, buy yourself a Chinese spider at the restaurant supply store. It's a skimmer with a long handle with what looks like a wire-mesh basket at the end of it. If you have your sauce and other ingredients ready in a wide pan, you can scoop the pasta out of the pot, directly into the sauce. This adds a little of the pasta water, which helps make the sauce more voluptuous.

Let the pasta sit in the sauce for five minutes without touching it, then stir it all up. You should have a great pasta dish on your hands.

fresh gluten-free pasta

Gluten-free fresh pasta? Easy peasy. Trust me. We made dozens of mediocre-to-bad batches until we landed on this one. Once we found this one under our hands, we stopped experimenting. This is ours. We hope it will be yours too.

255 grams All-Purpose Gluten-Free
    Flour Mix (page 31)

1 tablespoon psyllium husks (see page 33)

Pinch ground nutmeg (freshly grated,
    if you can)

1 teaspoon kosher salt

3 large egg yolks

2 large eggs

1 to 2 tablespoons extra-virgin olive oil

1 to 2 tablespoons lukewarm water

MAKING THE DOUGH IN THE FOOD PROCESSOR. Combine the flour, psyllium husks, nutmeg, and salt in the bowl of the food processor to combine and aerate the flours. In a small bowl, mix together the egg yolks, eggs, 1 tablespoon of the oil, and 1 tablespoon of the water. Pour the liquid mixture into the flour mixture in the processor. Pulse the processor 8 to 10 times, then look at the dough. If the dough has formed crumbs that look like dry cheese curds, you're done. If they are a little too dry, add the remaining oil, pulse, look, then add more water, if necessary. If the dough looks a bit too wet, add another tablespoon of flour. Turn the pasta dough out onto a dry, clean surface.

MAKING THE DOUGH BY HAND. Combine the flour, psyllium husks, nutmeg, and salt in a bowl. Whisk them together for a few moments to combine and aerate the flours. Pile the flour mixture into a small mound on a clean, dry surface and make a well in the center. In a small bowl, mix together the egg yolks, eggs, 1 tablespoon of the oil, and 1 tablespoon of the water. Pour the liquid mixture into the flour mixture. Using a fork, rubber spatula, or your fingers, stir the liquids gently, bringing in a bit of flour from the outside walls with each turn. When most of the egg mixture is blended with the flour, bring the rest of the flour into the middle with your hands. If it feels too dry—flour flaking off the ball of dough—add the remaining oil, then water. If the dough feels too wet—if it squelches when it touches the board—add another tablespoon of flour.

Take a few moments to knead the dough, gently. Push forward on the ball of dough with your hand, then fold the ball back on itself toward you. Rotate the dough and repeat until the dough feels supple and smooth.

Once you have your ball of dough, whether you made it with the food processor or by hand, wrap up the dough in plastic wrap. Let it sit for 30 minutes at room temperature.

Spread flour on your work surface. Cut the ball of pasta dough into 4 equal pieces. Working gently, roll out the dough, backward and forward, side to side, until it is as thin as it will go.

Using a sharp knife, cut the pasta into noodles of your desired width. Move the noodles onto a plate and cover them with a damp cloth as you finish the other noodles.

If you have a pasta machine, roll out the ball of dough to an oval about 3 inches long and 3 inches wide. Then, put the pasta through the rollers, starting at the first setting, then moving up until the dough is as thin as you desire and not breaking. Continue with the cutting steps above.

FEEL LIKE PLAYING?

You can play with different flours for different flavors. I really love raw buckwheat flour, corn flour, and millet flour in pasta. As much as I love teff for baking, I don't love the way it turns pasta dark brown and just a tiny bit slimy. A touch of garbanzo flour in the mix adds a deep savory flavor but using all garbanzo makes the pasta taste like a mouth full of beans. Almond flour and coconut flour are too filled with fats to work here. So, play with your own favorite set of flours.

You may now cook your pasta. Fill a large pan with water and enough salt to make it taste like the ocean. When the water is boiling, gently nudge your noodles into the water and cook until they are soft but still have a bit of a bite, 2 to 3 minutes. (Don't overcrowd the pan. You might have to cook this in 2 batches.) Drain immediately, reserving a bit of the cooking water for any sauce you might be making. Toss the noodles with a bit of oil to coat.

Eat.

Feeds 4

FEEL LIKE PLAYING?

If you want the kale softer here, then blanch it before putting it into the pot.

We really love this dish with another pasta called casarecce, which is like little twirled sticks. Here they work beautifully together.

fusilli with italian sausage and dark greens

You can get fancy with pastas. Or you can throw some of your favorite ingredients into a pot and just go.

8 ounces gluten-free fusilli pasta

¼ cup extra-virgin olive oil

½ pound sweet Italian sausage, sliced

1 medium onion, peeled and diced

2 cloves garlic, peeled and chopped

1 teaspoon fennel seeds

Pinch red pepper flakes

1 bunch Lacinato kale, leaves removed from the stems and cut into ribbons (you can also use chard, mustard greens, or collard greens)

1 cup freshly grated Parmesan cheese

Cooking the pasta. Set a large pot over high heat. Fill it with hot water and enough salt to make it taste like the ocean. When the water comes to a boil, add the fusilli. Cook until the pasta is tender but still has a bite, 7 to 10 minutes, depending on the brand of pasta you have.

Cooking the sausage. While the pasta is cooking, set a Dutch oven over medium-high heat. Add 2 tablespoons of the oil. When the oil is hot, lay the sausage slices flat on the bottom of the skillet. Cook until the bottoms are browned, about 3 minutes. Flip over the sausages and brown the other side, about 3 minutes. Remove the sausage from the skillet.

Cooking the onions and spices. Add the onion and garlic to the Dutch oven and cook, stirring, until the onion has softened, about 5 minutes. Add the fennel seeds and red pepper flakes and cook until their scents are released, about 1 minute. Add the kale and cook, stirring fast, until it's wilted, about 3 minutes. Add the sausage back to the pot.

When the pasta is done, move it over to the pot with the onions and sausages, bringing some of the pasta water with it. Cover the pot and let the entire concoction sit for 5 minutes. Take off the lid and stir it up. Top with the Parmesan and serve.

Feeds 4

shells with fresh ricotta, chives, and arugula

This pasta dish takes only a few moments to make but it's memorable far beyond the end of the meal. Wilted arugula, a little bite of chives, the zip of lemon zest, and warm fresh ricotta, mingled with good pasta? Call me to the table now.

Ricotta is best when it's warm. But we also make fresh ricotta to keep in the refrigerator for busy nights we want to make a pasta dish like this. We try to remember to pull it out in time to have room-temperature ricotta as we begin cooking the pasta. For this pasta dish, you'll use half the fresh ricotta, which leaves you with leftovers. This is not a problem!

1 pound gluten-free pasta shells

1 large bunch arugula, torn into pieces

2 tablespoons chopped fresh chives

1 large lemon, zested (you can use the lemon you juiced for the ricotta)

1 recipe Fresh Ricotta Cheese (recipe follows), still warm

Kosher salt and freshly ground black pepper

COOKING THE PASTA. Set a large pot over high heat. Fill it with hot water and enough salt to make it taste like the ocean. When the water comes to a boil, add the pasta shells. Cook until the shells are tender but still have a bite, 5 to 9 minutes, depending on the brand of pasta you have. Drain, reserving some of the pasta cooking water for adding below.

FEEL LIKE PLAYING?

You can use store-bought ricotta here but be sure to bring it to room temperature before you begin cooking the pasta. The key to this dish is all that warmth and watching the arugula wilt in its spell.

FINISHING THE DISH. Add the arugula, chives, and lemon zest to a large, wide-mouthed bowl. Top with half the warm ricotta. Move the hot pasta, along with a splash of the pasta water, on top of the rest of the dish. Let it sit for 5 minutes. Toss to combine. Season with salt and pepper to taste.

Serve immediately.

Feeds 4

fresh ricotta cheese

The first time I made ricotta, I couldn't believe how easy this was and how much better it tasted than that stuff in the tub. I could just eat fresh warm ricotta with a spoon.

One note before we begin: you have to use a lightly pasteurized milk, not an ultrapasteurized milk, to make ricotta. The ultrapasteurization process changes the milk proteins, which means it won't be able to make curds. So, no ricotta. And that would be sad.

2 quarts whole milk
(use lightly pasteurized)

1 pint heavy cream

1 teaspoon kosher salt

1 large lemon, juiced

MAKING THE RICOTTA. Line a colander with several layers of cheesecloth and let it sit in a large bowl. Set a Dutch oven over medium heat. Pour in the milk, cream, and salt. Cook, stirring occasionally to prevent scorching on the bottom of the pan. When the milk and cream start to steam and show the first signs of simmering (this will take from 8 to 12 minutes), stir in the lemon juice. Keep stirring the milk until curds begin to form, 1 to 2 minutes. There should be little bubbles along the edges of the pot and thick, creamy curds in the middle of the pot. (If you don't have many curds at this point, add a bit more lemon juice or an acid like apple cider vinegar. That should start the curds moving.)

Use a slotted spoon or spider to scoop the curds out of the pot and into the prepared colander. The whey will drain out into the bowl, leaving only fresh warm ricotta in the cheesecloth. (Keep the whey! See glutenfreegirl.com for suggestions.) Move the cheesecloth gently to form a ball of ricotta. Refrigerate the ricotta in an airtight container if you are not going to use it all right away.

Makes 1½ cups

FEEL LIKE PLAYING?

This method will give you warm, creamy ricotta immediately. If you want a tighter ricotta, tie up the cheesecloth and let it hang over the faucet in the kitchen sink to cool. Let the ricotta drain until it has formed a tight ball, 20 to 25 minutes. You'll use half the ricotta here for the shells recipe. What to do with the rest? Spread it on toast in the morning. Use it to top pizza. Stuff mushrooms with it. Or, make Lemon-Ricotta Pancakes (page 39).

penne with shrimp and lemon-parsley butter

Danny cooked a version of this dish at a restaurant in Denver called Papillon. It was a huge seller. One of his first days there, one of the cooks told Danny: "You'll make more of this dish than you can shake a stick at." He made hundreds and hundreds of orders of it in his time there. And he ate his fair share too. "It was one of those dishes that, if you were hungry in the middle of service and didn't have time to eat, you made yourself a little extra and wolfed it down on the line."

The first time we made this together, I looked at him and said, "I could bathe in this sauce." He grinned and said, "I love when my wife says this."

8 tablespoons (1 stick) unsalted butter, at room temperature

$\frac{1}{2}$ large lemon, zested and juiced

1 tablespoon finely chopped fresh Italian parsley

Kosher salt and freshly ground black pepper

2 ounces pine nuts

8 ounces gluten-free penne

$\frac{1}{4}$ cup extra-virgin olive oil

$\frac{1}{2}$ medium onion, peeled and sliced

4 ounces clam juice

12 ounces large shrimp, peeled and deveined

2 cups chopped spinach

3 ripe plum tomatoes, cut in half

MAKING THE LEMON-PARSLEY BUTTER. In the bowl of a stand mixer with the paddle attachment, whip the butter until it has tripled in volume. Add the lemon zest and juice, parsley, and a pinch of kosher salt and pepper. Mix until they are thoroughly combined. Taste and adjust the seasonings if necessary. Set aside.

TOASTING THE PINE NUTS. Set a small skillet over medium-high heat. Add the pine nuts and let them heat in the skillet, shaking it frequently, until they smell toasted and have browned, about 7 minutes. (Pine nuts are expensive and burn easily, so watch!)

COOKING THE PASTA. Set a large pot over high heat. Fill it with hot water and enough salt to make it taste like the ocean. When the water comes to a boil, add the penne. Cook until the penne is tender but still has a bite, 7 to 10 minutes, depending on the brand of pasta you have.

Making the sauce. As the pasta is cooking, set a Dutch oven over medium-high heat and pour in the oil. When the oil is hot, add the onion and cook, stirring frequently, until it's softened, about 5 minutes. Add the lemon-parsley butter and clam juice. Let the butter melt and simmer the sauce for 2 minutes. Salt to taste.

Add the shrimp and cook for 1 minute. Add the spinach and tomatoes. Turn off the heat. Using a slotted spoon or spider, move the hot pasta, along with a splash of the pasta water, into the pot of sauce. Let the pasta and sauce sit for 5 minutes. Stir in the toasted pine nuts and serve.

Feeds 4

FEEL LIKE PLAYING?

If tomatoes are not ripe, use ½ cup of sun-dried tomatoes here. Add them just after you put the pasta in the pot to give the sun-dried tomatoes time to soften in the heat.

This lemon-parsley butter is good on everything. Okay, maybe not ice cream, but everything else. We'd suggest you make a double batch and use the remaining butter on other pasta dishes, on top of rice, on roasted chicken, or anywhere you might like a flavored butter.

If you can't find pine nuts at a decent price, I think toasted walnuts here would be great.

zucchini noodles with spinach pesto, feta, and sunflower seeds

Want pasta in the middle of the hot summer without having to turn on the stove? Here it is.

2 cups chopped spinach

$1/2$ cup pine nuts

2 cloves garlic, peeled and chopped

1 large lemon, zested and juiced

$1/2$ cup grated Gruyère

1 cup extra-virgin olive oil

3 large ripe zucchini

$1/4$ cup crumbled feta cheese, crumbled (we prefer French feta)

$1/4$ cup sunflower seeds

MAKING THE PESTO. Add the spinach, pine nuts, garlic, and lemon zest and juice to the bowl of a food processor. Whirl them up until everything is broken down into small pieces. Add the Gruyère and run the processor. You should have a great-smelling paste by now. With the food processor running, slowly drizzle in the oil until you have rich green pesto.

SLICING THE ZUCCHINI. Grab a zucchini with your left hand. Using a vegetable peeler, grate long, even strips of the zucchini until you have reached the fleshy center and can peel no longer. (You can eat the outer skin, of course.) Repeat with the remaining zucchini.

ASSEMBLING THE DISH. Toss the zucchini noodles so they are all separated. Plop a couple of tablespoons of pesto into the noodles and toss them together. If you want more pesto, add a tablespoon at a time. You don't want to overpower the zucchini. When you have dressed the noodles to your liking, add the feta and sunflower seeds. Toss and serve.

Feeds 4

> ## FEEL LIKE PLAYING?
>
> I love these zucchini noodles for a quick, hot-weather meal. You can toss them in some extra-virgin olive oil in a hot pan, dollop on some tomato sauce, and sprinkle them with Parmesan.
>
> You can play with any number of pestos here. I like the Walnut-Kale Pesto on page 181.

fettuccine with walnut-kale pesto, cannellini beans, and roasted tomatoes

A dish with this many components in the title might sound like an arduous task. It's actually quite easy to make. And, if you make each of the parts early in the week (cook a big pot of beans, make some roasted tomatoes and store them in a jar in the refrigerator, make a batch of pesto), this dish would only take as long to make as it takes to cook the pasta.

15 ounces assorted ripe tomatoes

1^1/$_4$ cups extra-virgin olive oil

Kosher salt

1 medium onion, peeled and chopped

5 cloves garlic, peeled and chopped

2 tablespoons chopped fresh thyme

1 cup dried cannellini beans, soaked in water to cover for at least 2 hours and drained

Freshly ground black pepper

2 cups chopped Lacinato kale (or use any kale you like)

^{1}/$_2$ cup walnut pieces

1 large lemon, zested and juiced

^{1}/$_2$ cup freshly grated Parmesan cheese

1 pound dried gluten-free fettuccine

ROASTING THE TOMATOES. Preheat the oven to 350°F. Line a baking sheet with parchment paper. Cut the tomatoes into quarters and put them in a large bowl. Coat the tomatoes with 2 tablespoons of the oil and season with salt. Lay the tomatoes onto the baking sheet evenly. Roast until the tomatoes start to wither into themselves and ooze juice, about 2 hours. Remove the tomatoes from the oven.

COOKING THE BEANS. Set a large pot over medium-high heat. Pour in 2 tablespoons of the oil. When the oil is hot, add the onion. Cook, stirring frequently, until the onion is softened, about 5 minutes. Add 2 tablespoons of the chopped garlic and the thyme and cook, stirring, until the scents are released, about 2 minutes. Add the beans and 4 cups of water. Cook until the beans are tender, 60 to 90 minutes. Taste the beans. Season with salt and pepper. Cook until the beans are evenly seasoned. Drain the beans and set aside.

continued...

MAKING THE PESTO. Add the kale, walnuts, the remaining garlic, and lemon juice and zest into the bowl of a food processor. Whirl them up until everything is broken down into small pieces. Add the Parmesan and run the processor. You should have a great-smelling paste by now. With the food processor running, slowly drizzle in the remaining 1 cup of oil until you have rich green pesto.

COOKING THE PASTA. Set a large pot over high heat. Fill it with hot water and enough salt to make it taste like the ocean. When the water comes to a boil, add the fettuccine. Cook until the fettuccine is tender but still has a bite, 7 to 10 minutes, depending on the brand of pasta you have.

Put the beans and tomatoes in a large, wide-mouthed bowl, along with a large dollop of the pesto. Add the drained fettucine on top and wait 5 minutes, then toss until it is evenly coated.

Feeds 4

FEEL LIKE PLAYING?

If you wanted to use a store-bought pesto, some canned beans, and sun-dried tomatoes, this would still be a delicious dish.

Those roasted tomatoes are a staple in our house. They're heavenly in summer with truly ripe tomatoes. But sometimes, when we need that tomato taste, we'll buy some hothouse tomatoes grown in British Columbia and intensify the taste by roasting them. We put roasted tomatoes on pizza, in sandwiches, on pasta, and anything that begs for a tomato.

One of my favorite quick meals for our daughter is pasta with this walnut-kale pesto, a handful of quick-wilted dark greens, and some grated cheese.

sweet potato macaroni and cheese

For years I made a complicated cheese sauce for macaroni and cheese. But then I had a toddler sitting on the kitchen counter, equally eager to help me cook and desperate to eat. Complicated cheese sauces went away. Luckily, I figured out that the starches from pasta slough off into the water while cooking, pasta water thickens a thin milk sauce into a silky smooth cheese sauce. Add some thin slivered sweet potatoes and you have Lucy's favorite pasta dish of all time.

4 tablespoons (½ stick) unsalted butter

1 cup whole milk (you can use low-fat, if you prefer)

1½ cups Cheddar cheese, grated

1 pound gluten-free elbow macaroni

Extra-virgin olive oil, for drizzling on pasta

Kosher salt and freshly ground black pepper

1 large sweet potato, peeled and thinly sliced

PREPARING TO COOK. Preheat the oven to 400°F. Set out the butter and milk. Grate the cheese.

COOKING THE PASTA. Set a large pot over high heat. Fill it with hot water and enough salt to make it taste like the ocean. When the water comes to a boil, add the macaroni. Cook until the macaroni is tender but still has a bite, 7 to 10 minutes, depending on the brand of pasta you have. Immediately drain the pasta, reserving some of the pasta water, and run cold water over it to stop the cooking. Drizzle the pasta with some oil and let it sit.

MAKING THE CHEESE SAUCE. Put the same pot over medium-high heat. Add the butter. When the butter is melted and starting to foam, add the milk. Add a third of the Cheddar and whisk vigorously. When it is fully melted and incorporated, add ¼ cup of the reserved pasta water. Whisk until the sauce is coherent then add another third of the Cheddar. Whisk until the sauce is thick and creamy.

FINISHING THE MAC AND CHEESE. Return the pasta to the pot and toss to coat with the cheese sauce.

Transfer a third of the macaroni and cheese to a 9 x 13-inch casserole pan. Top it with sweet potato slices. Spoon in another layer of macaroni and cheese, followed by sweet potato slices. Finish with the last layer of macaroni and cheese. Top with the remaining Cheddar.

Bake in the oven until the cheese on top is fully melted and starting to brown, about 15 minutes.

Feeds 4

spaghetti and meatballs

Danny still hasn't seen *The Godfather* (I know!), but every time I eat spaghetti and meatballs, I think of that movie. I love the scene where some of the mafia guys make spaghetti and meatballs together, the image of the giant pot of red sauce, the twirls of spaghetti coming off the fork, the fat fists of meatballs atop it all. I'm getting hungry just thinking about it.

There are a dozen great ways to make tomato sauce for spaghetti. My favorite here is based on Marcella Hazan's recipe, partly because it's so easy and partly because it's rich and slippery with the butter and Parmesan rind. The meatballs here are based on a recipe from our friend Molly Wizenberg, who got it from Café Lago, a great Italian restaurant in Seattle. I love how a recipe stands alone on a page but the connections that led to it being here are like a room packed full with mafia guys eating spaghetti and meatballs.

For the sauce (makes enough to coat 1½ pounds pasta)

- Two 28-ounce cans whole peeled tomatoes, drained
- 8 tablespoons (1 stick) unsalted butter
- 1 large onion, peeled and cut in half
- 1 rind good Parmesan cheese
- ½ teaspoon kosher salt
- 1 sprig fresh basil, chopped

For the meatballs

- 1 cup gluten-free breadcrumbs
- ⅓ cup whole milk
- 1 pound ground beef (not extra-lean), at room temperature
- 1 pound ground pork, at room temperature

- 1 cup freshly grated Parmesan cheese
- 2 cloves garlic, peeled and finely chopped
- ¼ cup finely chopped fresh Italian parsley
- 1 teaspoon kosher salt
- ¼ teaspoon freshly ground black pepper
- 2 large eggs, at room temperature
- ⅛ teaspoon ground nutmeg (freshly grated, if you can)
- 2 tablespoons fresh lemon juice
- 3 tablespoons extra-virgin olive oil

For the spaghetti

- 2 tablespoons kosher salt
- 1 pound gluten-free spaghetti

MAKING THE SAUCE. Set a Dutch oven (or large pot) over medium heat. Pour in the tomatoes. Nestle the butter in the tomatoes, along with the onion and Parmesan rind. Sprinkle in the salt. Cook, stirring occasionally, at a very slow simmer, until the onion has softened and started to fall apart, about 45 minutes to 1 hour.

TAKE OUT THE ONION. Chop it as finely as you can. Add it back into the sauce, along with the basil. Simmer for 5 more minutes, breaking up any lumps of tomato that feel too large to you. (You could use the immersion blender to smooth out the sauce, but I think it's better a little chunky.)

SOFTENING THE BREADCRUMBS FOR THE MEATBALLS. Combine the breadcrumbs and milk in a small bowl and stir them together. Let sit for 10 minutes.

MIXING THE MEATBALLS. In a large bowl, add the beef, pork, Parmesan, garlic, parsley, salt, and pepper. In a small bowl, whisk the eggs with the nutmeg and add them to the meat mixture. Pour the lemon juice over the meat. Squeeze all the milk from the breadcrumbs, reserving the milk. Add the breadcrumbs to the meat mixture. Mix with your hands, taking care to not smoosh the ingredients together; this is not like creaming butter and sugar together. Instead, fold the ingredients over each other, gently, until they are just combined.

MAKING THE TASTER. Set a large cast-iron skillet over medium-high heat. Pour in 1 teaspoon of the oil. Form a small patty with the meat and put it in the hot oil. Cook until the patty is firm and browned on both sides, about 2 minutes per side. Let it rest out of the pan for a moment to cool. Taste. Adjust the seasonings of the raw meat mixture, if necessary.

CHILLING THE MEATBALLS. Put the meat mixture into the refrigerator, along with the reserved milk. Chill for at least 30 minutes, and preferably up to 1 hour.

MAKING THE MEATBALLS. Measure out 2 ounces of the meat mixture. Moisten your hands with some of the reserved milk and roll the meat into a ball. (These will be large balls, the size of golf balls. If you want smaller meatballs, try 1 ounce of meat.)

BROWNING THE MEATBALLS. Set the skillet over medium-high heat again and add the remaining oil. When the oil is hot, add the meatballs. (You might not be able to fit all the meatballs into the pan.

continued...

If not, don't scrunch them—cook the meatballs in 2 batches instead.) Cook the meatballs until the bottoms are browned, about 5 minutes. Flip over the meatballs.

Add the tomato sauce to the pan. Bring the sauce to a simmer and turn down the heat to medium-low. Cook until the meatballs are firm to the touch and fully cooked inside, 15 to 20 minutes.

Cooking the spaghetti. While the meatballs are simmering in the sauce, set a large pot over high heat. Add the salt and 8 cups of water. When the water has come to a boil, add the spaghetti. Stir the spaghetti within the first minute, then let it cook until the spaghetti has softened but still has a bit of a bite to it (al dente), 6 to 10 minutes, depending on the brand of spaghetti you have bought. (If you are making fresh pasta, you will find it cooks much faster than dried pasta, so watch!)

FEEL LIKE PLAYING?

You might have some sauce and meatballs left over, but that wouldn't be a problem, would it? Make up another batch of spaghetti the next night. It doesn't get much better than spaghetti and meatballs.

Take the meatballs out of the simmering sauce. With a slotted spoon or spider, move the cooked pasta to the sauce, along with a splash of the pasta water. Let the pasta sit for 5 minutes. Toss to coat with the tomato sauce. Stir.

Pile some spaghetti on each plate, then add the meatballs.

Feeds 4

capellini carbonara with smoked paprika and kale

Pasta carbonara is one of the great comfort wonders of the world. Don't listen to the voices that say theirs is the only authentic way to make it. Just make some. Here, we like pancetta, smoked paprika, Lacinato kale (thanks to Francis Lam for that suggestion), and cashew cream. This dish is far from boring. It's unctuous and silky, a wonderful weeknight meal.

8 ounces gluten-free capellini

2 large egg yolks

$\frac{1}{2}$ cup cashew cream (page 102)

1 tablespoon extra-virgin olive oil

6 ounces pancetta, cut into small pieces

2 cloves garlic, peeled and sliced

1 bunch Lacinato kale (or any type of kale), cut into ribbons

1 teaspoon smoked paprika

3 ounces freshly grated Parmesan cheese

6 scrapings of fresh nutmeg

COOKING THE PASTA. Set a large pot of salted water on high heat. Bring the water to a boil and add the capellini. Give the pasta a good stir after it has settled in the pot, then let it cook until the pasta yields somewhat reluctantly to a fork.

MAKING THE EGG CREAM. As you are cooking the pasta, combine the egg yolks and cashew cream in a bowl. Whisk together until silky. Set aside.

MAKING THE CARBONARA. Set a large skillet over medium-high heat, then pour in the 1 tablespoon of the oil. Add the pancetta pieces to the hot oil. Cook, stirring occasionally, until they start to brown, about 4 minutes. Add the garlic and cook, stirring, until the kitchen smells like garlic, about 2 minutes. Add the kale ribbons and cook, stirring occasionally, until they have begun to wilt, about 3 minutes. Stir in the smoked paprika and cook until it releases its fragrance, about 1 minute.

Add the cooked pasta to the skillet. Move the cooked pasta, along with some of the pasta water, over to the sauce. Let the pasta sit for 5 minutes and stir until the pasta is coated. If the sauce is not yet silky, add more of the reserved pasta water and stir until a silky sauce forms. Top with the Parmesan and nutmeg. Stir well. Serve.

Feeds 4

vermicelli rice noodles with sunflower-sesame sauce

You know what's good about this dish, besides everything? (1) Rice noodles are perfect for kids because they don't require cooking. You pour boiling hot water over them, let them sit for 3 minutes, and they're ready. (2) This sauce is addictive. I'm not kidding. If you make a big batch—you'll have some left over after making this pasta—you might start drizzling it on salads, on rice, on crusty bread. It's ridiculously good. (3) Trust me. It's good.

$^1/_4$ cup sunflower seed butter

$^1/_3$ cup rice wine vinegar

$^1/_4$ cup tahini

3 tablespoons hot water

3 tablespoons gluten-free tamari

3 tablespoons maple syrup

¼ cup peanut oil

2 tablespoons sesame oil

2 tablespoons dry sherry

2 teaspoons finely chopped garlic

2 teaspoons grated fresh ginger

$^1/_2$ teaspoon red pepper flakes

Kosher salt

1 pound firm tofu, cut into 1-inch cubes

Freshly ground black pepper

1 pound vermicelli rice noodles

MAKING THE SUNFLOWER-SESAME SAUCE. Add the sunflower seed butter to a blender, along with the vinegar, tahini, hot water, tamari, maple syrup, 2 tablespoons of the peanut oil, the sesame oil, sherry, garlic, ginger, red pepper flakes, and a pinch of salt. Blend until smooth. Taste. Season with more of whatever you feel is missing.

Let the sauce sit in the refrigerator for at least 1 hour before using.

ROASTING THE TOFU. Preheat the oven to 450°F. Line a baking sheet with parchment paper. Toss the tofu in the remaining 2 tablespoons peanut oil and season with salt and pepper. Put the tofu cubes on the baking sheet, allowing space between the cubes. Roast until the bottoms are dark-golden brown, about 15 minutes. Flip the tofu and roast until the second side is dark-golden brown and the cubes have puffed up, about 10 minutes. Take the tofu out of the oven.

continued . . .

Cooking the rice noodles. Bring a pot of hot water to boil. Put the rice noodles in the boiling water. Let them sit for 3 minutes and drain thoroughly.

Place the drained noodles in a large bowl. Cover with the sunflower-sesame sauce and toss to coat. Top each serving with some of the roasted tofu.

Feeds 4

FEEL LIKE PLAYING?

If you can't find vermicelli rice noodles, then linguine would do well here too.

This sauce is great on plain white rice, as a marinade for grilled chicken, as a topping for rice and beans. Anything, really.

the meat chapter

THE WAY WE EAT MEAT, AND HOW MUCH MEAT WE EAT, HAS CHANGED PRETTY DRAMATICALLY over the past few years. We don't have many dinners with a hunk of meat in the middle of the plate, with a baked potato and couple of pieces of broccoli on the side. Sometimes. But we don't have that dinner often anymore.

Instead, we're far more likely to cook up some quinoa, add hazelnuts and wilted kale, then toss in a couple of ounces of roasted pork, cut into cubes. Toss with lemon tahini dressing and you're set.

We are inspired by what changes. We get genuinely geeky jazzed about fava beans coming into season or asparagus from Washington finally appearing in the grocery store. We think vegetables first because that's what changes from week to week. If January is celery root, then July is eggplant. If we based our meals on meat, we would end up eating the same meals over and over again.

But it's also because we made the conscious decision to buy only meat that comes from a source we trust. You've heard all those *E. coli* pink slime stories in the past few years. Big factory farm meat is often off-putting. It may be cheap but it doesn't taste like much. And where does it come from?

So, as soon as our daughter was able to eat meat, we realized we wanted to buy pork shoulder from a butcher we like, one who carries meat from a local farm who lets the animals roam more freely than in the typical fashion. And then we grind it ourselves to make sausage. We buy beef cheeks and braise them for hours until they are tender, instead of splurging for the immediately tender tenderloin.

This really isn't so unusual. This is how people used to eat meat in this country.

And because buying meat from a source we know is a little more expensive than picking up the plastic-wrapped package at the grocery store, we compromise. We eat less meat than we did before. You might notice that at least a third of the recipes in this cookbook are vegetarian. That wasn't intentional. We love great flavors. If those flavors come from caramelized onions instead of bacon, those meals satisfy just as well.

We know that most folks in this country eat more meat than we do. Maybe we'll inspire you to look at how you eat it too? But we're not vegetarians. We do love a good Moroccan lamb burger in the summer, beef and bison chili in the fall, some cottage pie in the dark winter days, and pork chops with prosciutto-spinach sauce when greens first hit the market again. We wouldn't want to go without these dishes. We think you'll like them too.

kale and sausage soup with chickpeas and tomatoes

After a food blogging conference in San Francisco we were a little exhausted. Luckily, the lovely Dianne Jacob welcomed us into her home. After days of decadent food experiences, we were thrilled to find she had prepared a simple kale and sausage soup for us. Danny and I both found it nourishing and hearty. With its chickpeas and tomatoes, this has more depth than most soups; it's hearty like a stew. Using everything fresh makes it taste bright and alive.

2 tablespoons extra-virgin olive oil

8 ounces pork sausage links (we like a mild Italian), cut into 3/4-inch slices

1/2 medium yellow onion, peeled and cut into small dice

2 cloves garlic, peeled and sliced thin

4 leaves fresh sage, cut into ribbons (use dried sage if you want to)

One 15-ounce can diced tomatoes, drained

One 15-ounce can chickpeas, drained and rinsed

2 cups chicken stock

Kosher salt and freshly ground black pepper

4 large leaves kale, stems removed, cut into chiffonade

Freshly grated Parmesan cheese (optional)

BROWNING THE SAUSAGES. Set a large saucepan on medium-high heat. Pour in the oil. Add the sausage slices to the hot oil. Cook, stirring occasionally, until the sausage is thoroughly browned. Put the sausage onto a paper towel–covered plate. Keep the fat in the pan.

COOKING THE ONION AND GARLIC. Add the onion and garlic to the hot fat in the saucepan. Cook, stirring occasionally, until they are softened and translucent, about 5 minutes. Add the sage and cook until it releases its fragrance, about 1 minute.

FINISHING THE SOUP. Pour the tomatoes and chickpeas into the saucepan. Cook until heated through, about 3 minutes. Pour in the chicken stock and bring it to a boil. Turn down the heat to medium and let the soup simmer for 5 minutes. Season the soup with salt and pepper to taste. Throw in the kale leaves and cook until they are wilted, about 2 minutes. Turn off the heat. Serve in large bowls with a bit of Parmesan cheese on top, if you wish.

Feeds 4

beef and bison chili

You're never going to find an agreement about what makes true chili. Some insist that it has to contain only beef, no beans. But is it ground beef or cubes or steak? Others think it's all beans. Or spicy-so-hot that your ears blow smoke like the cartoons. Or mild and pleasing, with green bell peppers and pineapple. (I hope nobody actually makes that one.)

We say there are plenty of ways to make chili and the best one is the hot bowl in front of you, the one you're sharing with friends. I adore the complexity of taste in the other chili in our book, the one with butternut squash, black beans, and kale. But when I want a hearty chili, something deeply satisfying when I'm craving protein? It's this one with bison and beef. If you can't find bison, try pork shoulder or more beef tri-tip.

2 tablespoons peanut oil

1 pound beef tri-tip, cut into $\frac{1}{2}$-inch cubes

1 pound bison sirloin, cut into $\frac{1}{2}$-inch cubes

2 onions, peeled and chopped

4 cloves garlic, peeled and sliced

1 tablespoon ground cumin

1 tablespoon ancho chile powder

1 tablespoon dried oregano

2 teaspoons smoked paprika

2 teaspoons berbere seasoning (page 229; optional)

2 teaspoons ground coriander

1 canned gluten-free chipotle pepper in adobo sauce, chopped

One 28-ounce can diced tomatoes, drained

2 cups tomato juice

2 cups beef stock

$\frac{1}{2}$ cup chopped fresh cilantro

2 tablespoons fresh lime juice

BROWNING THE MEAT. Set a Dutch oven over medium-high heat. Pour in 1 tablespoon of the oil. When the oil is hot, add the beef and bison. (If the meat does not all fit comfortably in the same pan, do this in 2 batches.) Cook until the bottom of each piece is browned, about 3 minutes. Cook on all sides until the meat is entirely browned, about 10 minutes total. Remove the meat to a plate.

COOKING THE ONIONS AND GARLIC. Pour in the remaining tablespoon of oil. When the oil is hot, add the onions and garlic and cook, stirring frequently, until the onions are softened and beginning to brown, about 5 minutes.

ADDING THE SPICES. In rapid succession, add the cumin, ancho chile powder, oregano, paprika, berbere (if you're using it), and coriander. Cook, stirring occasionally, until the spices have released their fragrance into the room, about 5 minutes. Add the chipotle pepper and stir.

FINISHING THE CHILI. Pour in the tomatoes and stir. Add back the meat. Cook, stirring, until the meat is hot again, about 3 minutes. Pour in the tomato juice and beef stock. Bring the liquids to a boil, then turn the heat down to medium-low. Simmer for at least 1 hour, stirring occasionally, and longer if you can. The longer you simmer, the more the flavor builds.

Just before serving, throw the cilantro and lime juice into the chili. Stir and serve.

Feeds 6

FEEL LIKE PLAYING?

Of course, this chili tastes better the next day. It always does. It freezes well too.

If you can't find bison in your area, simply do all beef.

If you want, you could also throw in some cooked beans (whatever pot of beans you made that week). Add 1 more cup of tomato juice if you choose to do that.

Please don't make that chili with green bell peppers and pineapple. That sounds awful.

cottage pie

"Shepherd's pie," we announced, and Danny set down a large pie plate filled with juicy meat, roasted vegetables, and bubbling browned mashed potatoes. Our friend, Alison, who has always loved Danny's food, said, "Oh I can't wait!" After a few bites, she informed us we weren't eating shepherd's pie.

"The shepherds watched sheep. That's why they ate lamb pie. In my country, when we make this with beef, as you have, it's called cottage pie." Of course, in her lilting Yorkshire accent, this hardly sounded like a chastisement. We just dug in and stopped calling it shepherd's pie after that. Cottage pie sounds better anyway, don't you think?

3 large Yukon gold potatoes, peeled

Kosher salt

$3/4$ cup whole milk

3 tablespoons unsalted butter, softened

4 tablespoons extra-virgin olive oil

Freshly ground black pepper

2 pounds ground beef

1 medium onion, peeled and chopped

2 cloves garlic, peeled and chopped

2 sprigs fresh rosemary, leaves removed and chopped

2 carrots, peeled and chopped

1 leek, white part only, sliced

3 cups white mushrooms, stems removed and chopped

1 tablespoon All-Purpose Gluten-Free Flour Mix (page 31)

2 cups beef or chicken stock

1 bunch Red Russian kale, stems removed and leaves cut into ribbons (use any dark greens you want here)

COOKING THE POTATOES. Chop the potatoes into 1-inch cubes. Any stubby ends left? Toss them— you want the potatoes to cook evenly. Set a Dutch oven filled three-fourths of the way with cold water on high heat. Add enough salt to make the water taste like the ocean and put in the potatoes. Bring the water to a boil, then reduce the heat to medium. Simmer the potatoes until you can slide a knife through one of the potato pieces easily, about 10 minutes. Drain the potatoes in a colander over the sink. Cool them to room temperature.

MASHING THE POTATOES. Push the potatoes through a food mill or potato ricer. (You can also push the potatoes through a fine-mesh sieve with the back of a ramekin.) Put the soft, fluffy potatoes back into the Dutch oven.

Set a small pot on medium heat. Pour in the milk and heat until it starts to steam and little bubbles form on the edges of the pot. Turn off the heat.

Add the butter to the potatoes. Slowly pour in the hot milk, stirring constantly with a rubber spatula, keeping in mind you may not need all the milk. You want the potatoes to be creamy without being moisture laden. When the potatoes are just creamy, pour in 2 tablespoons of the oil and fold it into the potatoes. Taste the potatoes. Season with salt and pepper. Set aside.

PREPARING TO BAKE. Preheat the oven to 450°F.

BROWNING THE MEAT. Set a Dutch oven over medium-high heat. Pour in 1 tablespoon of the oil. When the oil is hot, add the ground beef in clumps. Let it sit for 1 minute, undisturbed, then begin turning it, breaking up the meat as it browns. When the meat is entirely browned, about 5 minutes, take it out of the Dutch oven.

COOKING THE VEGETABLES. Pour in the remaining tablespoon of oil. Add the onion and garlic and cook, stirring, until the onion has softened, about 5 minutes. Stir in the rosemary and cook until the scent is released, about 1 minute. Add the carrots and leek and cook, stirring, until the carrots are soft, about 3 minutes. Add the mushrooms and cook until they start to soften and squeak a little, about 3 minutes.

> ### FEEL LIKE PLAYING?
>
> If you want to make this with lamb, you have shepherd's pie.
>
> The kale isn't typical for cottage pie, but since we put it in everything, we thought it would be nice here. You could try any leafy dark green in its place.
>
> If you can't eat dairy, you can easily use a nondairy milk in the mashed potatoes.

FINISHING THE FILLING. Add the beef back into the Dutch oven. Add the flour and stir it up. Cook until everything is browned, about 2 minutes. Add the stock. Bring the liquid to a boil, then reduce the heat and simmer everything for 5 minutes. Toss in the kale and stir.

BAKING THE COTTAGE PIE. Put the beef filling into a 9-inch pie pan. Top with the mashed potatoes. Bake until everything is hot and bubbly, about 10 minutes. Turn on the broiler and cook until the mashed potatoes are browned, about 5 minutes.

Feeds 4

pork chops with spinach-prosciutto sauce

Danny and I talk about food. Usually, over breakfast with our daughter, we're talking about lunch or the dishes we will test that day or what's coming in at the farm stand that week. We never really stop talking about food, because food is how we structure our day.

I thought Danny had told me about every dish he had made at a restaurant that he loved. Casually, one afternoon, he mentioned pork chops in a spinach-prosciutto sauce. "What?" I said to him. We made it for dinner that night. It did not disappoint.

4 bone-in pork chops

Kosher salt and freshly ground black pepper

2 tablespoons canola oil

5 slices prosciutto, rolled up and sliced

1 medium onion, peeled and chopped

2 cloves garlic, peeled and chopped

2 tablespoons finely chopped fresh rosemary or 1 tablespoon dried

$^1/_2$ cup cashew cream (page 102) or heavy cream

2 cups chopped spinach

PREPARING TO COOK. Preheat the oven to 450°F.

COOKING THE CHOPS. Season the pork chops with salt and pepper on both sides. Set a large skillet over medium-high heat. Pour in the oil. Lay the chops in the pan and let them cook, undisturbed, until the bottoms are browned, about 5 minutes. Flip the chops and put them in the oven. Cook until they reach an internal temperature of 145°F, about 5 minutes. Take them out of the oven and put them on a plate to rest.

MAKING THE SAUCE. Put the same skillet back on medium-high heat. Add the prosciutto and cook, stirring occasionally, until it is crisp and has released some of its fat, about 5 minutes. Remove the prosciutto from the skillet. Add the onion and garlic and cook, stirring, until the onion has softened, about 5 minutes. Stir in the rosemary and cook until the scent is released, about 1 minute. Pour in the cashew cream. When it comes to a boil, toss in the chopped spinach. When the spinach wilts, add back in the prosciutto. Taste and season with salt and pepper if necessary.

Put the pork chops on serving plates and drizzle with the sauce.

Feeds 4

lamb sausage

Sometimes, out of convenience, when I have a toddler in the cart who's begging to play in the toy aisle and needs to go home for dinner that minute and I can't quite remember what is in this recipe for lamb sausage I grab some packaged links. Fair enough. But when I have the time I tuck this recipe in my purse for that moment in the store.

1 pound ground lamb, at room temperature

$^1/_2$ cup finely chopped pitted marinated green olives

$^1/_2$ cup gluten-free breadcrumbs

2 tablespoons Dijon mustard

2 tablespoons fennel seeds

2 tablespoons chopped fresh thyme or 1 tablespoon dried

Kosher salt and freshly ground black pepper

2 tablespoons extra-virgin olive oil

Mixing the sausage. In a large bowl, combine the lamb, olives, breadcrumbs, mustard, fennel seeds, thyme, and a good pinch of salt and pepper. Mix them together with your hands until all the breadcrumbs are incorporated and the ingredients evenly distributed. Ideally, you'd refrigerate the sausage mixture for at least an hour here, giving the flavors a chance to meld.

Cooking the sausage. Take the sausage out of the refrigerator and let it rest on the counter until it's close to room temperature. Grab a 2-ounce ball of the sausage meat and form it into a smooth, evenly shaped patty. Repeat with the rest of the sausage meat.

Set a large skillet over medium-high heat. Pour in the oil. When the oil is hot, add the patties. Give each of them a little pat down with a spatula, to ensure the entire surface of the patty is on the skillet. Cook until the bottoms are browned, about 4 minutes. Flip over the sausages and brown the other side, about 4 minutes more. This should take the patties to medium. If you want them well done, cook them for a few more moments.

Feeds 4

FEEL LIKE PLAYING?

You could use these sausages for pizza, to make meatballs out of them, or cook them up for breakfast with roasted potatoes and dark greens.

These have a distinctive Mediterranean flavor to them. You could easily switch up the spices to make them Mexican or Thai or French instead. Switch the meat to pork and it's another round of playing.

chorizo-stuffed pork loin

The presentation of this dish looks impressive—that lovely spiral slice of roasted meat, stuffed with chorizo. But Danny taught me that it's not nearly as hard to make as it looks. (He also wrapped a USB cord around my forearm to demonstrate trussing to me so I could write it here. I'll always think of that when I make this recipe.) If you would like to see Danny demonstrate how to butterfly the pork loin, see our website for a video.

2 large red bell peppers

6 tablespoons extra-virgin olive oil

1 pound pork loin

Kosher salt and freshly ground black pepper

4 ounces fresh chorizo sausage

1 medium onion, peeled and chopped

2 cloves garlic, peeled and chopped

$\frac{1}{2}$ teaspoon fresh oregano or 1 teaspoon dried

PREPARING TO ROAST. Preheat the oven to 450°F.

ROASTING THE PEPPERS. Coat the red peppers lightly with 2 tablespoons of the oil on a baking sheet. Slide the sheet into the oven. Roast the peppers, turning every 10 to 15 minutes with tongs, until mostly black and the skin starts to separate like an air pocket, about 30 minutes. Remove the peppers from the oven, put them in a large bowl, and cover it tightly with plastic wrap.

BUTTERFLYING THE PORK. Lay the pork fat-side down on a cutting board. Make a lengthwise slice from the top of the loin to the bottom, about three-fourths of the way through the loin. Open up the loin like you are opening a book. Slice lengthwise again to open the loin more fully. Slowly, turn the pork loin 180 degrees. Slice down the length of it again to open up the loin a little more each time.

POUNDING THE MEAT. Put the unfurled tenderloin between large pieces of plastic wrap. Flatten out the pork loin by using a meat pounder. Pound the entire loin evenly to make a flat surface. Season the loin on both sides with salt and black pepper.

STUFFING THE LOIN. Put the chorizo in the middle of the tenderloin, patting it down, and leaving about 1 inch on all sides of the loin. (If you put chorizo over the entire tenderloin, it will spill out the sides during the cooking.)

continued . . .

TRUSSING THE LOIN. Bring a large piece of kitchen string—twice as long as the loin—under the loin, at the bottom end. Make a loop on the top of the loin and tie it. Make a loop with the remaining string and bring it over the top end. Slide it down the loin until it is about 1 inch from the first loop. Tie it. Repeat with the rest of the loin. When you reach the end of the loin, turn the loin over and tuck the string under all the loops on the bottom of the loin. Tie the end piece of the string onto one of the loops.

ROASTING THE LOIN. Put the loin into a large skillet or roasting pan. Coat it with 2 tablespoons of the oil. Slide it in the oven. Cook the loin until it has reached an internal temperature of 145°F, about 1 hour.

MAKING THE SAUCE. Unwrap the roasted red peppers. Peel the skin with your fingers. Remove the stem and seeds. Do not rinse the peppers under water, as tempting as that is, because water will wash away the flavors. Set aside the peppers.

Set a skillet over medium-high heat. Pour in the remaining extra-virgin olive oil. When the oil is hot, add the onion and garlic and cook, stirring, until the onion has softened, about 5 minutes. Stir in the oregano and cook until the scent is released, about 1 minute. Add the peppers and ½ cup hot water. Cook until everything is softened, hot, and smelling good.

Pour the pepper mixture into a blender. Puree until smooth. Season to taste.

To serve, slice the loin into 1-inch-thick slices. Drizzle with the roasted red pepper sauce.

Feeds 4

> ## FEEL LIKE PLAYING?
>
> Any number of sauces would work well with this pork. My other favorite? The Ginger-Scallion Sauce (page 248)!
>
> Should I mention that the leftovers of this make tremendous sandwiches? Yes, I should.

moroccan lamb burger

I love lamb burgers. I feel like they're far juicier than beef burgers. (Have you noticed how most grocery store beef is labeled "Super Lean" or "Extra Lean"? What happened to "Not That Lean"?)

When I think of lamb, I think of Morocco. I don't know that I'll ever get to Morocco—maybe someday—but these burgers hit the spot.

1 tablespoon extra-virgin olive oil

1 small white onion, peeled and finely chopped

1/3 cup chopped fresh Italian parsley

2 tablespoons finely chopped fresh mint

1 1/2 teaspoons ground coriander

1 1/2 teaspoons ground cumin

1/4 teaspoon ground cinnamon

2 pounds ground lamb

1/4 cup chopped preserved lemons (page 96)

1/4 cup gluten-free breadcrumbs

1 large egg

Kosher salt and freshly ground black pepper

COOKING THE ONION. Set a skillet over medium-high heat. Add the oil. When the oil is hot, add the onion and cook, stirring, until softened, about 5 minutes. Scatter the parsley, mint, coriander, cumin, and cinnamon over the onion and cook, stirring occasionally, until the scent is released, about 2 minutes. Take the skillet off the heat and allow to cool to room temperature.

MAKING THE BURGER PATTIES. Add the cooled onion mixture to the ground lamb in a large bowl, along with the preserved lemons, breadcrumbs, and egg. Season with salt and pepper. Use your hands to mix them until everything is incorporated; do not overmix the meat. Divide the meat mixture into 4 parts. Form each part into a large patty.

GRILLING THE BURGERS. When the grill is hot, lift the lid and lay the patties down gently on the grill. At first, the patties are going to cling to the grill. Don't worry. Close the lid and wait 1 minute. When enough grease has dripped from the burgers to loosen the grip on the grill, flip the burgers. Repeat on the second side.

Now, grill each burger for 2 to 3 minutes. Flip the burgers one more time and cook until the internal temperature reaches 140°F for rare (150°F for medium-rare). Remove them from the grill and serve.

Feeds 4

FEEL LIKE PLAYING?

These burgers are even more flavorful when you get lamb shoulder from the store and ask your butcher to grind it fresh for you.

For a Moroccan vegetarian burger, switch the spices in the veggie burger (on page 110) for these. Play until it tastes right to you.

pork adobo

Our dear friend Tamiko is half Japanese, half Filipina. She introduced me to chicken adobo. The sauce enveloping the meat was a sweet briny salty complicated deliciousness. When I made it at home, we switched to pork adobo and we were happy, sitting at the table together, slurping up pork shoulder with this sauce.

1 cup apple cider vinegar

¾ cup gluten-free tamari

10 cloves garlic, peeled and finely chopped

¼ cup packed dark brown sugar

¼ cup black peppercorns

2 bay leaves

One 3-pound pork shoulder, cut into 2-inch cubes

2 tablespoons grapeseed oil

Cooked rice, for serving

MAKING THE MARINADE. Combine the vinegar, tamari, garlic, brown sugar, peppercorns, and bay leaves. Add the pork to the marinade. If the cubes are not entirely covered in the marinade, add a little water and stir. Allow the pork to marinate for at least 1 hour. (For an even stronger flavor, set up the marinade in the morning and let sit in the refrigerator to be ready to cook for dinner.)

COOKING THE ADOBO. Set a Dutch oven over medium-high heat. Pour the marinade and pork through a fine-mesh sieve into the Dutch oven. Transfer the pork into the Dutch oven. Cook, stirring occasionally, at a gentle simmer until the pork cubes are firm to the touch (internal temperature of 135°F), 30 to 40 minutes. (Boiling the sauce will make the meat tough so do simmer this slowly.)

BROWNING THE MEAT. Pull the pork pieces from the Dutch oven. Set a large skillet over medium-high heat. Pour in the oil. When the oil is hot, add the pork. Cook the pork pieces until the bottoms are browned, about 3 minutes. Flip over all the pieces and brown the other side. Remove from the heat when done.

REDUCING THE SAUCE. While the pork is browning, cook the remaining sauce, stirring occasionally, until it has reduced by half its volume.

Serve the pork with the reduced sauce poured over it. We like to eat it with brown basmati rice.

Feeds 4

moussaka

The length of this recipe might persuade you to save it for a long weekend afternoon. There's no need. It's not nearly as hard as it seems. The first time I made this, I had two three-year-olds at my feet in the kitchen, bickering about who was allowed to ride on the plastic car at that moment. And still, it came out great. (I sat them both on the kitchen counter and asked them to cut up onions with plastic knives. That helped.) You can do this.

2 large eggplants

Kosher salt

2 large Yukon gold potatoes, peeled and sliced ¼ inch thick

¼ cup extra-virgin olive oil

1 large white onion, peeled and chopped

2 cloves garlic, peeled and sliced

1½ pounds ground lamb

¼ teaspoon allspice

½ teaspoon freshly grated nutmeg

¼ teaspoon cinnamon

1 bay leaf

2 tablespoons tomato paste

One 14-ounce can diced tomatoes, drained

¼ cup tomato sauce

2 tablespoons red wine vinegar

2 cups whole milk

4 tablespoons (½ stick) unsalted butter

6 tablespoons All-Purpose Gluten-Free Flour Mix (page 31)

1 ounce feta cheese

½ cup grated Mizithra cheese

SALTING THE EGGPLANTS. Cut the eggplants in half and peel them. Cut into ¼-inch-thick slices and lay them on a couple of plates. Liberally crunch salt over the slices and let sit for at least 30 minutes. You'll notice little beads of moisture on the eggplant. Wipe them off.

PARBOILING THE POTATOES. Meanwhile, set a pot of cold salted water over high heat and add the potatoes. Bring to a boil and continue boiling until a knife inserts semi-easily into the potato, 5 to 7 minutes. Turn off the heat and drain the potatoes.

ROASTING THE EGGPLANTS AND POTATOES. Turn on the broiler. Lay the eggplant and potato slices on baking sheets and drizzle them with 2 tablespoons of the oil. Broil until the eggplant and potato slices have browned and started to crisp, 5 to 8 minutes. Set them aside.

continued . . .

MAKING THE MEAT SAUCE. Set a large skillet over medium-high heat. Pour in the remaining 2 tablespoons of oil. When the oil is hot, add the onion and garlic and cook, stirring frequently, until the onion has softened, about 5 minutes. Add the lamb and cook, breaking up the meat and stirring it, until the meat is entirely browned, about 5 minutes. Stir in the allspice, half the nutmeg, and the cinnamon. Cook until the scent of the spices wafts through the room, about 1 minute. Nestle the bay leaf in the meat. Add the tomato paste and cook, stirring, until it is fully incorporated into the meat mixture. Add the tomatoes and cook, stirring, until the tomatoes have started to soften, about 3 minutes. Pour in the tomato sauce and vinegar and simmer the mixture over low heat while you make the béchamel sauce.

MAKING THE BÉCHAMEL SAUCE. First, relax. This isn't as hard as it sounds. Set a small pot over medium heat. Bring the milk to a simmer. Turn it down to the lowest setting and cover it.

In another pot on the stove, melt the butter. Sprinkle the flour over the melted butter and whisk. This will not look like a traditional roux. Instead, it will be bubbling and somewhat liquidy. Keep whisking. Cook until the butter-flour has browned just a bit. Pour in ½ cup of the warm milk. The roux will immediately thicken, tremendously. That's good. Keep whisking. Add more milk and whisk. The ball of roux will thicken before it begins to relax into a liquid state. Add a pinch of salt and the remaining ¼ teaspoon nutmeg. Stir and stir. Continue to add milk until you have a thick, milky gravy. Stir in the feta cheese.

PREPARING TO BAKE. Preheat the oven to 400°F.

ASSEMBLING THE MOUSSAKA. Layer the bottom of a 9 x 13-inch casserole pan with the roasted potatoes, followed by the roasted eggplant. Remove the bay leaf and scoop in the meat sauce and pat it evenly over the potatoes and eggplants. Pour the béchamel sauce over it all. Sprinkle on the Mizithra cheese.

> ### FEEL LIKE PLAYING?
>
> If you can't find Mizithra in your area, grated Parmesan would be fine here. The feta is optional too.
>
> Béchamel sauce is pretty versatile. You could make some with four different cheeses for a decadent macaroni and cheese. It works well in lasagna as well. Add Cheddar cheese, dry mustard, and some Worcestershire sauce for a great cheese sauce on top of roasted broccoli. Spoon some Dijon mustard into a béchamel for a mustard sauce for fish.
>
> This meat sauce alone would be fantastic on pasta!

Bake in the oven until the top is bubbling with melted cheese and the smell of the moussaka is almost too good to bear, 45 minutes to 1 hour.

Feeds 8

lamb curry with eggplant

Danny cooked a version of this dish at Café Cielo in Seattle in the early '90s. He still gets dreamy eyed thinking about it.

1 large eggplant

Kosher salt

2 tablespoons extra-virgin olive oil

1 pound boneless lamb shoulder steaks, cut into 1-inch cubes

1 large onion, peeled and chopped

3 cloves garlic, peeled and sliced

2 teaspoons Madras curry powder

1 teaspoon fennel seeds

One 15-ounce can whole tomatoes, drained

One 14-ounce can full-fat coconut milk

$1/4$ cup chopped fresh cilantro

1 tablespoon fresh lemon juice

Cooked rice or noodles, for serving

SALTING THE EGGPLANT. Peel the eggplant. Cut the eggplant into 1-inch cubes. Lay the cubes on a plate and sprinkle liberally with salt. Let it sit for 30 minutes. There will be beads of moisture on the eggplant. Wipe them off.

BROWNING THE LAMB. Set a large skillet over medium-high heat. Pour in 1 tablespoon of the oil. When the oil is hot, add the lamb cubes. Cook until the bottom of each piece is browned, about 3 minutes. Turn the lamb and cook until each side of the cubes is browned, about 10 minutes total. Remove the lamb to a plate.

COOKING THE EGGPLANT. Add the remaining oil. Add the onion and cook, stirring, until softened, about 5 minutes. Add the eggplant cubes and cook until they've begun to soften, about 4 minutes. Add the garlic and cook, stirring, for 1 minute. Stir in the curry powder and fennel seeds and cook until they release their scent, about 1 minute.

COOKING THE CURRY. Pour in the tomatoes and cook until they begin to soften, about 2 minutes. Add back the lamb, pour in the coconut milk, and bring to a mild boil. Reduce the heat and simmer until the coconut milk is reduced and thickened, about 5 minutes.

FINISHING THE CURRY. Toss in the cilantro and lemon juice and cook just long enough to heat them up, about 1 minute. Take the curry off the heat. Serve over rice or noodles.

Feeds 4

breaking down a chicken

FOR YEARS I SPENT A LOT OF MONEY ON PLASTIC-WRAPPED PACKAGES OF BONELESS SKINLESS chicken breasts. They didn't have a lot of taste or inspire me to cook anything new. They certainly didn't look as though they came from an animal.

It wasn't until I met Danny that I discovered I could buy a whole chicken for far less money than the component parts. He taught me how to break down that chicken into two breasts, two legs and thighs, two wings, and have the carcass left for making stock. Even when we buy the more expensive, organic chicken, we still get three full dinners out of that one chicken, generally for the price of one package of boneless, skinless breasts.

Each week, we buy a local chicken, one that has roamed free and been fed what chickens like to eat. Why? The taste.

Some commercially produced chicken is injected with a saltwater solution that not only adds sodium to the meat but also means the chicken you are buying could be 15 percent water weight. These oversize chickens with blown-up breasts are all blowzy and no substance.

When we buy a chicken that actually tastes like something—dark meat that asserts itself, chicken breasts that aren't watered down—we don't need a lot to make a meal. We roast the whole chicken and make chicken enchilada casserole with the breasts. The next day, lunch is roasted chicken salad with apples and golden raisins from the legs. And the roasted chicken carcass makes a tremendous stock for chicken soup with coconut milk and mushrooms.

We roast chicken breasts with lemon and pistachios. Or make gluten-free chicken strips to dunk into smoked paprika-chipotle sauce. We roast the legs slathered in coconut oil and the Ethiopian spice blend berbere (see page 229).

Buying and using the entire chicken makes sense financially. You get more good meals on your table with one chicken than the package of parts.

FEEL LIKE PLAYING?

Some folks insist that trussing the chicken is the way to ensure crisp skin. I agree it helps a bit, but I often forget to do it. I don't think it's necessary. If you feel comfortable trussing, however, do it.

Thomas Keller's method of roasting chicken is to truss it, salt it liberally, and put it in a 450°F oven until it's done. You pour the juices over the top, followed by herbs, and let it rest. Again, this is great. However, Danny feels like the lower temperature makes the chicken juicier.

roasted chicken

Let me start off by telling you this: I used to be anxious about roasting a chicken. In my mind, there was one right way I had to find, a technique I had to know before I could slide that chicken into the oven and have it come out honey-golden with crackling skin in the end.

Truth is, you could roast a chicken a dozen ways and still have it come out great. The key is the chicken itself. Most grocery store chickens, especially the ones produced in huge factory farms, are pretty tasteless. They're more water than anything else. So, if you can find a local chicken, raised in a way that lets them move? Your roasted chicken is already good.

We like this method best in our house.

One 3- to 3½-pound chicken
    (preferably free-range)

Kosher salt

1 tablespoon oil (coconut, peanut,
    or sesame)

2 tablespoons unsalted butter

2 tablespoons finely chopped
    fresh thyme

PREPARING TO ROAST. Preheat the oven to 375°F. Pull the chicken out of the refrigerator and allow it to come to room temperature before you roast it. Use paper towels to pat the chicken dry, inside and out. (This will help the skin to crisp.)

PREPPING THE CHICKEN. Put the chicken breast side up in a large ovenproof skillet. Season the chicken liberally with salt, inside and out, then coat the skin in the oil.

ROASTING THE CHICKEN. Put the chicken in the oven. Roast for 30 minutes, then spread the butter on top of the chicken breasts. Return the chicken to the oven and roast until the juices run clear and the legs have reached an internal temperature of 185°F, 20 to 30 minutes more.

FINISHING THE CHICKEN. Pull the chicken out of the oven. Carefully, holding the chicken with a fork, tip all the juices out of the pan into a large measuring cup with a spout. Immediately pour all the juices over the top of the chicken. Sprinkle with the thyme. Let the chicken sit for 20 minutes before you carve it.

Feeds 4

chicken enchilada casserole

My mom used to make an enchilada casserole for dinner when I was a kid. Chicken pieces nestled with green chiles from a can, wrapped in flour tortillas. Those were nudged against each other in a blue glass casserole pan and smothered in a white sauce. (She insists it wasn't a white sauce but some kind of green sauce made with the chiles.) Handfuls of Monterey Jack cheese bubbled on top. It was always one of my favorites.

When I set out to make some version of it, I realized I wanted to roast my own chicken and use chipotle peppers instead of the green ones in the can. I simmered a sauce of onions, tomatoes, and chicken stock until it had reduced enough to blanket the top of the enchiladas. I wonder how Lucy will remember this one when she's an adult.

2 tablespoons chili powder

1 tablespoon smoked paprika

1 tablespoon Mexican oregano

Pinch red pepper flakes

One 3½-pound chicken

Kosher salt and cracked black pepper

¼ cup extra-virgin olive oil

1 large onion, peeled and chopped

2 small red bell peppers, chopped

2 cloves garlic, peeled and sliced

1 teaspoon ground cumin

One 14-ounce can diced tomatoes, drained

1 canned gluten-free chipotle pepper in adobo sauce

1 quart chicken stock

16 corn tortillas

4 cups grated Monterey Jack cheese

1 lime, zested

ROASTING THE CHICKEN. Preheat the oven to 375°F. Combine the chili powder, paprika, oregano, and red pepper flakes in a small bowl. Pat dry the chicken with paper towels and season it with salt and black pepper. Pour 2 tablespoons of the oil over it and rub the spice mixture all over the chicken. Roast the chicken according to the instructions on page 215. When it has cooled to room temperature, cut off the breasts and shred the meat. You might have some spice mixture left over. That's great! Save it for tortilla soup (page 74).

Preparing to make the enchiladas. Turn up the heat of the oven to 400°F.

Cooking the filling. Set a deep skillet over medium-high heat. Pour the remaining 2 tablespoons oil into it. When the oil is hot, add the onion, red peppers, and garlic and cook, stirring occasionally, until the onion has softened, about 5 minutes. Stir in the cumin and cook until the scent is released, about 1 minute. Add the tomatoes and chipotle pepper and cook, stirring, until it is heated through, about 2 minutes. Add 3 cups of the roasted chicken into the skillet, followed by the chicken stock. Bring the liquid to a boil, then turn down the heat to medium-low and cook for 15 minutes.

Strain the filling through a fine-mesh sieve, reserving the stock. Set the chicken filling on a plate. Return the stock to the skillet and turn up the heat to medium. Allow the chicken stock to reduce while you are preparing the tortillas.

Heating the tortillas. If you have a gas stove, put the flame on high. Toss a tortilla right on the flame. Let it heat until it is a bit charred at the edges, about 1 minute. Flip the tortilla with tongs and heat the other side. Remove the tortilla to a plate. Repeat with the remaining tortillas. (If you don't have a gas stove, use a cast-iron skillet to heat the tortillas.)

Making the enchiladas. Take a heated tortilla. Add about 3 tablespoons of the chicken filling into the bottom half of the tortilla. Roll the tortilla tightly around the filling and put it, seam side down, into a 9 x 13-inch casserole pan. Continue with the rest of the tortillas and filling until you have finished.

Pour the reduced chicken stock over the enchiladas. Cover with the Monterey Jack cheese and lime zest.

Baking the enchiladas. Bake the enchiladas until the cheese has melted and bubbled over the top, starting to brown, about 30 minutes.

Feeds 4 to 6

> ### FEEL LIKE PLAYING?
>
> These really don't have much heat, apart from the nudge of chipotle peppers. If you want more of a kick, I'd try poblano peppers or red jalapeños. Or, you could glug some hot sauce in the chicken stock before it reduces. However, think of the kids here.

chicken strips

You couldn't pay me to eat chicken strips or nuggets from a fast-food joint. No thank you. But homemade chicken strips made from juicy breast meat from a chicken I trust, a crisp crust that shatters on the teeth, and a smoked paprika-chipotle dipping sauce? Heck yeah!

We tried making these a few different ways. It wasn't until we read a recipe for fish sticks from Canal House Cooks that we saw the light. They used panko, but panko crumbs have gluten in them. After trying ground-up crackers and breadcrumbs, we hit upon the solution: tortilla chips. If you grind up tortilla chips for a long time in a food processor, they are nearly indistinguishable from panko.

Chicken strips for everyone!

2 cups tortilla chips

140 grams All-Purpose Gluten-Free
    Flour Mix (page 31)

3 large eggs, at room temperature

1 pound boneless chicken breast

Kosher salt and freshly ground black pepper

2 cups sunflower, safflower, or canola oil,
    for frying

Smoked Paprika–Chipotle Sauce (recipe
    follows), for serving

PULSING THE TORTILLA CHIPS. In the food processor, pulse the tortilla chips until they have become fine crumbs, about 5 minutes. Pour them into a wide-mouthed bowl, and then pour the flour into another wide-mouthed bowl. Beat the eggs in another wide-mouthed bowl and set all the bowls next to each other.

PREPARING THE CHICKEN. Cut the chicken into strips ¾ inch thick by 3 inches long. (Yes, we really did take out the ruler for this recipe! But you can approximate.) Making sure the chicken strips are about the same size will ensure that each is cooked well. Season them with salt and pepper.

FEEL LIKE PLAYING?

Here's the good news. If you want to make fish sticks? Simply replace the chicken with a firm-fleshed fish like halibut or cod, use the same recipe, and you have fish sticks that will disappear from the table immediately.

Any time you have a leftover bag of tortilla chips that are going a little stale? Pulse up those chips and keep them in a jar. They'll keep as crumbs for quite a long time, so you can make these or anything you want to give a crisp crust.

DREDGING THE CHICKEN. Coat each chicken strip in the flour, then dip in the eggs, then the tortilla chip crumbs. Put the coated chicken strips on a cooling rack and let them rest for at least 15 minutes, and up to 1 hour.

COOKING THE CHICKEN. Set a large skillet over medium heat. Pour in oil to a depth of 1 to 2 inches. Heat the oil until it hits 350°F on a candy thermometer. Carefully add 5 to 6 chicken strips to the hot oil. (You'll probably have to cook these in 2 batches.) The oil will sizzle and bubble immediately. That's how you'll know it's hot enough, besides the thermometer. Cook until the coating on the chicken is golden brown and crisp, 4 to 5 minutes. Remove the chicken strips from the oil and put them on a paper towel–covered plate to drain.

REPEAT WITH THE REMAINING CHICKEN STRIPS. Remember that the temperature of the oil will have risen, so be careful with the second batch. You might also need to add some more oil for the second batch.

Serve immediately with the smoked paprika–chipotle sauce.

Feeds 4

smoked paprika–chipotle sauce

We love our vivacious friend Tami for many reasons. That she gave us this sauce is one of them. We really can't take much credit. She was kind enough to introduce it to us and then let us introduce this sauce to you.

Tami started making this because her sister waxed poetic about the tortas with addictive smoked paprika sauces she was eating in small shops in Brooklyn. Tami made her describe every taste, down to the slightest nuance. She fiddled and played until she had made the sauce you see here. By the time she visited her sister, she found that she liked her own sauce better than the ones she ate in Brooklyn. Believe me, we approve of her fiddling.

Tami uses Vegenaise with this because her daughter is allergic to eggs. However, you can use homemade or store-bought mayonnaise. Just be careful when you choose the chipotles in adobo sauce. Many brands contain wheat flour. You don't want to feel sick after eating this sauce.

4 cups mayonnaise

1 to 3 canned gluten-free chipotle peppers in adobo sauce, depending on your taste for heat

3 tablespoons smoked paprika

2 cloves garlic, peeled

3 slices preserved lemons (page 96)

MAKING THE SAUCE. Combine all the ingredients in a blender and let it run. When the sauce is bright orange in color and smooth, take a taste. Maybe you want more lemon or another chipotle pepper. Play with your own taste.

Makes 2½ cups

FEEL LIKE PLAYING?

Keep this sauce in the refrigerator and use it any number of ways: spread on a veggie burger, dolloped on rice, schmeared on corn tortillas for quesadillas. If you thin it out with some rice wine vinegar, you'll have an addictive salad dressing. Make some and find your own favorite ways to eat it.

roasted lemon chicken with pistachios

Roasted chicken with a warm pan sauce might seem intimidating. It's easy once you try it. Your friends will be impressed. Your bellies will be happy. And you will grin, knowing it didn't take you nearly as long to make this as they think.

Chicken, lemon, and pistachios are best friends—like that trio of girls in middle school who were inseparable. (However, there's no meanness or insecurity here.) The flavors of this dish mingle and build as you roast, then reduce the sauce. Try this once and we think you'll make it again.

1 lemon

2 chicken legs

2 boneless chicken thighs

2 boneless chicken breasts, cut in half lengthwise

Kosher salt and freshly ground black pepper

8 tablespoons extra-virgin olive oil

1 medium onion, peeled and diced

1 tablespoon chopped fresh thyme

$1/2$ cup dry white wine

1 cup chicken stock

1 tablespoon unsalted butter

$1/4$ cup pistachios

$1/4$ cup golden raisins

PREPARING TO COOK. Preheat the oven to 375°F. Remove the top and bottom of the lemon. Cut into 4 lengthwise slices. Cut each of those in half and dice them up, leaving the skins on. Season the chicken pieces with salt and pepper on both sides.

BROWNING THE CHICKEN. Set a large skillet over medium-high heat. Pour in 4 tablespoons of the oil. When the oil is hot, add the chicken legs and thighs. Sear the legs and thighs until they are browned on the bottom, 3 to 4 minutes. Move them to a roasting pan. Add 2 more tablespoons of the oil and sear the chicken breasts the same way.

ROASTING THE CHICKEN. When all the browned chicken is in the roasting pan, put it in the oven. Roast the chicken until the breasts reach an internal temperature of 150°F, 10 to 12 minutes, and the thighs and legs reach an internal temperature of 180°F, 12 to 15 minutes. (Keep checking.)

continued . . .

Caramelizing the onions and lemons. While the chicken is roasting, set the same skillet over medium-high heat. Add the remaining oil. When the oil is hot, add the diced onion and cook, stirring frequently, until it starts to lightly caramelize, 10 to 12 minutes. Add the lemon pieces and cook, stirring occasionally, until the lemons have begun to caramelize too, about 5 more minutes.

Making the sauce. Stir in the thyme and cook until it releases its fragrance, about 2 minutes. Deglaze the pan by stirring in the wine. Cook until the wine has reduced by half its volume, about 3 minutes. Add the chicken stock. Simmer, stirring occasionally, until the sauce begins to thicken, about 5 minutes.

Pull the roasted chicken from the oven. Put it onto plates to serve.

Finishing the sauce. Add the butter to the sauce and stir until it is fully incorporated. Just before serving, add the pistachios and raisins to the sauce and stir. Season with salt and pepper to taste. Give the sauce one last stir.

Pour the sauce over the roasted chicken. Serve.

Feeds 4

FEEL LIKE PLAYING?

If you use this recipe as a template, you can make up your own chicken dishes every time you cook. Instead of lemon and thyme, try orange juice and tarragon. Instead of white wine, try port or Madeira. Instead of chicken stock, try water if the other flavors you are using are dominant. Walnuts instead of pistachios, dried sour cherries instead of golden raisins. It's easy to make this one your own.

curry-braised chicken legs

Here's one of the fun parts about being married to a chef. When I asked Danny what we should do with chicken legs for this chapter, he didn't hesitate before saying: "Let's make curry-braised legs." I assumed he had made it before at a restaurant. Nope. It just came to him, and then he moved into the kitchen and made this dish.

I think I'll keep him around.

3 cups chicken stock

2 tablespoons finely chopped fresh ginger

2 tablespoons curry powder

1 tablespoon grated lime zest

1 teaspoon coriander seeds

$^1/_2$ teaspoon kosher salt

4 chicken legs

2 tablespoons coconut oil

1 yellow onion, peeled and chopped

2 stalks celery, chopped

2 carrots, peeled and chopped

2 cloves garlic, peeled and sliced

$^1/_2$ cup dry white wine

2 tablespoons unsalted butter

PREPARING TO COOK. Preheat the oven to 400°F. Set a small pot on the stove and bring the chicken stock to a simmer.

BROWNING THE CHICKEN LEGS. In a small bowl, mix together the ginger, curry powder, lime zest, coriander seeds, and salt. Rub the mixture evenly on the chicken legs.

Set a large skillet on medium-high heat. Add the oil. When the oil is melted, lay down the chicken legs. Cook until the bottoms of the chicken legs are browned, about 5 minutes. Flip the chicken legs and brown the other side, about 5 minutes. Remove the chicken legs from the skillet, leaving the oil in the skillet.

COOKING THE VEGETABLES. Add the onion, celery, carrots, and garlic to the hot oil in the skillet. Cook, stirring frequently, until the onion has softened, about 5 minutes. Pour in the wine to deglaze the browned bits on the bottom of the skillet; scrape them up and stir. Cook until the wine has reduced in volume by half, about 3 minutes.

continued . . .

BAKING THE LEGS. Transfer everything in the skillet to a 9 x 13-inch casserole pan. Lay the chicken legs on top. Pour the warm chicken stock over it all. Cover the pan with aluminum foil.

Cook until the internal temperature of the chicken legs has reached 180°F, 20 to 25 minutes. Take the pan out of the oven.

Set the chicken legs on a plate. Strain the liquid in the pan through a fine-mesh sieve into a pot on the stove. Over medium-high heat, reduce the liquid by half its volume, about 5 minutes. Add the butter and stir until it is fully incorporated into the sauce.

Serve the chicken legs with some of the sauce dribbled over them.

Feeds 4

FEEL LIKE PLAYING?

You could easily do this with 8 legs, if someone wanted more than 1 chicken leg for dinner. Just nestle them in among each other.

Friends of ours who tested this recipe loved the flavors but wanted the sauce a little creamier. So they whisked in a little cashew cream (page 102) before the liquids reduced and reported they were deeply satisfied by this.

roasted chicken salad with apples, golden raisins, and tarragon

I must admit something embarrassing. Whenever I think of chicken salad, I think of the recipe for Waldorf salad that a customer keeps screaming at Basil Fawlty: chicken, apples, celery, and walnuts! I have that frantic scene locked in my head. Chicken salad = *Fawlty Towers*. Except, I went back to see that scene again to write this headnote (and get a little comic relief) and realized there's no chicken in a Waldorf salad. Oops. Well, this one's still great.

3 cups cubed cooked chicken, taken from roasted legs and thighs

2 large green apples, peeled and cubed

½ cup golden raisins

2 tablespoons finely chopped fresh tarragon

1 cup mayonnaise

2 tablespoons rice wine vinegar

2 tablespoons cold water

Grated zest of 1 lemon

Kosher salt and freshly ground black pepper

Butter lettuce leaves, for serving

Assembling the salad. Combine the chicken, apples, raisins, and tarragon in a large bowl.

Making the dressing. In a small bowl, whisk together the mayonnaise, vinegar, water, and zest. Season with salt and pepper. (We like lots of pepper here.)

Finishing the salad. Dollop the dressing on the chicken salad and toss to coat. Refrigerate for at least 1 hour before serving in lettuce cups.

Feeds 4

FEEL LIKE PLAYING?

I really like this salad best in cold butter lettuce cups, as you can see here. However, it's also great on sandwich bread (page 48) or pita bread (page 281). You can't go wrong with either one.

berbere-roasted drumsticks

The first time I ate Ethiopian food, it was as though my head was expanding. Not only was the eating experience different—a communal table without silverware, all the food dolloped on a giant injera bread—but the flavors were also unfamiliar. I wanted more.

Berbere is the spice mix ubiquitous in Ethiopian cuisine. Every household makes a slightly different blend, of course, so there is no one taste to berbere. But there's a smokiness, a slight sweetness, something fiery, something calming. We can't get enough of it around here. Even plain roasted chicken is memorable with berbere.

8 tablespoons (1 stick) unsalted butter

2 tablespoons fresh lemon juice

2 tablespoons Berbere Seasoning (recipe follows)

$1/2$ teaspoon each kosher salt and freshly ground black pepper

8 chicken legs

PREPARING TO ROAST. Preheat the oven to 450°F. Line a baking sheet with parchment paper.

SEASONING THE CHICKEN. Set a large skillet over medium-high heat and add the butter. When the butter has melted, add the lemon juice, berbere seasoning, and the salt and pepper and stir. Using your tongs, bathe each chicken leg in the berbere sauce and transfer to the baking sheet. Brush the rest of the berbere sauce over the chicken legs on the baking sheet.

FEEL LIKE PLAYING?

You can make these roasted chicken legs with any seasoning or spice rub. Herbes de Provence. Preserved lemon. Smoked paprika. Ginger and fish sauce. Go wild.

ROASTING THE LEGS. Roast the legs in the oven until the internal temperature reaches 180°F and the juices run clear when you poke one of the drumsticks with a knife, 30 to 40 minutes. If you want to crisp up the skin even more, turn on the broiler and cook for another 3 to 5 minutes.

Feeds 4

berbere seasoning

Berbere is a blend of spices and seasonings that make up the taste of Ethiopian food. It's a little bit spicy, slightly sweet, partly familiar, and mostly new to the American palate. From what I understand, every household in Ethiopia makes a slightly different version than their neighbor's. Feel free to come up with your own combination. However, making it fresh ensures the taste is particularly bright and earthy.

2 teaspoons fenugreek seeds

1 teaspoon coriander seeds

1 teaspoon black peppercorns

2 cardamom pods

4 dried chiles de arbol, stemmed and seeded

1 tablespoon smoked paprika

2 tablespoons paprika

1 tablespoon dried basil

1 teaspoon kosher salt

$\frac{1}{2}$ teaspoon ground ginger

$\frac{1}{2}$ teaspoon ground cinnamon

TOASTING THE SEEDS. Set a small skillet over medium-high heat. Add the fenugreek, coriander, peppercorns, and cardamom pods. Toast the spices, moving the skillet around the burner constantly, until the smells are released, 4 to 5 minutes.

GRINDING THE SEASONING. Let the toasted spices cool. Add them in a clean spice grinder along with the chiles and grind fine.

FINISHING THE SEASONING BLEND. Pour the ground spices into a bowl. Stir in the smoked paprika, paprika, dried basil, salt, ginger, and cinnamon.

This will keep in an airtight container for 3 months. You're going to be using it often, however.

Makes $\frac{1}{2}$ cup

avgolemono

I grew up eating chicken noodle soup out of a can: thick noodles, bits of chicken, all of it just a little too salty. Still, comforting, because it's what I knew. When I was sick, I sort of craved it. However, the first time I went to Vios, a great little Greek café in Seattle, I ordered a bowl of avgolemono soup. I must admit—I ordered it for the name. (Words run rampant in my head sometimes, meaning I have to repeat them.) Then I had my first bite.

It took me a while to realize this Greek chicken soup was egg (*avgo*) and lemon (*lemono*) with chicken and rice. The bright hints of lemon make this the perfect comfort food for a cold winter's day.

One 3-pound chicken, breasts removed and set aside

2 carrots, peeled and chopped

2 stalks celery, chopped

1 onion, peeled and cut in half

3 cloves garlic, peeled and sliced

1 tablespoon dried oregano

Kosher salt

1 cup calrose medium-grain rice

3 large eggs

3 large lemons, juiced

Grated lemon zest and fresh oregano (optional), for garnish

MAKING THE CHICKEN STOCK. Set a stockpot over high heat. Add the chicken, without the breasts, and the carrots, celery, onion, garlic, and oregano. Pour in enough water to cover everything by 1 inch. Bring the water to a boil, then turn down the heat to medium to medium-low so it's at a gentle simmer. (You should only see a few bubbles popping at the surface every minute or so.) Skim the frothy stuff that will rise to the top of the pot on a regular basis. Simmer for at least 1 hour, preferably more like 2 to 3 hours.

Strain the stock through a fine-mesh sieve into another large pot. Now you have chicken stock. (You can play with the flavors, taking out the oregano or the garlic, if you wish. For a simple stock, you really only need onions and carrots. That's enough. You can also make a good stock with a chicken carcass without any meat on it. It's the bones that matter here.)

continued . . .

POACHING THE CHICKEN BREASTS. Set a Dutch oven over medium heat and add the chicken breasts. Add enough of the chicken stock to cover by 1 inch. Add about a teaspoon of salt. Bring the stock to the start of a gentle boil and turn down the heat to medium-low. Simmer the chicken breasts at a very small simmer until there is no pink inside, 10 to 15 minutes. Remove the chicken from the stock and allow it to cool to room temperature before cutting it into 1-inch cubes.

MAKING THE SOUP. Set a large pot on medium-high. Pour in the remaining chicken stock. Bring it to a gentle boil, then turn down the heat to medium. Add the rice. Let it simmer until the rice is tender, about 10 minutes.

Beat the eggs and lemon juice together in a large bowl. Slowly, in a steady stream, drop 1 ladleful of chicken stock into the eggs and lemon. Whisk briskly. Repeat this 2 more times, then pour the egg mixture into the stock.

Add the cubes of poached chicken. Simmer until everything is heated, about 3 minutes.

Serve with a garnish of lemon zest and fresh oregano, if you wish.

Feeds 4

FEEL LIKE PLAYING?

Of course, you can make this with boxed chicken stock and already cooked chicken, if you're in a rush. It won't taste the same but it will be much better than that canned chicken noodle soup.

We like calrose medium-grain rice here because we just love calrose medium-grain rice. You can use any kind you like but the thickness of the soup will vary depending on how starchy your rice is.

FEEL LIKE PLAYING? > > > > >

We like this stew served over quinoa. The nutty taste of it blends well with all these flavors.

If you can't find fennel near you, then leave it out and add some thinly sliced cabbage at the end of the cooking time, after the chicken is cooked.

I love black Mediterranean olives here too. Pretty much every cheese but the stinky kinds would work well as a topping for this stew.

chicken stew with tarragon and fennel

This is the kind of hearty stew I love to make on a winter afternoon.

¹/₄ cup extra-virgin olive oil

6 boneless chicken thighs

1 bulb fennel, thinly sliced (on the
    mandoline, if possible)

2 large shallots, peeled and finely chopped

2 cloves garlic, peeled and finely chopped

2 tablespoons finely chopped fresh tarragon

2 tablespoons champagne vinegar

6 ripe plum tomatoes, diced, or one
    28-ounce can diced tomatoes, drained

1 bay leaf

¹/₂ cup pitted green Cerignola olives
    (any good green olive will do)

2 cups chicken stock

2 ounces crumbled feta cheese

SEARING THE CHICKEN THIGHS. Set a large skillet over medium-high heat. Add 2 tablespoons of the oil. When the oil is hot, lay down 3 of the chicken thighs and cook until they are browned on the bottom, about 5 minutes. Flip them over and brown the other side, about 5 minutes more. Repeat with the remaining thighs.

COOKING THE AROMATICS. Add the fennel, shallots, and garlic to the hot pan. Cook, stirring occasionally to scrape up the bits from the bottom of the pan, until the shallot is softened and beginning to brown, about 5 minutes. Stir in the tarragon and cook until the scent is released into the room, about 1 minute.

BUILDING THE STEW. Pour in the vinegar and vigorously scrape the bottom of the pan. Add the tomatoes and bay leaf and cook until the tomatoes have begun to soften, about 3 minutes. Nestle the chicken thighs in among the tomatoes. Add the olives. Pour in enough chicken stock to cover the chicken.

FINISHING THE STEW. Cook the stew until the liquids have barely come to a boil. Reduce the heat to medium-low, cover the skillet, and simmer until the thighs have reached an internal temperature of 180°F, about 20 minutes. Remove the bay leaf before serving.

To serve, drizzle each bowl with a bit of the remaining 2 tablespoons oil and some of the feta.

Feeds 4

chicken soup with coconut and mushrooms

Just about the same time I was slurping spoonfuls of this intensely flavored soup at my favorite Thai restaurant in Seattle, Danny was working at one of Jean-Georges Vongerichten's restaurants in New York, making this soup. Known as *tom yum gai* in Thai, this soup will cure you of the sniffles and any temporary ills. The combination of lemongrass, ginger, and chicken stock alone make it worth cooking. Once you have reached halfway through the bowl, however, you're going to find yourself spooning it into your mouth faster and faster. Slow down. You want to savor this.

1 tablespoon coconut oil

1 large onion, peeled and chopped

2 cloves garlic, chopped

1 tablespoon red curry paste

1 stalk lemongrass, end removed and middle part chopped

One 1-inch piece fresh ginger, peeled and chopped

4 cups chicken stock

2 cups coconut milk

12 ounces chicken breast, cut into cubes

2 cups sliced white mushrooms

1 lime, zested and juiced

2 tablespoons gluten-free fish sauce

$\frac{1}{2}$ cup finely chopped scallions

$\frac{1}{2}$ cup finely chopped fresh cilantro

Cooking the aromatics. Set a large Dutch oven over medium-high heat. Add the oil. When it has fully melted, add the onion, garlic, curry paste, lemongrass, and ginger and cook, stirring, until the onion is softened and everything smells tremendous, about 7 minutes.

Finishing the soup. Pour in the chicken stock and stir. Bring the stock to a vigorous simmer but do not boil it. After 15 minutes, add the coconut milk, chicken, and mushrooms. Cook until the chicken cubes feel firm to the touch, about 5 minutes.

Stir in the lime zest and juice and fish sauce and let the soup simmer for another 2 minutes. Taste the soup. Add more lime juice or fish sauce, if you wish.

Serve the soup topped with the scallions and cilantro.

Feeds 6

fire up the grill

OUR FRIENDS QUINN AND ALISON HAVE A HUGE, BEAUTIFUL GRILL ON THE DECK OF THEIR LOVELY
home. On summer days, they have parties during which every inch of that grill is covered in ribs or kebabs or
hamburgers. We all gather happily around the grill, smelling the smoke. In the winter, they still use the grill to cook
dinner. Even though they love to talk about and eat food as much as we do, these two folks we adore will be the first
to tell you that they aren't very confident cooks. Many nights, they throw a piece of marinated chicken on the grill
for dinner for their daughter.

We love those dinners. There's no shame in a good piece of grilled chicken, some brown rice, and some roasted
vegetables. But if you have it every night, you're going to grow a little bored with food.

So, Quinn and Alison, this chapter is for you.

Let's throw some vegetables on the grill in high summer and stew them a bit for grilled vegetable ratatouille.
That salmon from Alaska we got at the seafood market today? Danny wants to grill lemons and jalapeños and bok
choy for a new relish. You're going to love these grilled sardines with avocado and ginger-scallion sauce.

Oh, and there's always grilled pizza, of course.

I made my own gluten-free hamburger buns for the barbecue. Want to try pork-turkey burgers this time?

And how about chicken breasts stuffed with gluten-free croutons for a new texture and taste?

In the middle of January, we're probably going to have a piece of meat braising in low heat in the oven. Or, I'll
marinate a piece of flank steak in lemongrass, mint, cilantro, and ginger all day and throw it on the grill even when
the weather's cold. But we all know that the grill is best when the weather is warm. And the smell of lamb kebabs on
the grill in the middle of summer, a cold yogurt-with-spiced dukkah dip waiting? It's pretty much heaven.

Hey Quinn and Alison, fire up the grill. We're bringing sausages and onions, fresh corn, tomatoes, and basil.
We can't wait to see you.

grilled pizza

This was inspired by Carol Field's recipe from *The Italian Baker*, one of the best baking books of all time. She's a genius.

Her dough called for up to eight hours of rising. I tried that here—not good. Because there's no gluten in these doughs, the structure that the proteins in the flours and the psyllium provide is pretty fragile. Eventually, the gas bubbles formed by the yeast poke apart the structure. I never let a gluten-free dough rise more than two hours. Generally, it's about an hour.

The only exception to this rule is when you let the dough rise overnight in the refrigerator because the cold makes the rise much slower. That practice builds extraordinary flavor.

And after all that work? Pizza dough for the grill.

750 grams All-Purpose Gluten-Free Flour Mix (page 31)

1 tablespoon whole or powdered psyllium husks (see page 33)

1 envelope ($2^1/_4$ teaspoons) active dry yeast

1 teaspoon sugar

1 teaspoon kosher salt

1 large egg, at room temperature

$^1/_4$ cup extra-virgin olive oil

$1^1/_2$ to $2^1/_2$ cups warm water, at about 110°F

MAKING THE DOUGH. Mix the flour, psyllium husks, yeast, sugar, and salt in the bowl of a stand mixer. With the stand mixer running, add the egg and oil.

Slowly, drizzle in half the water and continue mixing the dough. Pour in more water and mix until you have a sticky ball of dough that slumps off the paddle when you stop the mixer. Do not add more flour. Gluten-free doughs are wetter than gluten doughs.

LETTING THE DOUGH RISE. Put the dough into a lightly greased bowl. Let the dough rise until the texture has firmed into something close to a traditional pizza dough, 1 to 2 hours.

SHAPING THE DOUGH. Oil your hands again. Gently turn the dough out onto a floured surface. Cut it into 6 equal pieces and form them into balls. Cover them with a damp cloth and let the dough rest for another 30 minutes.

continued . . .

Grilling the pizza. Fire up the grill. Get it as hot as you can. (If you have a thermometer on your grill, it should read over 700°F.)

Roll out each of the balls of dough into an oval about 6 inches long. (It might help to roll them out between 2 pieces of lightly greased parchment paper, to avoid sticking.) Place the oval of dough, oil side down, onto the grill. Repeat with the remaining dough. (If you have a small grill, you may have to do this in batches.) Put the lid on the grill and cook until the bottom of the pizzas are set and have grill marks, 4 to 6 minutes. Pull the pizza crusts off the grill.

This is where you top your pizzas. Of course, you may use anything. However, I like to keep it simple. Brush the grilled side with extra-virgin olive oil and tomato sauce and put the pizzas back on the grill for 3 minutes. Add some fresh mozzarella you have torn with your hands. Close the cover of the grill and let the pizzas cook until the mozzarella has melted. Take the pizzas off the grill and toss on some fresh basil leaves and a sprinkle of kosher salt.

Eat.

Feeds 6

FEEL LIKE PLAYING?

If you want, you can make this the night before you want to cook it, with cool water, and put it in the refrigerator. Let the dough come to room temperature before you grill it. You can take out a hunk of dough to make a little pizza every night for a week.

This pizza also bakes up great in the oven. Set your oven on as high as it can go and preheat for 30 minutes. If you have a pizza stone, please put it in before you turn on the oven. You can use a pizza tray, a large piece of parchment paper, or put the pizza dough directly onto the pizza stone. Use half the dough this recipe yields for a 12-inch pizza.

Also, you can use this dough to make gluten-free naan (see page 277) and gluten-free pita bread (see page 281).

FEEL LIKE PLAYING? > > > > >

Of course, you can top these with anything you like. But I like lettuce, a tomato (when they're in season), some sharp white Cheddar, pickles, and a swipe of the Smoked Paprika–Chipotle Sauce on page 220.

Play with the seasonings here. You could work with spices that you feel go well with turkey or pork.

turkey-pork burgers

The secret to a great burger—whether it's beef or a combination of meats like this turkey-pork burger—is coarsely ground meat. Choose a cut like chuck or top round for beef, shoulder for pork, and turkey breasts, then ask your butcher to grind it for you. The difference in taste and juiciness between those cuts and already ground meat is pretty astonishing.

We use breadcrumbs and egg here to help bind the burger. Ground turkey can get a little mushy and you don't need that in your burger.

1 pound ground turkey, at room temperature

1 pound ground pork, at room temperature

$1/4$ cup gluten-free breadcrumbs

1 large egg

1 teaspoon smoked paprika

1 teaspoon chopped fresh rosemary, or $1/2$ teaspoon dried

$1/2$ teaspoon celery seeds

Kosher salt and freshly ground black pepper

MAKING THE BURGERS. In a large bowl, combine the turkey, pork, breadcrumbs, egg, paprika, rosemary, and celery seeds, as well as a couple of big pinches of kosher salt and a pinch of pepper. Using your hands, gently mix them together until just combined. You don't want to overwork the meat.

FORMING THE PATTIES. Divide the meat mixture into 4 pieces. Working quickly, form each ball into a patty. Even out the edges with your fingers and put down the patty. Repeat with the other meat balls. Let the meat rest while you heat up the grill.

GRILLING THE BURGERS. When the grill is as hot as you can make it go, lift the lid and lay the patties down gently on the grill. At first, the patties are going to cling to the grill. Don't worry. Close the lid and wait 1 minute. When enough grease has dripped from the burgers to loosen the grip on the grill, flip the burgers. Repeat on the second side.

Now, grill each burger for 2 to 3 minutes. Flip the burgers one more time and cook for 2 to 3 minutes. You can tell the burgers are done when they feel firm to the touch with just a little give. Remove them from the grill.

Feeds 4

gluten-free hamburger buns

I looked for gluten-free hamburger buns that satisfied my cravings for years. I wanted a bun that was soft and springy, with enough bite to hold up and not fall apart on the patty. Commercial buns were always too much like cardboard for my taste, probably because they were trying to duplicate typical grocery store buns. But I never liked the starchy-stiff buns available in the bread aisle anyway. I wanted home-baked buns.

Danny and I came up with some buns we liked, including ones based on the focaccia recipe from our first book. However, after I figured out the sandwich bread, I poured that thin batter into our hamburger bun pan on a whim. And there they were: soft, pliable, with a crisp crust that didn't fall apart. Easy-peasy, it turned out.

3 tablespoons unsalted butter, melted, plus extra for greasing pan and sprinkling on top

1 recipe Gluten-Free Sandwich Bread dough (page 48)

6 tablespoons sesame seeds

$\frac{1}{2}$ teaspoon kosher salt

PREPARING TO BAKE. Preheat the oven to 400°F. Grease a hamburger bun pan.

RISING THE HAMBURGER BUNS. The dough for the sandwich bread will be as pourable as pancake batter. Pour in enough to fill each well about halfway. Distribute the rest of the batter evenly among the wells. Allow the batter to rise until it is just under the lip of the pan, about 45 minutes to 1 hour.

BAKING THE HAMBURGER BUNS. When the batter has risen, the tops will have stiffened into something akin to traditional bread dough. Gently, very gently, brush the melted butter on top of each bun, then sprinkle with the sesame seeds and salt. Bake until the tops are browned and set, and the internal temperature of the bread reaches 180°F, about 20 minutes.

Allow the hamburger buns to cool entirely on a cooling rack before slicing them open.

Makes 6 buns

grilled salmon with lemon-jalapeño-bok choy relish

One day, Danny grilled lemon slices for a fish special at the restaurant where he worked at the time. I sort of went nuts when I tasted it. What is this? It never occurred to me to grill lemons.

Add grilled baby bok choy, jalapeño, and fresh cilantro to those grilled lemons—on top of grilled salmon—and you have a pretty decadently healthy meal for summer. During salmon season, from May to October here, we will eat this as often as possible.

1 lemon, cut into $\frac{1}{2}$-inch slices

1 jalapeño pepper, sliced lengthwise and seeded

2 baby bok choy, halved

6 tablespoons extra-virgin olive oil

1 teaspoon finely chopped fresh basil

1 teaspoon finely chopped fresh cilantro

Kosher salt and freshly ground black pepper

1 pound salmon fillet, skin left on

GRILLING THE VEGETABLES. Fire up the grill. When it's as hot as it will go, coat the lemon slices, jalapeño, and baby bok choy in 2 tablespoons of oil and lay them on the grill. Cook until they are charred on one side. Flip them over and char the other side. Take the vegetables off the grill and let them cool.

MAKING THE RELISH. When the vegetables are cool to the touch, chop them up roughly. Toss them into the bowl of a food processor with the basil, cilantro, and 2 tablespoons of the oil. Pulse until it forms the texture of a chunky salsa. Taste. If you want, season with salt and black pepper. Set aside.

FEEL LIKE PLAYING?

If you can't find baby bok choy, regular bok choy will do here. Slice a head of bok choy in half lengthwise, then cut it in half again and grill those pieces.

This relish works well with grilled chicken or other fish like halibut as well.

continued . . .

GRILLING THE SALMON. Run your hand over the top of the flesh of the salmon. If you feel any pinbones, remove them with a pair of tweezers. Season the salmon with salt and black pepper. Coat the skin with the remaining 2 tablespoons oil.

Lay the salmon skin side down on the hot grill. When the skin loosens its grip on the grill, after about 2 minutes, carefully lift one edge of the salmon with the fish spatula. Wiggling a bit, gently move the fish spatula up the length of the salmon and flip the salmon. If some of the skin comes off, it's no big deal. Put the lid on the grill. Grill until the salmon has reached a temperature of 120°F for medium-rare, about 5 minutes. (You can cook the salmon a few more minutes for well done, but the salmon will be at its juiciest and most flavorful at medium-rare.) Take the salmon off the grill.

When the salmon is cool enough to touch, slice the fillet into 4 even pieces. To serve, put a salmon fillet on the plate and top with the lemon-jalapeño relish.

Feeds 4

grilled ratatouille

A few foods say summer to me: blackberries just off the vine, a ripe peach, the first slice of watermelon with salt and feta. And now, this grilled ratatouille, this fish, with most of the cooking happening on the grill, is worth a few minutes of standing inside in front of the hot stove. With ripe eggplants, summer squash, tender zucchini, and tomatoes in their four-week window of ripeness, the flavors are as intense as that bright August sun.

1 medium eggplant

Kosher salt and ground black
    pepper

1 large yellow squash, cut in half lengthwise

1 zucchini, cut in half lengthwise

1 red bell pepper, seeded

1 large ripe tomato, cut in half

$\frac{1}{4}$ cup extra-virgin olive oil

2 cloves garlic, peeled and sliced

1 tablespoon chopped fresh thyme

SALTING THE EGGPLANT. Cut the eggplant in half lengthwise. Sprinkle the cut sides with a liberal amount of salt. Allow the eggplant to sit for 1 hour, which will draw out some of the moisture and cut the bitterness.

GRILLING THE VEGETABLES. Wipe the moisture away from the eggplants. Season the squash, zucchini, red pepper, and tomato with salt and black pepper. Coat them all with 2 tablespoons of the oil. Heat the grill. When the grill has come to heat, grill all the vegetables until they have char marks, 3 to 8 minutes, depending on the vegetable. Flip them over and char the other side. Remove from the grill.

CHOPPING THE VEGETABLES. Take the skins off the eggplant, red pepper, and tomato. Chop all the vegetables the same size (about 2-inch cubes, roughly).

FINISHING THE RATATOUILLE. Set a Dutch oven over medium-high heat. Add the remaining 2 tablespoons of oil. Add the garlic and cook, stirring frequently, until it softens and the smell begins to permeate the room, about 3 minutes. Throw in the thyme and cook until the scent releases into the room, about 1 minute. Add the grilled vegetables and cook, stirring, until everything is mingling together, about 3 minutes.

Feeds 4

grilled sausage and onions with tomato-corn salad

The summer Lucy turned three, we went out to the small garden in our backyard every morning, checking on the tomatoes. We were reading a very dear book called *First Tomato* nearly every day. When she spotted the first tiny green tomato, she shouted, "Our first tomato, Mama!" The few tomatoes that actually swelled in size and blushed a deep red? They went into this meal.

4 sweet Italian sausages (about 12 ounces)

2 large red onions, peeled and sliced into 1-inch-thick rings

5 tablespoons extra-virgin olive oil

3 large ears corn, shucked and kernels cut off the cob

1 pint each red and yellow cherry tomatoes, quartered

3 sprigs fresh basil

1 tablespoon champagne vinegar

1 teaspoon Dijon mustard

Kosher salt and freshly ground black pepper

BLANCHING THE SAUSAGES. Set a large pot of water over high heat. Add the sausages and cook until they have turned color, about 5 minutes. Drain them.

GRILLING THE SAUSAGES AND ONIONS. Turn up the grill as high as it will go. Coat the sausages and onions in 2 tablespoons of the oil. Lay them down on the grill and cook, turning the sausages and onions occasionally, until the sausages have reached an internal temperature of 145°F. Take them off the grill.

MAKING THE SALAD. Toss the corn and tomatoes together. Take the basil leaves off the stem and stack them on top of each other. Roll up the leaves like a cigar and cut into thin slices. Toss these ribbons of basil into the salad.

Add the vinegar, mustard, a pinch of salt and pepper to a jar. Put on the lid and shake it up. Add the remaining 3 tablespoons of the oil, put on the lid, and shake it up again. Dress the salad.

Serve each person a grilled sausage, a handful of onion rings, and some of the salad.

Feeds 4

grilled sardines with ginger-scallion sauce

Sardines are such a sadly overlooked fish. They are relatively cheap and packed with good nutrients and healthy oils. Fresh sardines are delightful but a good brand of canned sardines is pretty great too. Grilled sardines? Addictive.

You know what else is addictive? This ginger-scallion sauce. I learned to make this from a slightly different version by my friend Francis Lam, one of the most passionate and singular food writers I know. Here's the sentence he wrote that convinced me to try it: "You can find the fragrant, salty, oily goodness of ginger scallion sauce wherever you find Cantonese barbecues, the places where roasted ducks and garish red strips of char siu pork are hanging in the window." Well, yes please!

It only occurred to me to combine the salty oily sauce with the salty oily fish one day when a pack of little kids were in the house. I set them to work making little boats of sticky rice. (Yes, there was rice all over the floor afterward. Oh well.) Afterward, each kid reached for one of the treats: rice topped with part of a sardine, a slice of avocado, and a drizzle of this ginger-scallion sauce. Every single kid ate at least three to seven of these. I kind of wish there had been a few left over for me.

Ginger-scallion sauce

One 2-inch piece fresh ginger, peeled and cut into thick coins

2 bunches scallions, chopped into 1-inch pieces

$\frac{1}{2}$ cup peanut oil

$\frac{1}{2}$ cup sesame oil

1 tablespoon gluten-free tamari

Grilled sardines

2 tablespoons peanut oil

1 teaspoon gluten-free tamari

10 whole sardines (that's about 3 cans, if you are using canned sardines)

To assemble and serve

1 recipe cooled Sticky Rice (recipe follows)

1 avocado, peeled, pitted and thinly sliced

Preparing the ginger and scallions for the sauce. Add the ginger slices in the bowl of a food processor. Whirl it up until the ginger is finely minced but before it's a paste, about 2 minutes. Transfer to a large bowl. Whirl up the scallions the same way. You want finely minced scallions so you don't later get a big bite of scallion, but don't let it become a liquid paste. Add the scallions to the same bowl as the ginger.

Heating the oil. Set a small pot on high heat. Pour in the peanut and sesame oils. Cook until the oils start to smoke, about 5 minutes. Trust me, you want it blasted hot.

Finishing the sauce. Pour the hot oils into the bowl with the ginger and scallions. Stand back and listen to that sizzle. It's really going to bubble up. When it's calm and cool in there, drizzle in the tamari and stir. You can use this immediately, but it's much better after you have refrigerated it for a day.

> ## FEEL LIKE PLAYING?
>
> Seriously, this ginger-scallion sauce is great on nearly anything savory. Rice and roasted chicken with a dribble of this? Yes. Indian flatbread dipped into this? You bet. Roasted tofu? Oh yeah.

Preparing to grill. Heat up your grill to screeching hot and scrape away any old bits.

Grilling the sardines. In a small bowl, mix the peanut oil and tamari together. Brush some onto each sardine, coating them completely. Lay the sardines on the grill. Cook until the skin on the bottom of the fish is crisp, about 2 minutes. Rotate the sardines and cook until the other side is crisp. Remove the sardines from the grill. Cut each sardine into 2 pieces.

Assembling. Grab about 2 tablespoons of the cooked rice. Squish the rice in your hand until you have shaped a little flat boat of rice. Repeat with the remaining rice.

Top each rice boat with a slice of avocado, a piece of grilled sardine, and a dribble of the ginger-scallion sauce.

Feeds 4 to 6

sticky rice

Honestly, the best and easiest way to make sticky rice is in the rice cooker. You set it up to cook and forget about it until it is done. However, if you don't have a rice cooker, steaming is the best way to cook it without it turning into a gloppy mess.

2 cups sweet rice (also called mochi rice or sticky rice)

1 tablespoon gluten-free tamari (optional)

1 tablespoon sesame oil (optional)

2 teaspoons rice wine vinegar (optional)

SOAKING THE RICE. Pour the rice into a large bowl and cover it with water. Let the rice soak for at least 1 hour before draining it to cook.

COOKING THE RICE. Set a large pot over high heat and fill it halfway with water. When the water has come to a boil, put the drained rice into a large strainer and set that over the pot. Cover the rice with a lid. Let the rice steam for 10 minutes, then check the consistency of the rice. It should be soft, with all the grains white instead of clear. If some of the rice grains on top are not fully cooked, flip the rice over and cook for 2 to 5 minutes more.

FLAVORING THE RICE. If you want to flavor the rice, combine the tamari, sesame oil, and rice wine vinegar. Drizzle this over the cooked rice. Flip the rice to make sure all the rice grains are coated.

COOLING THE RICE. Line a baking sheet with parchment paper. Spread out the cooked rice on the baking sheet. Allow the rice to cool.

Makes about 3 cups

papillon flank steak

Danny made this as a weekly lunch special at a restaurant in Denver called Papillon. He made it for years but he still likes it now. That tells you something about how good this tastes. This marinade would work really well with chicken thighs or a meaty fish like halibut. Marinating a whole side of Alaskan salmon with this overnight, then grilling it, would make a great barbecue.

1/2 stalk lemongrass, bashed

2 tablespoons chopped fresh mint

1/4 cup chopped fresh cilantro

3 cloves garlic, peeled and chopped

One 1-inch piece fresh ginger, peeled and chopped

2 tablespoons gluten-free tamari

Pinch red pepper flakes

2 tablespoons sesame oil

1 medium kaffir lime leaf (optional)

2 pounds flank steak

Kosher salt and freshly ground black pepper

MAKING THE MARINADE. Add the lemongrass, mint, cilantro, garlic, ginger, tamari, red pepper flakes, 1 tablespoon of the oil, and the lime leaf, if using, to the bowl of a food processor. Whirl them up until you have a thick, liquidy paste.

MARINATING THE FLANK STEAK. Spread the marinade over both sides of the flank steak. Put any remaining marinade in the middle and roll up the flank steak. Put it in a plastic bag and marinate for at least 12 hours.

GRILLING THE FLANK STEAK. Heat the grill as high as it will go. Use a paper towel to wipe off the marinade from the flank steak. Season the steak with salt and black pepper. Add the remaining oil to the steak.

Lay the flank steak on the grill. Grill for 3 to 4 minutes, then turn the steak horizontally at a 90-degree angle and cook for another 3 to 4 minutes. Flip the flank steak over and cook until it reaches an internal temperature of 135°F, about 5 minutes. Take it off the grill and let it rest for 5 minutes before cutting it up and eating.

Feeds 4 to 6

grilled lamb kebabs with dukkah-yogurt sauce

I've become very partial to an Egyptian spice mix called dukkah. Nutty and warm, spiced with unexpected flavors, it's good on almost everything: tossed on top of baked potatoes, scattered across the top of a bowl of soup, shaken onto a salad. Roasted vegetables with extra-virgin olive oil and salt are suddenly exciting with this on top. And if you have dukkah around, you can make pasta with butter and a handful of the spice mix for a quick dinner.

However, when you really want to plan ahead, try making these lamb skewers with dukkah-yogurt sauce. Marinating the lamb overnight makes the lamb tender. With a good sear from the grill, the hot kebabs cool down beautifully with the yogurt sauce.

If you want to serve these with warm gluten-free pita bread, dunked into extra-virgin olive oil and a little bowl of dukkah, I bet no one would mind.

Dukkah

½ cup hazelnuts (you could also try raw almonds)

¼ cup coriander seeds

2 tablespoons cumin seeds

3 tablespoons sesame seeds

1 tablespoon black peppercorns

1 teaspoon fennel seeds

1 teaspoon sumac (optional)

1 teaspoon kosher salt

½ teaspoon dried lemon zest

The lamb and yogurt sauce

2 cups whole milk yogurt

One 2-pound leg of lamb, chopped into 2-inch pieces

Kosher salt and freshly ground black pepper

Extra-virgin olive oil

MAKING THE DUKKAH. Set a large skillet over high heat. When the skillet is hot, add the hazelnuts. Toast them, moving them around the pan occasionally to avoid burning, until they have browned a bit and smell heavenly toasty, 3 to 5 minutes. Remove the hazelnuts from the pan and cool them to room temperature.

continued . . .

Toast the coriander and cumin seeds in the same manner. Remove from the skillet. Toast the sesame seeds, peppercorns, and fennel seeds in the same manner. Remove from the skillet.

Put the toasted hazelnuts, coriander, cumin, sesame seeds, peppercorns, fennel seeds, sumac (if using), salt, and lemon zest in the bowl of a food processor. (If you use a mortar and pestle, that's even better.) Pulse until everything is broken up but before it all becomes a paste.

MAKING THE MARINADE. Mix 1 cup of the yogurt and 3 tablespoons of the dukkah in a large bowl. Put the lamb pieces into the yogurt, making sure they are submerged. Marinate for at least 1 hour, preferably overnight.

GRILLING THE LAMB. Turn on the grill as high as it will go. Take the lamb pieces out of the yogurt. Gently shake off any excess yogurt but do not wipe it off. Stick the lamb onto skewers (5 to 6 pieces per skewer). When the grill is fully heated, lay the lamb skewers onto the grill. Grill each side until it is nicely browned, 3 to 4 minutes, then turn and continue to brown on all the sides. When the lamb has reached an internal temperature of 160°F, take off the grill.

MAKING THE DIP. In a bowl, combine the remaining 1 cup of yogurt with another 3 tablespoons of the dukkah. Season with salt and pepper. Top with a healthy dollop of oil and serve with the kebabs.

Feeds 4

FEEL LIKE PLAYING?

As you can imagine, everyone makes a different version of dukkah. Our friend Llysa gave us most of her spice combinations for this recipe. She prefers almonds and we like hazelnuts better here. Other spices you can play with and substitute for others: dried chickpeas, chili powder, cinnamon, marjoram, mint, nigella, red pepper flakes, and thyme. Go crazy and play!

Imagine a thick crust of dukkah on a piece of roasted chicken, or a hearty fish, and even tofu.

grilled lemon-tahini chicken stuffed with bread cubes

Lemon-tahini dressing is possibly my favorite dressing in the world. I love the mouth pucker of lemon and warm nuttiness of tahini together, especially on dark greens. However, once Danny taught me how to make this grilled chicken, I stopped thinking about salads.

He used to make this at a restaurant called Café Sport, many years ago in Seattle. The crisp bread cubes start to melt a bit into the grilled chicken, but they still have a bite. It's an unexpected texture, and that's hard to find with chicken recipes now. With the lemon-tahini brushed on before and during grilling, this is a bright summer recipe.

$^3/_4$ cup tahini

3 large lemons, zested and juiced

3 tablespoons champagne vinegar

1 teaspoon kosher salt, plus more for seasoning chicken

$1^1/_2$ cups extra-virgin olive oil

4 slices Gluten-Free Sandwich Bread (page 48)

4 bone-in, skin-on chicken breasts

Freshly ground black pepper

MAKING THE LEMON-TAHINI DRESSING. Add the tahini, lemon zest and juice, vinegar, and salt to a blender. Run the blender until the ingredients form a thick paste. With the blender running, slowly drizzle in the oil until the dressing is smooth. Taste. If the dressing needs a little more salt, dissolve it in a tablespoon more of lemon juice and then add it. Blend again.

GRILLING THE BREAD. Heat the grill until it's hot. Brush some of the lemon-tahini dressing onto both sides of all 4 slices of bread. Put the bread onto the grill. When the bread has grill marks, about 3 minutes, flip the bread slices and grill the other side.

Remove the bread and let it cool to room temperature. Cut each slice into $^1/_2$-inch cubes.

STUFFING THE CHICKEN BREASTS. Season the chicken breasts with salt and pepper. Gently, separate the skin from the chicken breast without tearing it off. Stuff each chicken breast with a quarter of the cubes. (If you have torn the skin, you can try anchoring the skin to the breast with toothpicks. Brush some lemon tahini dressing onto both sides of each piece of chicken.

continued . . .

GRILLING THE CHICKEN BREASTS. When the grill is as hot as you can make it go, lift the lid and lay the chicken breasts down gently on the grill. At first they will cling to the grill. Don't worry. Close the lid and wait for 1 minute. When enough grease has dripped from the chicken breasts to loosen the grip on the grill, flip them. Repeat on the second side.

Now, grill each chicken breast for 3 to 5 minutes. Flip the breasts one more time and cook until they have reached an internal temperature of 155°F, 3 to 5 minutes more. Remove them from the grill and serve immediately.

Feeds 4

FEEL LIKE PLAYING?

I like lemon-tahini dressing on nearly everything but particularly on a warm bowl of brown basmati rice.

And of course you can use commercially produced gluten-free bread for this.

buffets

ONE OF MY FAVORITE TIMES GROWING UP IN CLAREMONT, CALIFORNIA, WAS THE LATE SUNDAY morning buffet at Griswold's. We didn't go every week. Maybe once a month? The power of memory is fuzzy at best. I remember turkey and gravy and mashed potatoes. My brother swears they only had that option one time, near Thanksgiving. We both agree that our favorite was the little Swedish meatballs, swimming in a thin brownish gravy, barely warmed in a chafing dish. I could eat a dozen of those in one sitting. Look, I'm not saying any of it was good. Even at the time we ate there, our family referred to it as "Greaseballs" instead of Griswold's. But oh man, my brother and I loved that experience.

This is why, when I told my brother about the idea for this cookbook, he immediately said, "You need a buffet chapter. Buffets always make Elliott excited about dinner." My nephew, one of the lights of my life, doesn't particularly care about food. However, if you tell him it's Italian antipasti night, and have roasted cauliflower with salsa verde, mushrooms stuffed with mozzarella, salami, prosciutto, olives marinated with lemon zest, and a lot of little ramekins with other foods, he'll eat well. He likes taking a little bit of each and making his own plate.

Come to think of it, he's right. Our daughter's favorite meal at the time of this writing? Tortilla soup (the recipe is on page 74). She loves saying "chipotles in adobo pepper." But she really loves the garnishes, all the choices in little bowls. She likes to chant: "avocado, lime juice, Jack cheese, sour cream, cilantro." (That her soup ends up being about half grated cheese may be part of it too.)

We love potlucks. We tell everyone we're having an Indian buffet. We make the flatbread, the spiced paneer, and the raita. Someone else brings the chana masala, someone else the chicken tikka masala, and another friend makes daal. Someone who was in a rush grabs a jar of simmer sauce at the store and heats up some leftover roasted chicken in it. Our neighbor brings a big pot of rice from next door. No one has to cook that much. We all share in the party.

Buffet nights are easy. Make a few of the dishes from scratch—you have our suggestions as to which ones in the form of recipes—and buy the rest at the store. Make the carnitas, the corn tortillas, and the pickled carrots and jalapeños because making those yourself really makes a difference. But buy the salsa, cheese, sour cream, avocados, and cabbage. Throw it all together on the table and let the kids have at it. You have fun too.

I'm pretty sure the buffet you make will be better than Greaseballs any day.

Taco Bar

CORN TORTILLAS, CARNITAS, PICKLED
CARROTS, AND JALAPEÑOS

We love tacos around here. One of Danny's work
colleagues from Mexico opened a taco truck on the
island last year, serving spicy pork tacos and carne asada
tacos, all on tortillas made that day. People line up in
the rain just to eat them.

As much as we love Jorge—and we do splurge
on some of his tacos weekly—we've learned to make
carnitas, tortillas, and pickled jalapeños and carrots we
love. Even Jorge loves them. You can make them too.

For this buffet, we make the tortillas. You can
always buy them if you run out of time. Heat them
up on the burner until they are softened and slightly
charred. Tacos taste better on those tortillas. We also
make the carnitas, planning ahead by a day to be
ready for taco night. (The anticipation makes them
taste better.) And the big batch of pickled carrots and
jalapeños we make ahead lasts for weeks, in case we
want taco night again soon.

Other than that, we buy Cheddar cheese, salsa
from a local company, sour cream, cilantro, and lots of
avocados. Now that's a feast.

corn tortillas

This is really a technique more than a recipe. I've given you measurements here, but you have to
trust the feeling of the dough more than the measurements. You'll have to make tortillas a dozen
times before you get some you really love. But don't worry. Even if they're a little too thick or
lopsided, they're still going to be a hundred times better than store-bought.

Tortillas turn out best if you have a tortilla press. Sure, you could press them down with a
heavy skillet. But a tortilla press doesn't cost much more than a stack of premade tortillas at the
store. Once you start making these, you probably won't stop.

And once you get going, they take so little time. From the moment I pull the masa down
from the pantry shelf until we are eating hot corn tortillas—about 15 minutes. Whenever Lucy
needs a snack, I can make her a quesadilla in no time at all.

130 grams corn masa

Pinch kosher salt

¹⁄₂ cup water, more or less warm water

continued . . .

MAKING THE DOUGH. Combine the masa and salt. Slowly, drizzle in the water, mixing it in with your hands as you go. This is such an important step. Don't just dump the entire volume of water on the masa and mix it up. Drizzle in the water until the masa looks a little too wet but comes together in a slightly moist, pliable ball when you are done. The final dough should feel a little like Play-Doh. If the dough is not pliable, it's not wet enough yet. Add water 1 teaspoon at a time, mixing with your hands as you go. Set a damp towel over the masa dough. Let the dough rest for 15 minutes.

HEATING THE SKILLETS. Set a small skillet (preferably cast-iron) over low heat and another over high heat. Let them heat as you make the dough.

PRESSING THE TORTILLAS. Lay a piece of wax paper or heavy plastic wrap over the bottom of the tortilla press. Pick up a ball of dough about the size of an unshelled walnut, knead it in your hands, and lay it flat on top of the wax paper in the tortilla press. Lay the other piece of wax paper over it and press hard until the tortilla is about $1/8$ inch thick. Peel the wax paper from the tortilla. If the tortilla sticks, it means your dough is too wet. If it crumbles, your dough is too dry.

COOKING THE TORTILLA. Put the tortilla in the skillet over low heat. Cook until the edges of the tortilla begin to lift from the skillet, just a bit, about 30 seconds. Flip it over and cook the other side for 30 seconds more. Transfer the tortilla to the skillet over high heat and cook until the bottom has the start of brown speckles, about 45 seconds. Flip the tortilla and cook the other side until the tortilla puffs a bit, about 60 seconds. Take the tortilla off the skillet. Repeat with the other tortillas.

Makes about 8 tortillas

FEEL LIKE PLAYING?

If your tortillas are sticking to the wax paper when you try to peel them, they're probably too wet. But you can also lightly grease the wax paper to make the tortillas easier to peel.

Once you start making tortillas from scratch, you can make homemade tortilla chips. Brush both sides of 10 tortillas with oil. Cut each tortilla into 4 pieces. Sprinkle them with salt and any spices you want to use. Cook them in a 375°F oven for 8 minutes, then flip them over and cook them for another 8 to 10 minutes. They'll be shatteringly crisp.

If you find yourself out of masa, and you have some leftover commercial corn tortillas in your freezer, simply heat up the tortillas on the hot skillet the same way you cook these. They'll be good.

carnitas

Danny made these carnitas for the members of a popular radio program in Seattle one Cinco de Mayo. He made them tacos filled with this tender meat filled with the tastes of garlic, chiles, and cumin swirled together with the cheese and salsa. Those tacos were gone in moments. The producer of the show told him later, "I have to tell you, I have eaten all over the world, and especially in Mexico, and I think this is the best carnitas I have ever eaten."

They're the best carnitas I have ever eaten too.

Don't let the length of this recipe intimidate you. Most of the work for this happens in the refrigerator or the oven. If you plan ahead, you can offer your family a taco bar they will never forget.

Making the brine

1 tablespoon ground cumin

1 tablespoon ground coriander

2 quarts water

$1/2$ cup kosher salt

$1/4$ cup sugar

1 medium canned gluten-free chipotle pepper in adobo sauce

1 tablespoon black peppercorns

1 bay leaf

4 sprigs fresh thyme

Pinch red pepper flakes

3 pounds boneless pork shoulder, cut into large chunks

Cooking the pork

Kosher salt and freshly ground black pepper

$1/2$ cup nonhydrogenated lard

2 cups chopped onion

3 cloves garlic, peeled and smashed

1 tablespoon chili powder

One 28-ounce can diced tomatoes, drained

1 quart pork or chicken stock

1 bay leaf

2 teaspoons ground cumin

2 teaspoons ground oregano

One 15-ounce can black beans, rinsed and drained

TOASTING THE CUMIN AND CORIANDER. The day before you are serving, set a small skillet over medium-high heat. Add the 1 tablespoon cumin and the coriander. Cook, tossing the spices in the pan once in a while, until they begin to smell toasty, about 3 minutes.

continued . . .

MAKING THE BRINE. Add the toasted cumin and coriander, water, salt, sugar, chipotle pepper, peppercorns, bay leaf, thyme, and red pepper flakes to a large stockpot. Bring to a boil. Boil until the salt and sugar are thoroughly dissolved. Turn off the heat and let the brine sit for 30 minutes.

Strain the brine through a fine-mesh sieve into a large container or bowl and let the liquid cool to room temperature. Add the pork to the container and let it sit for 12 to 24 hours in the refrigerator.

PREPARING THE PORK. Remove the pork from the brine. Pat it dry, thoroughly. Season with salt and pepper. Preheat the oven to 350°F.

BROWNING THE PORK. Set a large skillet over high heat. Add 2 tablespoons of the lard. When the lard has melted, add the pork pieces. (You might want to do this in batches. Don't overcrowd the pan.) Cook until the bottom of the pork is browned, about 5 minutes. Flip over the pork pieces and brown the other side, about 5 minutes. Transfer the pork to a Dutch oven.

COOKING THE AROMATICS. Add 2 tablespoons of the lard to the skillet. Add 1½ cups of the onion and half of the garlic. Cook, stirring frequently, until the onion is softened and beginning to brown, about 5 minutes. Stir in the chili powder and cook until the scent is released, about 1 minute. Pour in half of the tomatoes and cook, stirring occasionally, until the tomatoes begin to soften, about 3 minutes. Add this to the Dutch oven.

COOKING THE PORK. Cover the pork and vegetables with the stock. Add the bay leaf.

Bring the stock to a boil and stir. Turn off the heat and slide the Dutch oven into the oven. Cook until the pork yields to a fork, 4 to 6 hours. (You can also cook this on the stovetop on a very low simmer, covered, or in a slow cooker.)

MAKING THE SAUCE. When the pork is done cooking, remove it to a plate to rest. Set the Dutch oven over medium-high heat. Bring the sauce to a boil, then turn down the heat to medium-low. Simmer the sauce until it has reduced by half its volume.

Meanwhile, set a large skillet over medium-high heat. Add 2 tablespoons of the lard to the pan. Add the remaining onion and garlic. Cook, stirring, until the onion has softened, about 5 minutes. Add the 2 teaspoons cumin and the oregano and cook, stirring, until the scent is released, about 1 minute. Add the beans and the remaining tomatoes and cook until they are hot, about 2 minutes. Add the simmering liquid. Cook the sauce until the kitchen smells insanely good, 20 to 30 minutes. Season with salt and pepper to taste.

CRISPING UP THE PORK. Set the Dutch oven back over high heat. Add the remaining 2 tablespoons of lard. Lay the pork in the melted lard. Cook until the bottom is browned, about 5 minutes. Flip over and sear the other side, about 5 minutes more. Take the pork out of the Dutch oven and shred it up with a fork. Add the shredded pork to the simmering sauce. Remove the bay leaf and serve.

Feeds 6

FEEL LIKE PLAYING?

If you wake up one morning and you simply must have tacos that night, you could make this without brining the pork. However, it might be worth having tortilla soup that night instead and waiting for the full experience.

This is a great dish for the slow cooker. Sear off the pork, cook all the onions and spices, and then put it all in the slow cooker to work its magic.

pickled carrots and jalapeños

There was a tiny Mexican take-out place down the street from the house where I lived when I first met Danny. On his days off from the restaurant, we'd walk down there hand in hand for tacos. Their tortillas were fresh, the meat nicely spiced, but the taste that made me keep going back was the pickled carrots and jalapeños.

I had never eaten these with tacos before I started going there. I haven't stopped.

2 tablespoons coriander seeds

1 teaspoon ground cumin

1 teaspoon mustard seeds

$\frac{1}{2}$ teaspoon black peppercorns

2 small carrots, peeled and cut into thin coins

2 jalapeño peppers, seeded and cut into thin coins

2 cloves garlic, peeled and sliced

1 cup white vinegar

1 cup water

1 teaspoon kosher salt

TOASTING THE SPICES. Set a small skillet over high heat. Add the coriander seeds, cumin, mustard seeds, and peppercorns. Cook until the spices fully release their scent, about 3 minutes, being sure to toss them around in the pan to avoid burning. Remove from the heat.

PREPPING THE VEGETABLES. Add the carrots, jalapeños, garlic, and toasted spices into a quart jar.

MAKING THE PICKLING LIQUID. Set a pot over high heat. Add the vinegar, water, and salt. As soon as the liquid comes to a boil, pour over the carrots and jalapeños in the jar. Put on the lid. Allow the liquids to come to room temperature and put the jar in the refrigerator.

Refrigerate for at least 3 days and up to 4 weeks.

Feeds 4

FEEL LIKE PLAYING?

Frankly, I'd eat these on almost anything. A warm tortilla with cheese and this is a really satisfying snack. Toss some onto the top of your tortilla soup (see page 74) or in with the roasted chicken in the chicken enchilada casserole (see page 216).

Antipasti Buffet

STUFFED MUSHROOMS AND ROASTED
CAULIFLOWER WITH SALSA VERDE

Danny and I both think fondly of our honeymoon in Italy. (Of course we do. Honeymoon! In Italy!) We saved up every penny we had to make it work. Maybe that's why we savored every day there so thoroughly. (Also, it was Italy.) One evening I remember in particular. It was so simple—we sat at a little table on a piazza in Foligno, on a warm evening, drinking Negronis and watching people pass by. We nibbled on a little antipasti platter: curlicues of house-cured coppa, prosciutto, and salame, with small slivers of cheese alongside the meat. In that moment, no meal had ever been so satisfying.

We still love antipasti nights here. Some good cured meats, some cheese. We heat up some extra-virgin olive oil, a little lemon zest, some red pepper flakes, and toss in good olives like Castelvetrano. Add these stuffed mushrooms and roasted cauliflower with salsa verde and we have the makings of a great meal.

stuffed mushrooms

My brother and mother have birthdays one after the other in the middle of January. When Andy was a kid, he always wanted the same meal for his birthday meal: Reuben sandwiches, bagels with cream cheese, ginger ale, and lemon cake. Luckily, he left behind the rigidity of that schedule long ago. So, this past year, when we offered to make a birthday meal for everyone, he gave us free rein to make whatever we wanted.

These stuffed mushrooms disappeared pretty quickly. My eight-year-old nephew gave them a thumbs-up. "You should put those in the cookbook, Shauna. They're good." Here they are, Elliott.

¼ cup sun-dried tomatoes (not oil-packed)

¼ cup pine nuts

1 pound cremini mushrooms

3 slices preserved lemon (page 96), pith removed

2 tablespoons finely chopped fresh basil

Pinch red pepper flakes

Kosher salt and freshly ground black pepper

½ pound mozzarella balls (known as bocconcini)

continued . . .

Soaking the sun-dried tomatoes. In a bowl, cover the sun-dried tomatoes with ½ cup boiling hot water. Let sit while you prepare the rest of the ingredients.

Toasting the pine nuts. Put the pine nuts in a small skillet. Slide it into the oven and set the oven to 350°F. Put the timer on for 10 minutes. Check the pine nuts, gently tossing them around in the pan, every 2 minutes until they smell toasty and are browning. Do not burn the pine nuts. Remove from the oven.

Preparing the mushrooms. Take the stems off the mushrooms and set them, cup side up, on a baking sheet covered in a parchment paper. Remove the sun-dried tomatoes from the water. Dry them with a paper towel, then chop finely. Chop the preserved lemons finely.

Combine the sun-dried tomatoes, toasted pine nuts, preserved lemons, basil, red pepper flakes, and a touch of salt and black pepper in a large bowl.

Fill each mushroom cup with a bit of the tomato–pine nut mixture, then top with a mozzarella ball. Slide the baking sheet into the oven and allow the mushrooms to bake for 5 minutes. Turn on the broiler and cook until the mozzarella is melting and starting to brown, about 2 minutes.

Feeds 8

FEEL LIKE PLAYING?

You could use any mushroom top that makes a cup. Portobellos or white button mushrooms would be great too.

If you can't find the little mozzarella balls in your store, you can chop up a larger ball of fresh mozzarella.

None of the kids at this party found these too spicy. But if your kiddos are sensitive to spice, you can leave out the red pepper flakes here.

FEEL LIKE PLAYING?   > > > >

Keep some salsa verde in the kitchen to make any simple dinner more delicious. Leftover roasted chicken on brown basmati rice with salsa verde is one of my favorite dinners. Toss some hot pasta with this and top it with cheese.

roasted cauliflower with salsa verde

Packed with fresh herbs, zingy from the lemon, and briny from the capers, this green sauce tastes good on everything. But roasted cauliflower is a particularly good pairing.

Salsa verde

1 cup chopped fresh Italian parsley

$1/4$ cup chopped fresh basil

1 clove garlic, peeled

2 anchovy fillets

1 teaspoon dried oregano

1 lemon, zested and juiced

$1/2$ cup extra-virgin olive oil

1 tablespoon capers, drained

$1/2$ teaspoon kosher salt

Cauliflower

1 large head cauliflower, cut into bite-size florets

2 tablespoons extra-virgin olive oil

$1/2$ teaspoon kosher salt

MAKING THE HERB PASTE. Add the parsley, basil, garlic, anchovies, oregano, and lemon zest to a food processor. Pulse until everything has broken down. With the food processor running, slowly add half the oil until you have a bright green paste.

FINISHING THE SALSA VERDE. Scrape the green paste into a large bowl. Crush the capers on a cutting board with the back of a large spoon. Add them to the salsa. Pour in the remaining oil and the lemon juice. Stir well. Taste. Season with the salt. Taste again. Season with more salt, if necessary.

Let the salsa verde sit in the refrigerator for at least 1 hour to build the flavor.

PREPARING TO ROAST THE CAULIFLOWER. Preheat the oven to 425°F. Line a baking sheet with parchment paper.

ROASTING THE CAULIFLOWER. In a large bowl, toss the cauliflower florets with the oil and salt. Spread them out in an even layer on the baking sheet. Roast until the cauliflower is tender to the touch and browning on the edges, 20 to 30 minutes.

Serve the cauliflower immediately, drizzled with some of the salsa verde.

Feeds 4

Spring Roll Buffet

MARINATED TOFU AND CASHEW
DIPPING SAUCE

On a warm summer day in our home, after shooting
video of us cooking and talking as a promo for our first
book, our friends Todd and Diane prepared us a feast.
They had been working so hard that we protested.
However, they wanted to give us this gift. Diane grew
up in Vietnam and she wanted to share her culture with
us. They took over the kitchen, marinated pork, cut up
vegetables, and stirred up a peanut dipping sauce. We
all sat together at our table outside, under the trees, and
wet the spring roll wrappers in a shallow bowl of warm
water for thirty seconds or so, until they were pliable.
Then we rolled bits of basil and cilantro, pork, lime
zest, sprouts, and lettuce into a tight wrapper. Heaven.

There are so many ways to make spring rolls. We
like this marinated tofu inside and the cashew sauce for
dipping. You can make them your own.

(If you would like to see exactly how to assemble
spring rolls, go to our website, glutenfreegirl.com.

marinated tofu for spring rolls

I love spicy pork in spring rolls, as well as some good roasted chicken. But I think I like tofu
best for its firm, chewy texture. Spring rolls are all about texture—the little tickle of cilantro, the
unctuous feel of cashew dip, the crunch of slivered carrots. Batons of roasted tofu play well with
them all.

1 large navel orange, zested and juiced

1 large lemon, zested and juiced

3 cloves garlic, peeled and minced

2 tablespoons finely chopped fresh mint

2 tablespoons sesame oil

2 tablespoons gluten-free tamari

1 tablespoon gluten-free fish sauce

$1/2$ teaspoon red pepper flakes

1 pound fresh firm tofu

MAKING THE MARINADE. In a bowl, combine the orange zest and juice, lemon zest and juice, garlic,
mint, oil, tamari, fish sauce, and red pepper flakes. Whisk together. Pour over the block of tofu in
another bowl and let marinate for at least 1 hour.

continued . . .

Roasting the tofu. Preheat the oven to 450°F. Line a baking sheet with parchment paper. Take the tofu out of the marinade. Cut the block into six long pieces, then slice each of those pieces in half lengthwise, ending up with 12 batons. Put the tofu batons on the baking sheet, allowing space between each. Pour the remaining marinade over each piece of tofu. Roast until the bottoms are dark-golden brown, about 15 minutes. Flip the tofu and roast until the second side is dark-golden brown and the batons have puffed up, about 10 minutes. Take the tofu out of the oven.

Feeds 4

FEEL LIKE PLAYING?

Feel free to use lime juice or rice wine vinegar in place of the citrus here. This happens to be a great marinade for pork or chicken as well.

cashew dipping sauce

Spring rolls are packed with interesting flavors and textures but they can be a little dry. With this dipping sauce, everything comes together. Besides, it's fun to dip.

Traditionally, this might be a peanut sauce. But I'm a limited fan of peanuts, to be honest. They're just a little gaudy for my taste. Cashews are more restrained. Plus, if you know anyone with peanut allergies, you want to be able to feed them.

2 cups raw cashews

2 to 3 tablespoons sesame oil

Kosher salt

2 tablespoons gluten-free tamari

1 tablespoon mirin

1 tablespoon rice wine vinegar

2 teaspoons finely chopped fresh ginger

MAKING THE CASHEW BUTTER. Add the cashews, 2 tablespoons of the oil, and a good pinch of salt to a food processor. Run the food processor until the nuts have broken down and begun to turn into butter, about 3 minutes. Stop the food processor and scrape down the sides. If the cashew butter feels too dry and is bunched into a ball instead of a smooth paste, add the remaining tablespoon oil, a little at a time. Process until the cashew butter is smooth and unctuous.

FINISHING THE SAUCE. In a bowl, combine the cashew butter with the tamari, mirin, vinegar, and ginger. Taste. Need more seasoning? Add it. You want a slightly thickened liquid dipping sauce, so if this feels too thick, add some hot water until you reach your desired consistency.

Makes 2½ cups

FEEL LIKE PLAYING?

Feel free to play with the seasonings here. I like lime juice instead of the rice wine vinegar or dry sherry in place of the mirin. You can adjust based on what you have in the house.

For an extra depth of taste, you can toast the cashews before making them into cashew butter.

Speaking of cashew butter, this is the method for making any nut butter you want: pistachio butter with a little lemon zest, walnut butter with cocoa powder and cinnamon, almond butter and honey. There's no need to buy jars from the store, really.

Indian Feast

RAITA, SPICED PANEER, AND
INDIAN FLATBREAD

There's a restaurant space on Vashon, right in the middle of town, which seems to have a strange curse. A few years ago, someone opened an Indian restaurant with great hopes. Apparently, it wasn't that good. When it failed, the brother-in-law of the owner of the first restaurant was determined he could do better. So, he opened another Indian restaurant in the same spot. It was good, but they tore down walls and made the space huge. No matter how good the food, they couldn't be successful. I missed their chicken tikka masala when it closed. The space was dark for a few months, and then people began talking. Something with fresh food in season? It was—ta-da! —another Indian restaurant. And it wasn't very good.

This is why we've learned to make Indian feasts at home. We make spiced paneer with clarified butter—so helpful for other foods too—raita, and Indian flatbread that closely resembles naan. For the main dish, we often make the Chana Masala you can find on page 162. Or, we buy an Indian simmer sauce at the store and heat up some leftover pork, chicken, or beans in it. Dinner's served.

raita

This little yogurt dip is cool, calm, and collected. If your chana masala is firing up your mouth, take a bite of flatbread and dip it into this. There, isn't that better?

1^1/$_2$ cups whole milk yogurt

1 long English cucumber, peeled and finely chopped

3 tablespoons finely chopped fresh cilantro

1 large lemon, zested and juiced

^{1}/$_2$ teaspoon garam masala

Kosher salt

MAKING THE RAITA. Mix together the yogurt, cucumber, cilantro, lemon zest and juice, and garam masala. Taste. Crunch in some salt and taste again.

Refrigerate for at least 1 hour before eating.

Feeds 4

FEEL LIKE PLAYING?

After you're done with your Indian feast, this is a great dip for vegetables. Lucy will dip carrots into this and be happy for a while, her legs swinging at her chair.

spiced paneer

This is a quick, surprising way to serve cheese at a party. Paneer is a fresh cheese, a little like firm ricotta or farmer's cheese. It's easy to make it yourself. (We have a recipe on our website.) However, if your store carries paneer, make it easy on yourself for this Indian buffet. With all these lovely spices, you're bound to make people's mouths happy.

Making clarified butter is easier than you may think. And we bet you will find a dozen uses for it in your kitchen after you make it the first time.

8 tablespoons (1 stick) unsalted butter

2 cloves garlic, peeled and finely chopped

1 large fresh green serrano chile, seeds removed and finely chopped

2 teaspoons coriander seeds

1 teaspoon cumin seeds

1 teaspoon garam masala

$^1/_2$ teaspoon ground cardamom

12 ounces paneer

CLARIFYING THE BUTTER. Put a few layers of cheesecloth in a fine-mesh strainer and set it over a large pot. Set a small pot over medium-low heat. Add the butter. As the butter melts, you'll notice a foam starting to form on the top. Allow the butter to melt and sputter and the foam to continue to rise. When the foam has stopped rising, take the pot off the heat. Skim the foam carefully, trying to capture it all. (You don't have to throw it away. It's butter. Save it for cooking rice or polenta.)

There will be a golden layer of butter in the pan, with darker milk solids at the bottom of the pan. Slowly, pour the butter through the cheesecloth into the pot below. The milk solids should stay in the cheesecloth. Transfer the clarified butter into a jar and refrigerate it until it has solidified.

SPICING THE PANEER. In a bowl, mix together the garlic, chile, coriander, cumin, garam masala, and cardamom. Gently but firmly press one side of the paneer down into the spice mix. Carefully, flip over the paneer and do the same on the other side.

COOKING THE PANEER. Set a small skillet over medium heat. Add 3 tablespoons of the clarified butter. When it is melted, lay one of the spiced sides of paneer into the clarified butter and cook for 1 minute. Gently, flip over the paneer and cook the other side. Serve immediately.

indian flatbread

This flatbread is crisp on the edges with little charred marks. Soft. Bendable. It is addictive on its own, especially when just off the hot skillet. I'm calling it flatbread instead of naan, for the purists. But dip it in something wonderful like chana masala or honeyed eggplant dip, and it doesn't matter what you call it.

1 recipe pizza dough (page 239), made and risen for about 1 hour

All-Purpose Gluten-Free Flour Mix (page 31), for shaping and rolling the dough

8 tablespoons clarified butter (page 276)

SHAPING THE DOUGH. Gently turn the dough out onto a floured surface. Cut it into 8 equal pieces and form them into balls. Cover the dough with a damp cloth and let rest for another 30 minutes.

ROLLING OUT THE DOUGH. Grab a ball of dough. Flour a clean counter. Roll out the dough to an oval about 6 inches long. Flour both sides of the dough.

COOKING THE FLATBREAD. Set a large cast-iron skillet over medium-high heat. Add 1 tablespoon of the clarified butter. When the butter is melted, brush both sides of the naan with a skim of water. Lay the oval of dough directly into the butter. Cook until the bottom is browned and even charred in a few places, 3 to 5 minutes. Flip the dough and cook the other side, another 3 to 5 minutes. Remove the flatbread from the heat to a waiting plate. Repeat with the remaining dough.

Makes 8 flatbreads

FEEL LIKE PLAYING?

Clarified butter has a high smoke point without the milk solids, so it's great for stir-fries, baking, and whenever you want the cooking abilities of oil but the taste of butter.

You can store clarified butter in the refrigerator for up to three months. Keep a jar around.

Mediterranean Buffet

SMOKED PAPRIKA HUMMUS, HONEYED
EGGPLANT DIP, AND GLUTEN-FREE PITA

Grilled zucchini, eggplant, and yellow squash, marinated mushrooms, smoked paprika hummus, honeyed eggplant dip, Greek salad, briny Greek olives, and a big dish of moussaka (see page 209), all sopped up with gluten-free pita bread. Now that sounds like a party to me.

smoked paprika hummus

Unless hummus is made the right way, it seems an awful lot like health food. It's one of those dishes you know you're supposed to love but have to work hard not to think of French fries instead.

The hummus at the restaurant on Vashon where Danny worked for a few years was like that. Good but grainy. Our friend Melissa Clark, who writes for the *New York Times*, gave us the secret: mix the lemon juice, garlic, salt, and spices before you add the chickpeas, tahini, and extra-virgin olive oil. All the flavors have a chance to mingle before you hit them with the cooked chickpeas. There hasn't been a grainy batch of hummus since then.

And smoked paprika? As you might have noticed here, I'm addicted. I swear it makes everything better.

2 cups dried chickpeas

1 large lemon, zested and juiced

2 cloves garlic, peeled

1¼ teaspoons kosher salt

1 teaspoon smoked paprika

½ teaspoon freshly ground black pepper

¼ cup water

½ cup tahini

½ cup extra-virgin olive oil

SOAKING THE CHICKPEAS. The night before you plan to eat, soak the chickpeas in a bowl with water to cover overnight. Before you are ready to make the hummus, cook the chickpeas in enough water to cover them by 2 inches. Bring to a boil, then reduce the heat and simmer until the chickpeas are soft, 45 minutes to an hour. Drain and set aside.

MAKING THE HUMMUS. Add the lemon zest and juice, garlic, salt, paprika, and pepper to the bowl of a food processor. Whirl them up. Pour in the water and whirl up the mixture.

Add the tahini and 2 cups of the cooked chickpeas and whirl up the ingredients. This will be thick. Slowly drizzle in oil with the food processor running. With just a bit oil remaining, stop the food processor and taste the hummus. If it needs more lemon juice, add some. If the hummus needs more salt, pinch it into the remaining extra-virgin olive oil, and stir it up before adding the oil.

Refrigerate for at least 2 hours before eating to allow the flavors to build.

Feeds 10

FEEL LIKE PLAYING?

Just because I'm addicted to smoked paprika doesn't mean you have to use it. More great flavors for hummus? Cumin. Coriander. Basil. Sage. For a real North African taste, use dukkah (page 252) here.

Of course, if you're in a rush, you can use 2 cans of chickpeas, rinsed and drained, instead of cooking the chickpeas.

honeyed eggplant dip

I've been inspired by Yotam Ottolenghi's cookbook, *Plenty*. Ottolenghi's food—deeply flavored, Middle-Eastern inspired, inventive—happens to be vegetarian. We've never considered a dish we've made from that book to be lacking anything. That's because he knows that a dish with something smoked, roasted, or pickled has a depth of flavor.

Plenty is where I learned how to roast an eggplant until it's a little charred to make this dip. The smooth dip has a little roasted taste, a little bitterness, a little honey sweetness, and a hit of garlic heat.

2 large eggplants	4 cloves garlic, peeled and chopped
¹/₂ cup tahini	2 tablespoons honey
¹/₂ cup hot water	2 teaspoons kosher salt
¹/₄ cup fresh thyme leaves	Freshly ground black pepper
¹/₄ cup pomegranate molasses	2 tablespoons extra-virgin olive oil
¹/₄ cup fresh lemon juice	

ROASTING THE EGGPLANTS. Preheat the oven to 450°F. Line a baking sheet with aluminum foil. Put the eggplants on the baking sheet and roast them, turning every 15 minutes to avoid too much burning, until the skins start to char and the eggplants slump into themselves in places, about 1 hour. Take the eggplants out of the oven and let them cool.

When the eggplants are cool enough to touch, remove and discard the skin. (I like to let the eggplant sit for hours until the skin is crackly dry and pries off easily.) If the eggplant feels wet, let it sit in a colander to drain for 30 minutes.

MAKING THE DIP. Add the tahini, water, thyme, pomegranate molasses, lemon juice, garlic, honey, and salt to the bowl of a food processor. Whirl them up until thoroughly mixed, about 5 minutes. Add the eggplants and whirl until the mixture is smooth, about 3 minutes more. Taste. Need more salt? Garlic? Honey? Add some, along with lots of freshly ground black pepper. Whirl up the mixture once more.

Refrigerate the dip for at least 1 hour, preferably overnight. Before serving, let the dip come to room temperature and drizzle the top with the extra-virgin olive oil.

Feeds 4 to 6

gluten-free pita bread

I never thought I'd eat pita bread again. I don't mean grocery store pita bread, all thin and crackery. I mean real, fresh-baked pita bread, warm and soft. But, because I'm stubborn, I kept trying to make pita bread without gluten. After watching a dozen videos of people making pita bread and trying the techniques suggested by every baker I know, I had some pretty decent pita bread. It still wasn't good enough.

That's when I have to throw out everything I know and listen to the dough. The day I had leftover pizza dough and started playing? That was a good day. (*Pizza* and *pita* come from the same root word, you know.) Once I had success with corn tortillas—watching them puff on a hot skillet—I knew what to do. It turns out that pita bread is far less about the gluten and far more about a hot oven or skillet and patience.

You may not get a huge puff from these. Don't worry. As long as you get a few spots that puff up, you'll have a pita bread into which you can cut a pocket. Have patience. Let the bread cool a bit before you cut. And then, the reward? Warm, soft pita for dipping and sandwiches. Yes!

**1 batch gluten-free pizza dough (page 239),
    made and risen for 45 minutes to 1 hour**

PREHEATING THE OVEN. Put a baking stone or cast-iron skillet in the oven on a rack in the middle of the oven. Preheat the oven to 500°F. (If your oven goes to 550°F, go there.)

MAKING DOUGH BALLS. Cut the dough into 12 pieces. Gently shape each piece into a ball. Cover the dozen dough balls with a damp cloth or oiled piece of plastic wrap. Let rest for another 20 minutes.

COOKING THE PITA. Roll a ball of dough into a disc about ¼ inch thick. (Here's a fun trick. If you have a tortilla press, put the ball of dough between 2 pieces of waxed paper in the tortilla press. Perfect flat circles every time.) Get your hands just a bit wet and touch both sides of the flat disc of dough. (If you have a spray bottle of water, you can spritz the dough from chest high.)

Lay the pita directly onto the scorching-hot baking stone or cast-iron skillet. Bake until the pita bread forms bubbles and puffs up in a few places and begins to brown, about 3 minutes. Take the pita out of the oven and let it rest for a few minutes. Repeat with the remaining dough.

continued...

When the pita breads have cooled to almost-room temperature, take a small paring knife to the first one. Cut the pita in half. Aim the tip of the knife to the biggest puffed-up bubble. Once you hit that air pocket, it should be pretty easy to slice across the length of the entire pita bread to form a whole pocket. If the bread feels doughy, wait for it to cool down more. Go slowly. There's no need to rush and possibly tear the bread.

When you're done, you should have 24 halves of warm, soft pita bread.

Makes a dozen pita breads, or 24 pita bread halves

FEEL LIKE PLAYING?

If you don't have a baking stone or cast-iron skillet, you can make these on a hot skillet. I might add a bit of extra-virgin olive oil to make sure the pitas don't stick, just a thin skim. Get the skillet hot on medium-high heat, add the extra-virgin olive oil, then lay the pita down on the skillet. Let the pita cook for about 30 seconds, then turn it until parts of the pita begin to puff. Turn the dough again and cook for another 2 minutes. Take the pita off the skillet and repeat.

If your balls of dough should grow dry while you are cooking the first pita breads, wet your hands and knead them again. You need these to be a little wet for the puff to happen.

If you want to make these more whole grain in nature, use half Whole-Grain Gluten-Free Flour Mix (page 32) and half the All-Purpose Gluten-Free Flour Mix (page 31).

sweetness at the end of the evening

I love baking almost more than I love breathing. (Of course, if I stopped breathing, I wouldn't be able to bake.) When I'm having a bad day, what do I do to pull myself out of the trance of that mood? I talk with my husband. I hug my daughter. I take a walk. Then, I pull out some teff and millet, a bit of buckwheat, and start weighing them on the scale. The softened butter by the stove goes into the stand mixer, followed by a small shower of sugar. Within moments—dough. Where there had been an empty counter, soon there will be a batch of warm cookies.

A few years ago, I spent several weeks of my life making gluten-free puff pastry work, dammit. It did, mostly. But I wouldn't want you to go through that on a Wednesday night. I wanted this chapter to be filled with weeknight desserts.

I wanted chocolate-cashew pudding. And fruit salad with a few twists. And blackberry-honey popsicles, because if your kids are anything like ours is, they're going to want to eat one of these every night through the hot weeks of summer.

I like desserts with layers of flavors, the zing of ginger or the soft whisper of orange flower water.

I love the seasons with my sweets as much as the savory foods. In the fall, a pear-walnut crumble at the end of the day makes everyone in my family happy. In the winter, I crave citrus. I also love the kind of simple elegance that a parfait of lemon curd, coconut whipped cream, and frozen berries provides.

That's what I want to share with you, here. A bit of sweetness at the end of the evening, created out of paying attention and friendship. These are the desserts we eat in our house. Truly. We hope you like them.

(As I was starting to work on this chapter, I had the great fortune of making a new friend. Anna Painter is a talented pastry chef who worked at Prune and Al Di La in New York. When she and her family moved to Seattle for her husband's job, mutual friends introduced us. We connected, immediately. As our daughters tried on dress-up clothes and danced, Anna and I talked about whole-grain flours, alternative sweeteners, and how much we love butter. Her whole-wheat peanut butter cookies became my whole-grain peanut butter and jam bars. This chapter simply couldn't exist without her.)

chocolate chip cookies with hazelnuts

There are only a few times I miss gluten at all anymore. Mostly I eat better than I ever did before I had to cut gluten out of my life. However, when friends of mine started raving about Kim Boyce's whole wheat chocolate chip cookies, I started to feel a little mopey. And then I did what I always do—converted them into something delicious that I can eat.

Kim Boyce's book, *Good to the Grain*, is one of my favorite baking books of all time. After leaving her pastry chef job at Spago, Kim set out to bake for her family. Realizing she didn't want to give them white flour and sugar all the time, she began working with whole-grain flours. Many of the flours she discovered are gluten-free. Everything I have made my own out of this book has been tremendous. But these are my favorite.

I'll never taste the whole wheat cookies, but I have a hunch these might be better. Teff has a slight chocolate taste to it, so it pairs beautifully with anything chocolate, as do hazelnuts. Teff + chocolate + hazelnuts = magic.

I feel privileged to know Kim. We talk about baking all the time, especially now that one of her daughters had to go gluten-free. She approves of these cookies. We think you will too.

210 grams Whole-Grain Gluten-Free
    Flour Mix (page 32)

1 teaspoon whole or powdered psyllium
    husks (see page 33)

$^3/_4$ teaspoon kosher salt

$^3/_4$ teaspoon baking powder

$^1/_2$ teaspoon baking soda

8 tablespoons (1 stick) cold unsalted
    butter, cut into 1-inch pieces

$^1/_2$ packed cup dark brown sugar

$^1/_2$ cup sucanat or white sugar

1 large egg, at room temperature

1 teaspoon vanilla extract

$1^1/_3$ cup bittersweet chocolate, roughly
    chopped into $^1/_2$-inch pieces

$^1/_2$ cup cracked hazelnuts

PREPARING TO BAKE. Preheat the oven to 350°F. Line a baking sheet with parchment paper.

COMBINING THE DRY INGREDIENTS. Whisk together the flour, psyllium husks, salt, baking powder, and baking soda until they have become one color.

continued . . .

CREAMING THE BUTTER AND SUGAR. Add the cold butter cubes to the bowl of a stand mixer. With the paddle attachment, run the mixer on medium speed until the butter is creamy and softened. Add the brown sugar and sucanat. Blend them together on medium speed until the mixture is light and fluffy, about 3 minutes. Use a rubber spatula to scrape down the sides of the bowl. Add the egg and mix until all traces of egg disappear into the batter. Mix in the vanilla.

FINISHING THE BATTER. With the mixer running, add the flour a scoop at a time. When all the flour has been added and all trace of flour has disappeared into the batter, scrape down the sides of the bowl. Add the chocolate and hazelnuts. Mix until just combined.

Turn the cookie dough out of the bowl onto a clean surface. If there is any flour, chocolate, or hazelnuts left in the bowl, mix them into the dough.

BAKING THE COOKIES. Scoop 30 grams of cookie dough into your hands. Shape it into a ball. Put it on the lined baking sheet, then flatten it a bit with your palm. Smooth out the edges of the cookie disc. Repeat until you end up with 6 cookies on the baking sheet with about 3 inches of space between them.

Bake until the edges are crisp and the center is still soft to the touch, about 12 minutes, turning the tray 180 degrees in the oven halfway through baking. Carefully move the parchment paper to a counter and bake the rest of the cookies.

Makes about 20 cookies

FEEL LIKE PLAYING?

Need I tell you that these cookies are best warm from the oven? However, you do need to let them cool a bit before you eat them. Hot out of the oven, they are still a little fragile. Just warm to the touch, they are heaven.

If you can't find hazelnuts, walnuts will do just fine.

These cookies also improve in flavor if you refrigerate the dough overnight. You can roll the dough into 3 logs, cover them in plastic wrap, and have cookie dough waiting to make a couple of cookies an evening, if you prefer.

citrus fruit salad with earl grey syrup and pomegranate seeds

In the dead of winter, it's hard to remember that there are days of ripe apricots and plums so juicy you need a napkin. Without good citrus fruit, I wouldn't survive the winter. At the end of most days, I don't need cookies or cake. (Danny would prefer that we eat something baked every night.) Give me some of this citrus salad, with the bergamot sweetness of Earl Grey syrup, and a few crunches of pomegranate seeds? I can survive the winter after all.

6 navel oranges

4 ruby red grapefruits

2 tangerines

1 cup water

$^1/_2$ cup sugar

2 tablespoons pomegranate molasses

2 bags Earl Grey tea

1 cup pomegranate seeds (from about 3 whole pomegranates)

PREPARING THE FRUIT. Peel all the citrus and take off those stringy white bits (the pith). Slice each citrus fruit into slices of the same size. Put in a bowl.

MAKING THE EARL GREY SYRUP. Set a pot over medium-high heat. Pour in the water, sugar, pomegranate molasses, and the tea bags. As the water comes to a boil, stir, gently, taking care not to burst the bags. Brush the sides of the pot with a pastry brush to remove any errant sugar. When the sugar has fully dissolved and the water has become slightly syrupy, about 15 minutes, remove the pot from the heat. Allow the syrup to cool to room temperature.

FINISHING THE SALAD. Drizzle the citrus with some of the Earl Grey syrup. Scatter the pomegranate seeds on top.

Feeds 4

FEEL LIKE PLAYING?

You won't need to use all the simple syrup you make here on the salad. Save the rest of it for another salad a few days later—the flavor only intensifies in the refrigerator—or mix it with club soda and ice cubes for a refreshing drink.

blackberry-honey yogurt popsicles

"Mama, may I have a popsicle for breakfast, please?" Normally, the answer to that would be no, of course. During her second full summer in the world, nothing brought Lucy more delight than popsicles. We started making pure fruit juice popsicles, which are wonderful. However, they contained too much sugar for me to feel comfortable giving them to her for breakfast.

These came to the rescue. Yogurt, honey, and blackberries? That sounds like a fine, frozen breakfast to me. It's a lovely dessert at the end of a long, hot day as well.

3 cups whole milk yogurt	⅓ cup honey
2 cups fresh blackberries	2 tablespoons finely chopped fresh basil (optional)

MAKING THE POPSICLES. Add the yogurt, 1 cup of the blackberries, the honey, and basil, if you are using it, to a blender. Blend until everything has turned purple and has a smooth texture.

FILLING THE POPSICLE MOLDS. Plop a whole blackberry into a popsicle mold. Pour a bit of the yogurt mixture into the mold. Plop in another blackberry and more of the mixture. Repeat until the mold is three-fourths full. Repeat with the remaining popsicle molds until they are filled.

Freeze until the popsicles are frozen through, about 1 hour.

Makes 1 dozen popsicles

FEEL LIKE PLAYING?

All summer long, we made popsicles with whatever fruit was in season that week. Golden raspberries, apricots, peaches, and cantaloupe—as long as they are ripe, these fruits make a great popsicle.

Danny and I both like a bit of fresh herbs in our popsicles, like basil or lemon thyme. Lucy's not as crazy about that idea, so we leave it optional.

If you don't have popsicle molds, then you can freeze these in little ramekins and make them frozen custards.

pear-walnut crumble

I love a good crumble. Honestly, other than pie, this is my favorite kind of dessert. Warm supple pieces of fruit surrounded by maple, oats, walnuts, and butter—need I say more?

Maybe just this: this is about the easiest weeknight dessert you can make. Your kids will be grateful too.

2 pounds firm Bosc or Bartlett pears

6 tablespoons maple syrup

$^1/_4$ teaspoon orange flower water (optional)

2 tablespoons fresh lemon juice

1 teaspoon grated lemon zest

$^3/_4$ cup gluten-free rolled oats

$^1/_2$ cup walnut halves

100 grams Whole-Grain Gluten-Free Flour Mix (page 32)

$^1/_4$ teaspoon ground cinnamon

4 tablespoons ($^1/_2$ stick) unsalted butter, cut into small pieces

PREPARING TO BAKE. Preheat the oven to 375°F.

PREPARING THE PEARS. Cut the pears in half. Peel and core them. Cut each pear half into 5 slices lengthwise, then dice them the other way.

MAKING THE FILLING. In a 9-inch pie pan, combine the diced pears, 3 tablespoons of the maple syrup, the orange flower water (if using), lemon juice, and lemon zest. Set aside.

TOASTING THE OATS. Set a small skillet over medium-high heat. Toss in the oats. Cook, flipping the oats in the pan occasionally, until they smell toasty, 5 to 10 minutes.

MAKING THE TOPPING. Put the walnuts onto a cutting board. Using a sharp chef's knife, chop the walnuts until they are very small pieces.

In a large bowl, combine the toasted oats, chopped walnuts, flour, and cinnamon. Add the butter. Work the butter into the flour mixture with your hands until the mixture is crumbly with some visible butter chunks. Drizzle it with the remaining 3 tablespoons of maple syrup and work that in. Plop the crumble topping over the pears in the pie pan, distributing it evenly.

BAKING THE CRUMBLE. Bake the crumble until the pears are knife-tender and the edges of the crumble are bubbling with hot juices, about 45 minutes.

Feeds 4

FEEL LIKE PLAYING?

If you can't eat oats, even certified gluten-free ones, try quinoa flakes here.

If you can't have nuts, try sunflower seeds, pulsed a bit. If you can eat nuts, we think hazelnuts would be wonderful here too.

Mix pears and apples together for even more warmth.

Orange flower water is the baker's secret weapon. Just the tiniest splash makes desserts like this mysteriously good to the people who eat it. "What is it? Why is this so good?" you'll hear them ask. You'll just smile and be grateful for that bottle of orange flower water in your pantry.

chocolate-cashew pudding

I adore elaborate baking projects and challenges like trying to figure out puff pastry. But on a weeknight, after a long day and a good dinner, nothing says comfort like homemade pudding.

A chocolate pudding recipe created by John Scharffenberger went the rounds of food blogs a few years ago. I meant to make it but life flew me away from its possibilities. Somehow, I thought pudding would be much more difficult than this. And the boon of having to use cashew cream for Danny? The combination of chocolate and cashew makes this taste like a candy bar.

$^1/_2$ vanilla bean (or $^1/_2$ teaspoon vanilla extract)

$^1/_2$ cup sugar

$^1/_4$ cup cornstarch

$^1/_2$ teaspoon kosher salt

3 cups cashew milk (page 102)

1 cup semisweet chocolate, chopped

PREPARING THE VANILLA. Slice open the vanilla bean, lengthwise. Scrape the flecks of fragrant black insides into a large saucepan. Then, toss in the rest of the bean.

HEATING THE MILK. Set the saucepan onto medium-high heat. Add the sugar, cornstarch, and salt and stir together well. Slowly, add the cashew milk, stirring the entire time. Cook, stirring and scraping the sides of the pan frequently, until the milk thickens. (At first, you'll think nothing is happening but trust and keep stirring.) Dunk a rubber spatula into the milk. If the thickened milk coats the back of the spatula, and you can run a finger down the middle and the trail stays, you are ready. This should take 15 to 20 minutes.

ADDING THE CHOCOLATE. Add the chocolate to the milk. Cook, stirring frequently, until the chocolate is fully incorporated into the milk and the pudding is silky smooth, 3 to 5 minutes.

FINISHING THE PUDDING. Pour the pudding through a fine-mesh sieve into a large bowl. Divide the pudding equally among 4 to 6 dishes, depending on how generous you want to be with the pudding. Chill entirely before serving. This should be at least one hour, preferably overnight.

Feeds 4 to 6

lemon yogurt cake

This classic French cake is a home cook's dream, nothing like the fancy-pants fondant-covered cakes of bakeries. It's moist from the yogurt, tart with the lemons, and has just enough sweetness to make you want another bite.

I bow down to Bill Yosses, the pastry chef at the White House, whose recipe for lemon yogurt cake inspired this one. As he wrote in his cookbook *The Perfect Finish*, this cake is an "elegant simplicity." Give me this cake over a fudgy frosted chocolate one any day.

½ cup grapeseed oil, plus a bit for greasing the cake pan

1½ cups white sugar

280 grams All-Purpose Gluten-Free Flour Mix (page 31)

1 teaspoon baking powder

½ teaspoon baking soda

½ teaspoon kosher salt

1 cup whole milk yogurt

2 large eggs, at room temperature

2 lemons, juiced

1 lemon, zested

1¾ cups powdered sugar

PREPARING TO BAKE. Preheat the oven to 350°F. Grease a 9-inch baking pan with some of the grapeseed oil.

COMBINING THE DRY INGREDIENTS. In a bowl, whisk together the sugar, flour, baking powder, baking soda, and salt until they are one color. Set aside.

COMBINING THE WET INGREDIENTS. In the bowl of a stand mixer, pour in the yogurt, eggs, remaining half cup of grapeseed oil, two-thirds of the lemon juice, and two-thirds of the lemon zest. Mix until blended into a silky liquid.

FINISHING THE BATTER. With the mixer running, add the dry ingredients slowly to the wet ingredients, about a quarter of the mix at a time. Allow the mixer to run for a few moments, until the batter is entirely smooth, with no visible flour remaining.

continued . . .

Baking the cake. Pour the batter into the prepared cake pan. Scatter the remaining lemon zest evenly over the top of the batter. Bake until the edges of the cake have begun to pull away from the pan and the top of the cake is springy firm to the touch, 30 to 40 minutes.

Remove the cake from the oven. Allow it to cool in the pan for 10 minutes. Turn the cake over onto a wire rack to finish cooling.

Glazing the cake. When the cake is completely cooled, in a bowl, mix together the powdered sugar and the remaining lemon juice until you have a slightly thickened glaze. Poke small holes on the top of the cake, then glaze the cake.

Feeds 6

FEEL LIKE PLAYING?

This cakes tastes just a bit different with every kind of citrus you use. Grapefruit yogurt cake has a slight bitterness, Meyer lemon cake has a lovely brightness, and a combination of all the citrus fruits you love will leave you especially happy.

FEEL LIKE PLAYING? > > > > >

I can't imagine I have to convince you to eat this in other ways. It's wonderful over vanilla ice cream, but it's also great spooned over thick Greek yogurt for breakfast.

If you can't eat dairy, try the coconut whipped cream (page 306).

If you want to make a dessert bar, put out a bowl of these cherries with a handful of hazelnuts, slivers of dark chocolate, some mascarpone cheese, or some soft chèvre.

cherries poached in sauternes
with crème fraîche

Growing up, the only poached fruit in syrup I knew was cling peaches in a can. By the time I started really cooking and baking, poached fruit seemed so. . . plain. Healthy. You know? The kind of dessert that you should eat on a weeknight.

However, as my friend Katherine said to me as I was figuring out what desserts to share here: "There is something so decadent about hot fruit. Don't let us forget about it!" And when that hot fruit is ripe cherries and poaching liquid is Sauternes, with a dollop of crème fraîche? Nothing plain here. Simple? Yes. Decadent? Absolutely.

1 bottle Sauternes wine

¾ cup sugar

4 cups pitted cherries

20 fresh basil leaves, finely chopped

½ cup crème fraîche

MAKING THE POACHING LIQUID. Set a deep pot over medium heat. Pour in the wine, sugar, and 2 cups of water. Simmer until the sugar has fully dissolved, about 5 minutes.

POACHING THE CHERRIES. Add the cherries and half the basil to the liquid. Simmer until the cherries are tender, about 5 minutes. Remove the cherries with a slotted spoon and put them in a large bowl.

FINISHING THE SYRUP. Continue simmering the liquid until it grows a little syrupy, about 30 minutes. Turn off the heat. Let the syrup sit until it has cooled completely.

MACERATING THE CHERRIES. Strain the syrup through a fine-mesh sieve and into the bowl of cherries. Add the rest of the basil. Let the cherries macerate in the refrigerator for at least 2 hours, preferably overnight.

To serve, scoop out some of the cherries, drizzle them with a little syrup, and top with the crème fraîche.

Feeds 4

coconut-cashew panna cotta with blueberry compote

Panna cotta intimidated me for a long time. It sounds hard, doesn't it? I love eating the smooth little puddings with a bit of a jiggle, but I didn't make them for years. When my friend Anna shared a recipe for the panna cotta she used to make at Al Di La, I stared at it. "That's it?" I kept saying.

Anna's recipe included heavy cream and crème fraîche, neither of which sit so well with Danny. So I flung myself into the flavors of coconut and cashew together. It turns out this is much more than a substitute. I love this panna cotta. It's so easy.

$^{1}/_{4}$ cup cold water

1 envelope (2 $^{1}/_{2}$ teaspoons) gelatin

1 vanilla bean

Neutral-tasting oil for coating ramekins

2 cups cashew cream (page 102), strained

One 14-ounce can full-fat coconut milk

$^{1}/_{3}$ cup sugar

Blueberry Compote (recipe follows), for serving

PREPARING TO MAKE THE PANNA COTTA. Combine the water and gelatin in a small bowl. Stir and set aside. Slice a line down the vanilla bean. Pry open the vanilla bean and scrape the dark flecks out of the bean. Lightly coat 8 ramekins with the oil.

HEATING THE CREAM. Set a large pot over medium-high heat. Pour in the cashew cream, coconut milk, sugar, and the vanilla bean scrapings and the bean. Cook, stirring frequently, until the sugar is fully dissolved and the liquids are starting to simmer, about 10 minutes. Take the pot off the heat.

FINISHING THE PANNA COTTA. Scrape the gelatin into the hot liquid. Whisk until the gelatin is entirely dissolved. Pour $^{1}/_{2}$ cup of the liquid into each ramekin. Chill in the refrigerator for at least 3 hours to give the panna cottas a chance to set.

Release a panna cotta from its ramekin onto a small plate. Spoon some of the compote over the panna cotta and serve.

Feeds 8

blueberry compote

2 cups fresh blueberries (frozen will do in
    the winter)

$^1/_2$ cup water

$^1/_3$ cup honey

$^1/_2$ teaspoon ground cinnamon

$^1/_2$ teaspoon kosher salt

MAKING THE COMPOTE. Set a pot over medium heat. Add the blueberries, water, honey, cinnamon, and salt. Stir until the blueberries start to break down a bit and the liquids begin to boil. Turn the heat down to medium-low and cook until the compote has thickened a bit, about 15 minutes. Turn off the heat and cool the compote to room temperature.

Makes $1^1/_2$ cups blueberry compote

FEEL LIKE PLAYING?

If you make your own cashew cream, remember to strain it before using it here. Otherwise the panna cotta will be slightly grainy on the tongue.

We like to top this with a warm fruit compote with whatever fruit is in season that week. Some of the Earl Grey simple syrup from the citrus salad (page 291) is also delightful.

You can make this for your vegan friends if you use agar agar in place of the gelatin.

peach brown butter buckle

Crumble? Crisp? Cobbler? Slump? Grunt? Buckle? One of my friends often tells this old joke: "I don't care what you call me, as long as you don't call me late for dinner!" Well, a buckle is so wonderfully good that I don't care what you call it. (But to be technical about it, a buckle has a soft cake on the bottom, fruit nestled in it, and a streusel topping.)

Baking a buckle is the chance to use slightly bruised fruit, the ones that have been sitting on the counter a bit too long. This isn't a tart, where the fruit needs to look perfect. You just want that ripe taste.

12 tablespoons (1½ sticks) unsalted butter

4 cups thick-sliced ripe peaches (from about 8 medium peaches)

1 teaspoon fresh lemon juice

1½ cups sucanat or white sugar

1 teaspoon ground cinnamon

265 grams Whole-Grain Gluten-Free Flour Mix (page 32)

1 teaspoon baking powder

1 teaspoon kosher salt

2 large eggs, at room temperature

⅔ cup milk (you can use nondairy milk here)

⅓ cup turbinado sugar or dark brown sugar

BROWNING THE BUTTER. Set a small skillet over medium-low heat. (In this case, don't use cast iron. You want a silver skillet so you can see the butter turning color.) The butter will start to foam and bubble. Don't touch it. The butter will turn clear for a moment then start to darken. It's easy for butter to burn quickly here. Watch. When the butter is browned and smelling wonderful, take the pan off the heat. Allow the butter to cool.

PREPARING TO BAKE. Preheat the oven to 350°F. Line a 9-inch cast-iron skillet with a circle of parchment paper, buttered on both sides.

MACERATING THE FRUIT. Add the peaches, lemon juice, two-thirds of the sucanat, and the cinnamon into a large bowl. Stir them together.

MAKING THE BUCKLE BATTER. In a bowl, whisk together 200 grams of the flour, the baking powder, and ¹/₂ teaspoon of the salt.

In another bowl, whisk together half of the browned butter and the remaining third of the sucanat. Stir in 1 egg at a time, whisking each one in fully before adding the next. Stir in the milk.

Sprinkle the flour mixture over the liquid mixture and stir them together with a rubber spatula until no visible flour is left. Pour the batter into the pan.

Arrange the peaches over the top of the batter. No need to be too fussy here. The streusel will cover them anyway.

MAKING THE STREUSEL TOPPING. Combine the turbinado sugar, the remaining 65 grams of the flour, and the remaining ¹/₂ teaspoon salt with the remaining brown butter. Stir until the mixture looks like large, damp crumbs. Arrange the streusel topping evenly over the top of the buckle.

BAKING THE BUCKLE. Bake the buckle until the top is golden brown and springy to the touch. If you insert a toothpick in the center and you come up with moist crumbs, you're done. (This should take 40 to 50 minutes.)

FEEL LIKE PLAYING?

There are so many endless variations on this buckle, based on the season. Try cherry-almond or blueberry-nectarine, a raspberry-strawberry, or an apple-pear buckle. Any fruits that are ripe at the same time will probably work together.

We also like fresh herbs instead of the cinnamon. Basil and apricot. Rosemary and pears. Lemon thyme and peaches are lovely together too.

Brown butter is pretty much good with anything.

Allow the buckle to cool for at least 15 minutes in the pan. You can invert the pan, then invert it again to slice up the buckle. Or, you could simply slice it out of the pan.

Feeds 8

peanut butter and jam bars

Think of a peanut butter sandwich. A great sandwich with fresh roasted peanut butter, thick homemade jam, and warm multigrain bread. That's what these cookies taste like. If you make them as we suggest here, in a springform pan and sliced up, they'll look like the sandwiches your mom might have made: little triangles with the crusts cut off.

I worked on these bars for a while, trying to make them work in a square baking pan. Then my friend Anna pointed me toward a shortbread recipe from Dorie Greenspan, in which she grated frozen dough into the pan to make a tender crust. I always trust Dorie. Oh, she was right.

175 grams Whole-Grain Gluten-Free
　　Flour Mix (page 32)

1 teaspoon baking soda

$^1/_2$ teaspoon kosher salt

8 tablespoons (1 stick) unsalted butter,
　　at room temperature

$^1/_2$ cup salted natural peanut butter, creamy

200 grams sucanat (or use half white sugar
　　and half dark brown sugar)

1 large egg

1 teaspoon vanilla extract

Baking spray or butter, for greasing pan

$^3/_4$ cup jam (flavor is your choice, of course,
　　but make it a thick jam)

COMBINING THE DRY INGREDIENTS. In a bowl, whisk together the flour, baking soda, and salt until they are one color. Set aside.

COMBINING THE WET INGREDIENTS. In the bowl of a stand mixer, beat the butter with the paddle attachment on medium speed. When the butter is creamy, add the peanut butter, followed by the sucanat. Whirl the mixer until everything is combined into a light fluffiness, about 3 minutes. Scrape down the sides of the bowl. With the mixer running, add the egg, followed by the vanilla. When the batter is one color, stop the mixer. Scrape down the sides of the bowl.

FINISHING THE DOUGH. With the mixer running, slowly add the dry ingredients to the wet ingredients, about a quarter of the mix at a time. When the dough is thoroughly combined, with no visible flour remaining, turn off the mixer. The dough will be slightly wet and tacky to the touch. That's okay. Don't add any more flour.

FREEZING THE DOUGH. Bring together the dough in your hands. (You might want to flour your hands first, to keep the dough from sticking.) Divide the dough in half and form each batch into a ball. Wrap each ball in plastic wrap. Freeze the balls of dough for at least 30 minutes, no more than 3 hours.

PREPARING TO BAKE. Preheat the oven to 350°F. Grease a 10-inch springform pan with baking spray or butter.

BAKING THE BARS. Remove one ball of dough from the freezer and unwrap the plastic. Using the large holes of a box grater, grate the ball of frozen dough directly into the bottom of the springform pan. Pat down the grated dough and even out the surface. Spread the jam over the dough, smoothing it with a spoon to make it even, leaving about a $1/2$-inch border around the edges. Grate the remaining dough over the layer of jam. Pat down the dough and even it out. Don't worry if there are a few holes and ragged patches.

FEEL LIKE PLAYING?

You can use any jam you want here, but we firmly recommend that it's jam instead of jelly. Thin, watery jelly will yield bar cookies that ooze and smoosh instead of making you happy.

Bake until the edges have begun to pull away from the pan and crisp up, with the center still soft, 20 to 30 minutes. Remove the pan from the oven and allow it to cool completely in the pan, set on a wire rack. Remove the outside circle from the springform pan, then cut the bars into wedges.

Feeds 10

lemon curd with coconut milk whipped cream and fresh berries

This lemon curd is sunshine on a spoon, the lift we need for the dark days of winter. Mouth-puckering and tart, this lemon curd has just enough sweetness to hold it together. Once you make the lemon curd, knowing you will have more than you need here for the parfait, you might find it hard not to just eat it straight out of the bowl and call it dessert.

Lemon curd (makes about 1 ½ pints)

1½ cups superfine sugar (also known as baking sugar)

6 large lemons, zested and juiced

6 tablespoons (¾ stick) unsalted butter, a bit softened

6 large eggs

6 large egg yolks

½ teaspoon kosher salt

½ teaspoon orange flower water (optional)

1 pint fresh berries (whatever is in season at the moment)

Coconut milk whipped cream

One 15-ounce can full-fat coconut milk

1 tablespoon white sugar

1 teaspoon vanilla extract

MAKING LEMON SUGAR FOR THE LEMON CURD. Add the fine white sugar and lemon zest to the bowl of a stand mixer. Mix until they are clumping together and smell like a bright winter day, about 5 minutes.

CREAMING THE BUTTER AND SUGAR. Add 4 tablespoons of the butter to the lemon sugar. Run the mixer until the butter and sugar are combined thoroughly and are fluffy, about 5 minutes.

With the mixer running, add the eggs one at a time, then the yolks one at a time. Pour in the lemon juice and mix, then the salt and orange flower water (if using). The mixture should be a thick liquid, quite yellow, and coherent.

COOKING THE LEMON CURD. Pour the liquid into a large pot set over medium heat. Cook, stirring frequently, until the liquid thickens. At first, you might think it will never happen. Keep stirring, constantly at this point, to avoid curdling. After 10 minutes or so, the curd will suddenly thicken, pull away from the edges of the pot a bit, and bubble vigorously. (You can also use a candy thermometer to take the curd to 170°F.) Stick a spoon into the curd. When you drag your finger down the back of the spoon, does it leave a clean trail? You're done. Pull the pot off the heat.

Add the remaining 2 tablespoons butter to the lemon curd and stir until the mixture is smooth (emulsified). Strain the curd through a fine-mesh sieve to remove the zest. (Skip this step if you don't mind the bits of zest on your teeth.) Refrigerate the lemon curd until it is cold, about 1 hour.

PREPARING TO MAKE COCONUT CREAM. Meanwhile, put the can of coconut milk and the bowl of a stand mixer in the refrigerator to chill at the same time as the lemon curd.

SCOOPING OUT THE COCONUT CREAM. Open the can of coconut milk and scoop out the firm layer on top. There will be a clear difference between this solid cream and the watery substance on the bottom. (Save the coconut water for smoothies or other desserts.)

MAKING THE WHIPPED CREAM. Pull the bowl of the stand mixer out of the refrigerator. Immediately pour the coconut cream into it and begin mixing. Whip the cream until it forms soft peaks, 3 to 5 minutes. Add the white sugar and vanilla and continue whipping for 1 more minute.

MAKING THE PARFAIT. Scoop some of the coconut cream in the bottom of a glass, then some of the lemon curd, then the berries. (Frozen ones work too, if you're doing this in winter.) Repeat, making as many layers as your glass will hold.

Feeds 4

FEEL LIKE PLAYING?

Every single kind of citrus you can imagine works in this dish: Meyer lemon, grapefruit, tangelo, tangerine, and satsumas. The winter is long. Play with them all.

You might have leftover lemon curd at the end of this. Oh dam. It stores well in the refrigerator for up to 2 weeks. You can also freeze it.

For a lemon-curd cream pie, use the dough recipe from the apple pie recipe (page 309). Bake it until it is browned and firm. Scoop in the lemon curd and top with the coconut whipped cream. Refrigerate before serving. (For a gluten-free pâte sucrée recipe, please see our website.)

apple pie

I love so many things about this crazy world. But, other than being with my daughter and husband, nothing makes me happier than making a pie. And apple pie is my favorite.

There's something wonderful about making a pie. It's meditation in the hands, silence in the sugar, a happy space of work and laughter. I know that many folks are scared of making pie dough. But here's the secret: gluten-free pie dough is much easier to work than gluten dough. You don't have to worry about the dough growing tough if you work with it too much. If it falls apart, you just pat it in the pan. Nothing to worry about here.

You want an apple that doesn't collapse into mush. It should be equal parts sweet and tart, with a big, bright apple taste. We like Gala, Pink Lady, Honeycrisp, and Jonagold apples. If you find a bag of Gravensteins, rush home to make pie.

What do you need to make a pie—your heart in your hands, your attention in the moment, and not much else. A happy baker makes a happy pie. Remember that. Don't be afraid. What's the worst that could happen? It's pie.

16 tablespoons (2 sticks) unsalted butter, plus 1 tablespoon cut into small pieces

420 grams All-Purpose Gluten-Free Flour Mix (page 31)

$1/2$ teaspoon kosher salt

$1/2$ cup cold water

3 tablespoons sour cream

8 large crisp apples (we like Gravensteins in season)

100 grams sugar

1 tablespoon fresh lemon juice

$1 \frac{1}{2}$ teaspoons ground cinnamon

$1/2$ teaspoon kosher salt

$1/4$ teaspoon ground nutmeg

1 large egg, beaten

Chilling the butter. Cut the 16 tablespoons of butter into 1-inch cubes. Put them in the freezer, on a saucer.

Making the dough. Add 350 grams of the flour and the salt to a large food processor. Pulse them together until the flour is fluffy and aerated. Add the chilled butter cubes to the food processor and

continued . . .

pulse 10 times. The flour and butter should look like a sandy mixture, with some butter chunks still visible.

In a small bowl, mix together the water and sour cream. Pour this into the food processor and pulse 5 times. The finished dough should look like curds of dry cottage cheese. You should also be able to pinch some of it between your fingers and have it stick together. If the dough is dry, add more cold water 1 tablespoon at a time. It's better to have a dough a little too wet than a little too dry.

Forming the dough into discs. Dump the dough onto a clean, cool surface. Gently, gather all the dough together in your hands. Working quickly, make half the dough into a ball and flatten it into a plump disc, about 2 inches tall. Wrap it in plastic wrap. Repeat with the remaining dough. Transfer the dough discs to the refrigerator to rest for 30 minutes.

Pulling out the dough. Take the dough discs out of the refrigerator. Let them sit for a few moments to soften while you make the filling.

Making the apple filling. Cut the apples in half lengthwise. Peel and core them. Cut each half into ½-inch slices.

Put the apple slices in a large bowl. Add the remaining 70 grams of flour, 90 grams of the sugar, the lemon juice, cinnamon, salt, and nutmeg and toss with the apples to combine. Let the filling sit on the kitchen counter while you roll out the dough.

Preparing to bake. Preheat the oven to 425°F.

Rolling out the dough. Put 2 pieces of wax paper on the kitchen counter. (You can also use parchment paper, a floured marble pastry board, or a floured countertop, if you wish.) To prevent sticking, lightly oil the sides of the wax paper that will be touching the dough.

Put one of the discs of dough between the pieces of wax paper. Pat down the disc a bit and lay the rolling pin on it. Imagine the dough is the face of a clock. Roll out once at 12 o'clock. Then, lift the rolling pin and roll out the dough at 12:10. Moving in "10-minute" increments, roll out the pie dough to slightly larger than your pie pan. Don't rush. Think of this as pie meditation. Roll out the dough evenly.

Lift the top wax paper. Put a 9-inch glass pie pan upside down on top of the dough. Flip the pan and dough over together. Carefully, strip away the remaining piece of wax paper. Pat the dough down into the pan, gently. If some of the pie dough sticks to the wax paper, no worries. Peel off that dough and pat it into the rest of the pie dough. There's no gluten so the pie crust won't get tough.

CRIMPING THE EDGES. Flour your fingers. Crimp the edges of the pie crust by pressing from the inside of the pie pan with the thumb and first finger on your left hand while pressing between those from the outside with the first finger of your right hand. Go slowly and enjoy it.

FILLING THE PIE. Fill the pie dough with the apple mixture. It should mound pretty high. Dot the top of the filling with the butter pieces.

PUTTING ON THE TOP CRUST. Roll out the remaining dough the same way as explained above. Lay the top dough onto the pie gently, as though you are putting a blanket on a sleeping child. Tuck the edges into the crimped crust. Make 2 or 3 small slits in the top crust to allow the steam out.

FEEL LIKE PLAYING?

When you feel comfortable with this pie, substitute half the volume of apples with pears. These two play really well together.

Cinnamon and nutmeg are my two favorite spices here. But I also love a pinch of cardamom, or a touch of allspice, or even a tiny bit of mace. Fresh vanilla bean scrapings will make this an even more extraordinary dessert.

Please make pie.

BAKING THE PIE. Brush the top of the pie crust with the beaten egg and sprinkle with the remaining 10 grams of sugar. Slide the pie into the oven.

Bake for 15 minutes. Turn down the heat to 375°F and bake the pie until the top crust is golden brown, the juices are sizzling on the edges of the crust, and the bottom crust is browned when you look at it from the bottom of the pan, about 45 minutes to 1 hour.

Allow the pie to cool to room temperature before serving, at least 2 hours. I know the wait is hard. It's worth it.

Makes one 9-inch pie

RESOURCES

We tried to use mostly ingredients that are available at most grocery stores in developing recipes for this book. However, there were cases when an ingredient like organic brown rice or heirloom beans made such a difference in the taste of the dish that we wanted to share them with you.

Living gluten-free means ordering ingredients online, especially flours in bulk. So, if you're putting together a food order online, we'd like to recommends some of these companies. (And then pester your grocery store to start stocking your favorites.)

ALTER ECO
www.alterecofoods.com

This fair-trade company buys directly from farmers in third-world countries and sells to consumers all over the world. We're fans of their quinoa, chocolate, rices, and teas.

ANSON MILLS
www.ansonmills.com

The heirloom grains grown and sold by Anson Mills are some of the finest grits, buckwheat, and polenta we have found. Not everything milled by Anson Mill is gluten-free, but they maintain good practices to keep the gluten-free grains separate from the gluten ingredients.

BOB'S RED MILL
www.bobsredmill.com

We could not live without Bob's Red Mill. Their huge array of whole grains, flours, and baking mixes make our lives better.

MASSA ORGANICS
www.massaorganics.com

This is the best brown rice I've ever eaten.

RANCHO GORDO
www.ranchogordo.com

Steve Sando created a lot of happy meals when he began growing and selling heirloom beans that were slowly slipping out of consumers' consciousness. Try one package and you might not go back to grocery store beans.

SPECTRUM ORGANICS
www.spectrumorganics.com

These are great cooking oils, most of them organic.

WHOLESOME SWEETENERS
www.wholesomesweeteners.com

This company produces sugars and sweeteners, such as coconut palm sugar and sucanat, which are not bleached or processed.

INDEX

Page numbers in *italics* indicate illustrations.